Educating the Emotions

*Bruno Bettelheim and
Psychoanalytic Development*

Educating the Emotions

Bruno Bettelheim and
Psychoanalytic Development

Edited by

NATHAN M. SZAJNBERG, M.D.

West Hartford, Connecticut

PLENUM PRESS • NEW YORK AND LONDON

Library of Congress Cataloging-in-Publication Data

Educating the emotions : Bruno Bettelheim and psychoanalytic
development / edited by Nathan M. Szajnberg.
      p.   cm.
    Includes bibliographical references and index.
    ISBN 0-306-43942-5
    1. Psychoanalysis.   2. Child psychotherapy--Residential treatment.
3. Educational psychology.   4. Bettelheim, Bruno.   I. Szajnberg,
Nathan M.   II. Bettelheim, Bruno.
    [DNLM: 1. Affective Disorders--in infancy & childhood.   2. Child,
Institutionalized--psychology.   3. Child Psychology.
4. Psychoanalytic Theory.   5. Psychology, Educational.   6. Teaching.
WM 460 E245]
RC509.E28   1992
616.89'17--dc20
DNLM/DLC
for Library of Congress   91-39116
                                                                  CIP

˙ ISBN 0-306-43942-5

© 1992 Plenum Press, New York
A Division of Plenum Publishing Corporation
233 Spring Street, New York, N.Y. 10013

Printed in the United States of America

To my parents, my past
To Debby, my love
To Sonia and Lily, my future

Contributors

ROBERT BERGMAN, M.D. • 2271 N.E. 51st Street, Seattle, Washington 98105

BERTRAM J. COHLER, Ph.D. • Committee on Human Development, University of Chicago, 5730 S. Woodlawn Avenue, Chicago, Illinois 60637

ELIO FRATTAROLI, M.D. • 168 Gramercy Road, Bala Cynwyd, Pennsylvania 19004

ROBERT M. GALATZER-LEVY, M.D. • The Institute for Psychoanalysis, 180 N. Michigan Avenue, Chicago, Illinois 60601

JOSEPH D. NOSHPITZ, M.D. • 3141 34th Street N.W., Washington, D.C. 20008

ROBERT A. PAUL, Ph.D. • Graduate Institute of Liberal Arts, Emory University, Atlanta, Georgia 30322

NATHAN M. SZAJNBERG, M.D. • 24 Chapman Road, West Hartford, Connecticut 06107

It is one's inner experience that permits gaining a full grasp of what is involved in the inner experiences of others, a knowledge which then can become the basis for theoretical studies. (Bettelheim, 1990, p. 36)

The great contribution he [Freud] has made to our understanding of literature . . . [is] what he says about the nature of the human mind: he showed us that poetry is indigenous to the very constitution of the mind. (Trilling, 1965, p. 92)

. . . Creativity . . . refers to a colouring of the whole attitude to external reality. It is creative apperception more than anything else that makes the individual feel that life is worth living. (Winnicott, 1971, p. 65)

The eternal aim of Art: to give expression to the myths we need to live by and to affirm life, both in tragedy and comedy. (Bettelheim, 1990, p. 120)

Humanist: A person having a strong . . . concern for human welfare, values and dignity. (*Random House Dictionary*, 1987)

Preface

Although Bruno Bettelheim died before this book was finished, he was present at its birth. In 1985, we felt we wanted to give him a gift for what he taught us: how to think critically about ourselves and our society; how to inform our emotions; how to move from self-knowledge to empathy for others, and how with such empathy, in turn, to enrich and expand our self-knowledge; and most important, how to integrate a sense of personal autonomy with a sense of responsible living with one's community.

For many of us, he was our Socrates. His best, most lively teaching was in the presence of a group of questioning, intellectually hungry students. We sought simple answers to our life problems, or those of our patients. He would press us, insisting that we not settle for stock phrases. The first place to learn was from within. He seemed to thrive on teaching those who were prepared to follow his example of demanding self-examination, often a painful process, with felt reasoning that could result in an informed heart.

Bettelheim treasured the written word. Fortunately, unlike Socrates, and despite believing that the best learning comes dialectically, he wrote. Several of us learned from him only through his writings. Early on he abjured the dry, passive-voiced, "professional" journals, filled with their English psychoanalytic argot that obscured more than clarified. These same journals refused to publish his account of his experience in Dachau, because they did not believe the horror of his account. Perhaps there was another important reason for his willingness to turn not only to writing books but also to such magazines as the *New Yorker*, *Redbook*, and the *Atlantic Monthly* for his voice. He believed deeply that psychology belonged to the lay public, not only rarefied psychoanalytic or psychological organizations. He believed deeply that matters of the soul, if they are true and if clearly stated, will be understood by the interested layperson. And the layperson would, of course, be interested in such matters, for they are matters of our daily life: raising and educating children, erasing prejudice, living autonomously in a mass society, enjoying fairy tales.

In 1985 we held a conference to present our thoughts to this man who engendered our ideas in such varied fields: anthropology, psychoanalysis, child development, education, milieu therapy, feminism, literature. This was the best gift we could offer him. He was reluctant to attend, not only because of his modesty, but also because of his concern that such a meeting might be a hardship on his friends. He agreed to join us only after we said we were going to hold the conference in any event. We met in the Judd Classroom at the University of Chicago, where he had taught all of his classes.

Surprisingly, when we agreed to rewrite these conference papers as chapters for this book, several publishers said they were interested only if we did not dedicate it as a *Festschrift*, since, we were told, *Festschriften* did not sell. It did not matter that our work was dedicated to Bettelheim's thoughts, that as good intellectual friends and colleagues our work would not be a hagiography but, as best we could manage, honest journeys beginning with his ideas as home ports, to whatever new lands we discovered on the vessels of psychoanalysis. We persisted, and through Theron Raines, Bettelheim's agent, found in Plenum a publisher who facilitated the birth of this volume.

Our task in this book is to recapture and develop the humanistic trends in psychoanalysis. This humanism withered as psychoanalysis was transplanted from Vienna to the fertile but alien soils of America. When one transplants great vineyard stock from the soils of Burgundy or Bordeaux to Napa Valley, the soil and climate may change the same wine—for better or worse. For psychoanalysis, the New World's soil changed the humanistic flavor to a technological one.

Those of us who wrote these chapters learned of this cultural task, educating or reeducating our emotions, from Bettelheim, as either teacher or colleague. When we wished to thank him for teaching us how to live a life with an informed heart—reason imbuing feeling—we felt that our best gifts would be our thoughts. It was daunting to capture his ideas and their influence on our respective, diverse fields, for his writings appear so diverse. His name is not simply connected to a single easily remembered idea, like the names of his equally humanistic colleagues, Erikson (the intimate connection of child rearing and societal values) or Peter Blos (the vicissitudes of adolescence).

Yet there is a unifying theme for Bettelheim and, we hope, for this book: how a humanistic psychoanalytic understanding of humankind deepens and enriches one's understanding of its cultural works. If humanism is our concern for values, welfare, and dignity, then culture is the shared representational manner in which we construct our lives, communally and intrapsychically. These cultural works include creating institutions for emotionally disturbed children; creating grammar schools or curricula; ameliorating prejudice or fostering tolerance; reading fairy tales; transmitting values, that is, educating the emotions of children whether in middle-class homes or in kibbutzim; understanding envy, whether it be of penis or womb; and creating or curing symptoms, those first creations of reflection.

The Nazi concentration camp profoundly marked Bettelheim: "It is death that endows life with its deepest, most unique meaning" (Bettelheim, 1979). When the Nazis entered Vienna on March 13, 1938, Bettelheim, an officer in the underground army, said all of Austria's "allies" turned away. He remained long enough to demobilize his men, then escaped to Czechoslovakia. The Czechs were only too pleased to detain him until the Nazis came. His one year in Dachau is recounted most directly in three volumes: *The Informed Heart* (1960), *Surviving* (1979), and *Freud's Vienna and Other Essays* (1990). These books bracket his life. The first sets its task to find and preserve autonomy in a mass age. The last closes with the admonition "We all must enlarge the feeling of community beyond our own group . . . because violence is as natural to man as the tendency toward order." These were his last published words.

When Bettelheim emigrated to the United States, he began, as he put it, the "better part of my life." He dedicated several decades of his life to demonstrating how ameliorating, how soul-saving, an institution can be for the emotionally damaged child. Four books recount his efforts: *Love Is Not Enough* (1950), an account of the structure of the day and the architecture of emotional education; *Truants from Life* (1955), an account of the children; and *A Home for the Heart* (1974), an account of the milieu staff. *The Empty Fortress* (1967) focused on his efforts to help autistic children, those most emotionally savaged. Because some adults objected to his description, following Leo Kanner, of the emotional coldness of some autistic children's parents, the substance of how these children were rehabilitated was also rejected.

While he worked with the most disturbed, Bettelheim's thoughts were never far from the vicissitudes of contemporary life, whether learning how to raise a child well (*Dialogues with Mothers* [1962], *A Good Enough Parent* [1987]), or understanding how prejudice bolsters self-esteem and the search for identity, explaining its stubborn endurance in the face of legislation or the usual "educative" approaches (*Social Change and Prejudice* [1964]).

As an emigrant, he was sensitive to how many different ways we can understand, find meaning, in the world, yet how we all share some fundamental anxieties and hopes. *Symbolic Wounds* (1954) grew out of his experience with four disturbed boys at the Orthogenic School at the University of Chicago, and the power of their envy of menses. He turned to anthropological data to confirm this as a common dynamic. *Children of the Dream* (1969) is more an ethnographic than anthropological undertaking. He felt that by learning how extraordinarily well children of the kibbutz were raised in a communal setting, we might learn about the possibilities for such approaches in American education. This book appeared at the time when the Head Start program was a new initiative in preschool community education for the underprivileged.

Finally, there are the books about language, the power of the word. *The Uses of Enchantment* (1977) was supposed to be part of Bettelheim's parenting book. As he recognized the importance of fairy tales and their attenuation in contemporary society, it became a volume of its own. It is about how language, reading, or better yet, story-telling can go well. *On Learning to Read* (1982) tells how reading pedagogy can go badly. Too many children are thought to be dumb, or, more politely, miswired or learning disabled, when in fact such children "misread" for good personal reasons. If we approach the children in this spirit, their "errors" often disappear. *Freud and Man's Soul* (1982) is a cautionary tale: even psychoanalysts may have their personal unconscious motives for mistranslating simple German words (*Ich, es, Uberich, Seele*) into emotionally distancing technological jargon (ego, id, superego, mind).

Thus, we have fifteen books that touch apparently disparate fields (anthropology, literature, psychoses, mental institutions, schools, the family), yet address one major issue: human meaning. This embodied duality—cross-disciplinary exploration driven by a desire to explore human welfare, values, and dignity—captures the era of the University of Chicago during Bettelheim's time. He, like Goethe, could experience an integrated sense of how he was influenced by and contributed to his intellectual community, in this case the University.

The University of Chicago prior to Bettelheim's arrival was guided by President Robert Maynard Hutchins's (Ashmore, 1989) insistence that the departmental divisions—dividing arts from sciences, dividing humanities from social sciences, or from physical sciences—interfered with the pursuit of knowledge, the mission of the university. An ideal university would have colleagues who belonged to no department, but to the disciplined pursuit of knowledge.

Bettelheim's professional home and primary appointment was in the Department of Education (not psychology, psychiatry, or psychoanalysis). During this era, the University gave safe haven to colleagues such as Paul Ricoeur, who was intrigued not only that Freud's dream work (Ricoeur,

1970) identified certain patterns of creativity in the human mind but also, and further, that there may be fundamental ways that humans create other works above the level of metaphor. At the level of narrative, he pursued drama, fiction (Ricoeur, 1970a, 1977, 1983, 1984, 1989), even music and the plastic arts (Ricoeur 1970b). These patterns of thinking creatively somehow are connected and perhaps translatable to each other.

The University was home to Mircea Eliade, who created a discipline, history of religions, that was both social science (he did some field work with shamans in Central Asia) and humanistic discipline (he and his students spend much time studying texts).

The University was a true intellectual refuge to Hannah Arendt. After describing the banality of evil that she discovered listening to Eichmann's trial—"his horrible gift for consoling himself with cliches," which helped avoid critical thinking; the language rules that cleansed emotionally laden words such as killing ("Final Solution"), or deportation ("resettlement"), or murder ("to grant a mercy death")—Arendt was critically beset by those who distorted her own words and thoughts to say that she sympathized with Eichmann and blamed the Jewish victims. Colleagues at the University including Hans Morgenthau, Richard McKeon, and Bruno Bettelheim personally consoled her and intellectually defended her (Young-Bruehl, 1982).

The University's administrative structure changed itself to facilitate the University's mission. It developed committees, autonomous of departments, to facilitate integration of only apparently varied intellectual approaches. For instance, the Committee on Social Thought included Saul Bellow, the novelist; David Greene, the classicist; and Henry Rago, the editor of *Poetry*. The University was large enough to offer elbow room for disparate, even dissenting viewpoints, yet small enough that it was a true intellectual community.

The college at the University was small enough to require an integrated faculty. Senior faculty, like Bettelheim, considered it an honor and responsibility to teach in the college. College students easily could elect graduate courses, often spicing them into liveliness. Faculty could be promoted and tenured in the college alone.

In a sense, Bettelheim, a refugee from Dachau concentration camp, found not only refuge, but also a true home in a university that considered itself an organic community obligated to reflect self-critically upon its own functioning in order to function. For Bettelheim, whose *Weltanschauung* was molded by the critical, yet careful personal reflection of psychoanalysis, this was the right place for him to develop.

Aristotle in his Lyceum would study the biology of fishes and write about rhetoric, poetics, and the movement of heavenly bodies. We have passed the era when a single scholar could engage in all these pursuits. The university is the organism that now contains such varied pursuits at the frontiers of the human mind and soul. If, however, this organism's scholars pursue their works independently in compartmentalized departments, walled off from their colleagues' understanding, then we no longer have a university, but some technical school, perhaps at best a "multiversity"—an institution, like Aristotle's misguided state, that may work at odds with itself (Booth, 1974, 1989).

However, when scholars engage each other, use good rhetoric to persuade colleagues of the value of their work (whether in psychoanalysis, astrophysics, or literary criticism), then we have a true organism with scholars who may have differentiated functions, but whose overall aim is to further knowledge, thereby invigorating the university.

We can return to Arendt to learn the role of humanism in the complex political organism, the university. "As humanists, we can rise above these conflicts. . . . We can rise in freedom above the specialties which we all must learn and pursue. . . . To the extent that we learn how to exercise our taste freely . . . a cultivated person ought to be one who knows how to choose his company among men, among things, among thoughts, in the present as well as in the past" (Arendt, 1968).

In this sense, we can understand how Bettelheim's *oeuvre* touched so many varied areas of human concern. He came with a *Weltanschauung*, psychoanalysis, to an intellectual climate that fostered cross-disciplinary exploration. This book is about Bettelheim's ideas and how they have furthered our thinking; it is also about the university community that helped this thinking flourish.

We invite the reader to join us in the larger intellectual community, unbounded by walls, that we hope this book embodies. It is in this spirit that we hope to "enlarge the feeling of community."

REFERENCES

Arendt, H. (1968). *Between Past and Future*, pp. 225–226. New York: Viking Press.

Ashmore, H. S. (1989). *Unseasonable Truths: The Life of Robert Maynard Hutchins*. Boston: Little, Brown.

Bettelheim, B. (1950). *Love Is Not Enough: The Treatment of Emotionally Disturbed Children*. Glencoe, IL: Free Press.

Bettelheim, B. (1954). *Symbolic Wounds: Puberty Rites and the Envious Male*. Glencoe, IL: Free Press.

Bettelheim, B. (1955). *Truants from Life: The Rehabilitation of Emotionally Disturbed Children*. New York: Free Press.

Bettelheim, B. (1960). *The Informed Heart: Autonomy in a Mass Age*. New York: Free Press.

Bettelheim, B. (1962). *Dialogues with Mothers*. New York: Free Press.

Bettelheim, B. (1967). *The Empty Fortress*. New York: Free Press.

Bettelheim, B. (1969). *Children of the Dream*. New York: Macmillan.

Bettelheim, B. (1974). *A Home for the Heart*. New York: Knopf.

Bettelheim, B. (1977). *The Uses of Enchantment: The Meaning and Importance of Fairy Tales*. New York, Knopf.

Bettelheim, B. (1979). *Surviving and Other Essays*. New York: Knopf.

Bettelheim, B. (1982). *Freud and Man's Soul*. New York: Knopf.

Bettelheim, B. (1987). *A Good Enough Parent: A Book on Child Rearing*. New York: Knopf.

Bettelheim, B. (1990). *Freud's Vienna and Other Essays*. New York: Knopf.

Bettelheim, B., and Janowitz, M. B. (1964). *Social Change and Prejudice*. Glencoe, IL: Free Press.

Bettelheim, B., and Zelan, K. (1982). *On Learning to Read*. New York: Knopf.

Booth, W. C. (1974). *Modern Dogma and the Rhetoric of Assent*. Chicago: University of Chicago Press.

Booth, W. C. (1988). *The Vocation of a Teacher*. Chicago: University of Chicago Press.

Random House Dictionary. (1987). New York: Random House.

Ricoeur, P. (1970a). *Freud and Philosophy: An Essay on Interpretation*. New Haven: Yale University Press.

Ricoeur, P. (1970b). Personal communication.

Ricoeur, P. (1974). *The Rule of Metaphor: Multidisciplinary Studies of the Creation of Meaning in Language*. Trans. R. Czerny, L. McLaughlin, and J. Costello. Toronto: University of Toronto Press.

Ricoeur, P. (1983). *Time and Narrative*, Vol. 1. Trans. K. McLaughlin and D. Pellauer. Chicago: University of Chicago Press.

Ricoeur, P. (1984). *Time and Narrative*, Vol. 2. Trans. K. McLaughlin and D. Pellauer. Chicago: University of Chicago Press.

Ricoeur, P. (1988). *Time and Narrative*, Vol. 3. Trans. K. Blaney and D. Pellauer. Chicago: University of Chicago Press.

Trilling, L. (1965). *Beyond Culture: Essays on Literature and Learning*. New York: Viking Press.

Winnicott, D. W. (1971). *Playing and Reality*. New York: Basic Books.

Young-Bruehl, E. (1982). *Hannah Arendt: For the Love of the World*. New Haven: Yale University Press.

Contents

CHAPTER 2

PSYCHOANALYSIS AND THE CLASSROOM:
INTENT AND MEANING IN
LEARNING AND TEACHING   41

BERTRAM J. COHLER and ROBERT M. GALATZER-LEVY

CHAPTER 3

HISTORY OF MILIEU IN THE RESIDENTIAL
TREATMENT
OF CHILDREN AND YOUTH   91

JOSEPH D. NOSHPITZ

CHAPTER 4

ORTHODOXY AND HERESY IN
THE HISTORY OF PSYCHOANALYSIS   121

ELIO FRATTAROLI

CHAPTER 5

BETTELHEIM'S CONTRIBUTION TO ANTHROPOLOGY   151

ROBERT A. PAUL

CHAPTER 6

FROM THE ORTHOGENIC SCHOOL TO
THE RESERVATION:
ACCULTURATION OF A PSYCHOANALYST   173

ROBERT BERGMAN

CHAPTER 7

SECRECY AND PRIVACY IN A PSYCHODYNAMIC MILIEU: THE INDIVIDUAL AND HIS COMMUNITY 193

NATHAN M. SZAJNBERG

Introduction

NATHAN M. SZAJNBERG

We wish to recapture a humanistic psychoanalysis, to explore and extend its place in American culture: our daily lives, institutions, and sense of community. We are taking a humanistic psychoanalysis as a worldview, a *Weltanschauung*, that educates us about our emotional lives. The reader will recognize that before we can develop a psychoanalytic matrix within our culture, we first need to explain how we can take psychoanalysis as a worldview when Freud decried such action.

For Bruno Bettelheim, who inspired this volume, psychoanalysis was a *Weltanschauung*: it discovers the meanings of our thoughts, feelings, and actions. It uncovers both the best and worst within us and between us without resorting to external explanatory powers. It defines the boundaries of our biological imperatives—the drives toward death or life, the degree of femininity or masculinity—thereby clarifying the wide range of autonomous or potentially autonomous decisions within an individual or society. Psychoanalysis explores the creativity that each culture uses to master these cross-cultural imperatives: death or life, femaleness or maleness, or maturational libidinal stages of orality, anality, and genitality.

How do we respond to Freud?

We could respond that Freud was cautious that psychoanalysis be considered a science rather than the belief system that *Weltanschauung* might suggest. Using the nineteenth century distinction of science (facts) versus nonscience (values), Freud believed that psychoanalytic discoveries were facts inherent in people. Today, following Michael Polanyi's (1962) and Thomas Kuhn's (1970) work on the history and philosophy of science, we know that the fact–value distinction does not separate science from nonscience. Scientific theory has been built not only on facts, but also on

1

values, such as which theory is more elegant or parsimonious. Therefore, if *Weltanschauung* carries with it the suggestion of value—which worldview is more aesthetically appealing—this in itself would not bar us from considering psychoanalysis as both *Weltanschauung* and science.

But Freud was more circumscribed about what in psychoanalysis was not a *Weltanschauung*. Late in his life, in the last chapter of the *New Introductory Lectures on Psychoanalysis*, he identified and counterposed science, religion, art, and philosophy as *Weltanschauungen*, defining the latter as

> an intellectual construction which solves all the problems of our existence uniformly on the basis of one overriding hypothesis, which accordingly leaves no question unanswered and in which everything that interests us finds its fixed place. (Freud, 1933, p. 158)

In an earlier work, he was even more specific:

> Many writers have laid much stress on the *weakness* of the ego in relation to the id and *of our rational elements in the face of the daemonic forces within us*; and they display a strong tendency to make what I have said into a cornerstone of a psychoanalytic *Weltanschauung*. (Freud, 1926, p. 151, my italics)

Freud does not want us to build a *Weltanschauung* on the cornerstone of the ego's weakness relative to the id. Yet, he places psychoanalysis within the scientific *Weltanschauung* (Freud, 1933).

We will not try to build an intellectual construction, psychoanalytic or otherwise, with "one overriding hypothesis" that solves our existential problems. We will suggest, however, that there are basic principles, theoretical underpinnings that facilitated the discovery and development of psychoanalysis. These principles have endured despite changes in psychoanalytic technique and even profound changes in psychoanalytic metapsychology. These principles establish a *Weltanschauung* in the sense of organizing our ideas about man's or woman's psychology.

Psychoanalysis assumes and demonstrates that there is meaning to our actions, thoughts, and feelings and that these meanings are constructed by us and motivate us. We need not seek motivation from greater external powers, whether these be religious—gods, devils, saints—or secular—goblins, ghosts, dybbuks, or genes. Psychoanalysis assumes that our inner meanings and motivations are mostly unconscious. They can become conscious in many ways: through dreams, actions, parapraxes, or art. That peculiar psychoanalytic innovation, the consulting room, provides a setting within which one can bring matters into consciousness in a mutative manner. This setting is an intimate, intense, frequent and lengthy dialectical enterprise, which provides access to one's inner world in a measured, titrated manner that can free one to have greater freedom of choices in one's inner life.

Psychoanalysis sees man as a rational animal. Consequently, a good life is informed by the rational, yet enlivened by the animal (libidinal, aggressive drives). Psychoanalysis sees development in discrete psychological stages, with mastery over specific tasks at each stage, and, overall, accommodating one's mind to the demands of and contributions from one's body. Finally, psychoanalysis believes that a better understanding of one's inner life can lead to a better understanding of what happens between people and ultimately to how we create and function in society, our greatest cultural creation.

Because psychoanalysis is a *Weltanschauung* in the sense that it guides our understanding of humanity, Bettelheim's works, like Freud's, ranged widely. Marked by his experiences in Nazi concentration camps, Bettelheim explored the depths of mass society and its institutions. He developed the principles of milieu therapy. Like Piaget, although he studied and wrote about children and child rearing, his thoughts were never far from human development. As an art historian, he returned to cultural works as they taught us about ourselves.

In this book, we pick up this task of how we transfer our values to our children and ourselves, how we educate our emotions.

We begin with the relationship between the individual and our institutions. How do we best construct institutions, particularly schools and mental institutions so that they best serve both the individual's and society's needs? What are those needs that foster greatest autonomy yet a sense of community in a democratic society? Szajnberg's chapter addresses the tension between autonomy and alienation as these are played out in settings such as public schools or mental institutions. He recounts what happens when individuals perceive that an institution's alleged values begin to stray from its actions. From Max Weber, we learn how bureaucratization is inherent to institutional development. A rationalized bureaucracy can help an institution function more efficiently and it can dehumanize the institution as the latter begins to fulfill its own needs rather than those it was established to serve. This chapter discusses psychoanalytically informed principles that protect us from the deterioration of an institution.

Cohler and Galatzer-Levy apply psychoanalytic principles to the classroom, particularly in higher education. They take the intriguing route of critically reviewing what psychoanalysis has learned about itself as an intellectual discipline: there has been a tendency to use experience-distant, emotionally removed language (ego, cathexis, libido) to study our innermost feelings. Cohler and Galatzer-Levy point out that this tendency to remove ourselves emotionally from new knowledge about ourselves or about our world will undermine both teaching and learning. They suggest that we attend to the subjective curriculum that is evoked by any objective curriculum in order to facilitate learning: we have feelings about what we are studying, whether about the origins of our universe, ourselves, or our feelings.

Noshpitz takes us on a journey from the seventeenth century to the present to learn how Western culture has cared for our troubling, troublesome, and troubled youth. He suggests that in contemporary America our cultural fascination with technology has influenced how we treat troubled youth. Institutions manipulate their behavior and expunge and ignore their feelings, so that these already alienated youth become further alienated from their "caretakers" and most tragically, sometimes from their own thoughts and feelings. He describes the brief hiatus after Bettelheim's pioneering work, when institutions for children were truly asylums of safety.

With Frattaroli's chapter, we turn to a broader exploration of a longstanding paradox in our human nature. In Western culture, we have had tension between thinking of ourselves as basically tragic (for instance, Job) or basically guilty (for instance, King Lear). Frattaroli demonstrates that Freud felt that same unresolved conflict, which for him was intrapsychic, but for his psychoanalytic disciples became interpersonal. Is man basically born good but befallen by tragedy, as the Kohutian self psychologists suggest, or is he born guilty and needing to repent, as the Kleinians (and others) insist? Frattaroli argues that in American culture, we have difficulty accepting ambiguity, the concordance of opposites, that man may be both guilty and tragic, depending on one's perspective of the moment. He discusses what implications this has for psychoanalytic thinking and, we suggest, for our daily lives.

Paul, an anthropologist, takes us across many cultures to point out that male envy of female menses and reproductive ability is found and denied in many cultures. He begins by reminding us that when Bettelheim first suggested this concept of womb envy in 1954, he was met by a resounding silence or an occasional criticism by professional anthropologists and psychoanalysts. In subsequent decades, ethnographic accounts from many cultures have spoken more loudly than those "experts."

In the last two chapters, we turn to how psychoanalysis helps us understand others outside of the consulting room. Bergman demonstrates how to transport the process of psychoanalysis into a foreign culture. By understanding communications and creating meanings, we emerge with a better understanding of others and ourselves.

Szajnberg discusses the power of secrecy and privacy in a community and how we can achieve a balance between a sense of simple solitude and a sense of community.

Each chapter is introduced by brief comments by the editor in order to provide "bridges" between chapters.

We hope that the reader's journey through this book will be both an exploration and an inward journey.

References

Bettelheim, B. (1954). *Symbolic Wounds: Puberty Rites and the Envious Male*. Glencoe, IL: Free Press.

Freud, S. (1926). Inhibitions, Symptoms and Anxiety. In J. Strachey (ed. and trans.), *The Standard Edition of the Complete Psychological Works of Sigmund Freud*, Vol. 20. London: Hogarth Press.

Freud, S. (1933). New Introductory Lectures on Psychoanalysis. In J. Strachey (ed. and trans.), *The Standard Edition of the Complete Psychological Works of Sigmund Freud*, Vol. 22. London: Hogarth Press.

Kuhn, T. (1970). *The Structure of Scientific Revolutions*. Chicago: University of Chicago Press.

Polanyi, M. (1962). *Personal Knowledge: Towards a Post-Critical Philosophy*. Chicago: University of Chicago Press.

The Individual and Society's Institutions

Autonomy and Integration

NATHAN M. SZAJNBERG

> It remains to ask whether we are to say that happiness is the same for the individual human being and for the state or not. The answer is obvious: all would agree that it is the same.
>
> (ARISTOTLE, *The Politics*, Book 7, i.i).

PSYCHOANALYSIS BEGINS TO ANSWER how an individual can maintain a sense of autonomy, or self-governance, yet a sense of integration with society's institutions. Vignettes from mental hospitals and public school systems are presented because these are designed specifically by society for our most dependent individuals. As Foucault (1973)* argued, those institutions offer a mirror of what society values and devalues. For example, it is no coincidence that society began to incarcerate its insane and irrationals at the rise of the Enlightenment: when the rational became highly valued, society needed to mark and set aside those who were not rational.

One vignette illustrates how children and staff in a mental hospital react when involved, involuntarily for the children, more voluntarily for the staff,

---

*Foucault, M. (1973). *Madness and Civilization: A History of Insanity in the Age of Reason*. New York: Vintage.

NATHAN M. SZAJNBERG • 24 Chapman Road, West Hartford, Connecticut 06107.

Educating the Emotions: Bruno Bettelheim and Psychoanalytic Development, edited by Nathan M. Szajnberg. Plenum Press, New York, 1992.

in research that they find anathema. In contrast, the hospital chief rationalized the study, condemning the staff's "unethical" engendering of discord among the children.

The second vignette portrays how different teachers' frames of mind fostered an atmosphere of autonomy in their classrooms despite a deep sense of alienation in a beleaguered public school system.

The last vignette portrays the differing reactions of therapists when an institution begins to sell its soul.

In each case, Szajnberg uses a psychoanalytic frame of reference to facilitate our understanding of how, as Aristotle suggested, happiness can be the same for the individual and society.

INTRODUCTION: MAINTAINING AUTONOMY AND INTEGRATION WITH SOCIETY'S INSTITUTIONS

Psychoanalysis is a recent accretion to Western intellectual thought. Freud first explored psychoanalysis as a new knowledge of one's inner life. But because this knowledge is developed initially in a dialectical setting, the consulting room, psychoanalysis also developed as a new knowledge about how two people develop, create, and explore mutual meanings and life narratives; how one person comes to understand another's feelings, wishes, and fears. Freud moved from this exploration between analyst and analysand to an exploration of what happens among individuals in a society and between individuals and society.

The problem of living among others, living a political life, was the purview of an older Western intellectual heritage: political philosophy. Before Aristotle blithely proclaimed that happiness is the same for both the individual and society, Socrates tragically and personally addressed the relationship between the individual and society: when jailed by his city-state for corrupting youth and sentenced to death, he resisted Crito's urge to escape and live in exile; he poisoned himself out of love for his Athens. Later, Aristotle escaped his fellow Athenians' wrath, preventing them from twice sinning against philosophy.

New disciplines developed to address and examine the social contract. In the eighteenth and nineteenth centuries, with an emphasis on liberty, equality, as well as fraternity, a *sociologie* was created by Comte and further developed by Weber, Simmel, and Durkheim (Levine, 1986) to study relationships among individuals, society, and its institutions. Another conceptual framework, cultural anthropology (and later, history of religions) at the turn of the present century, began to examine the belief systems that influence our daily existence. These disciplines tend to portray individuals as passive recipients or responders to cultural and social milieus. Even a pragmatic sociologist such as Goffman (1961) focused on how individuals either adapt or maladapt to an institution's structure. Modern philosophy, for the most part, seemed to recede from the challenge of examining man's active life in a political community, portraying a sense of anomie or nausea (Arendt, 1978).

Arendt, deeply affected by the Eichmann trial, raised the need for critical thinking for man in secular society. Critical thinking protects us from:

> [The] cliches, stock phrases, adherence to conventional standardized codes of expression, and conduct [that] have the socially recognized function of protecting us against reality, that is, against the claim on our thinking attention that all events and facts make the virtue of their existence. (Arendt, 1978)

Here, psychoanalysis, as a study of meaning created among people, can make contributions. Psychoanalysis has honed self-critical thinking. It is based on honest self-reflection, and has from early in its history attempted to examine, even prescribe, how one can live not only with oneself but also with society. Freud extended psychoanalysis's conceptual framework to explore society's miseries. For instance, Freud was deeply affected by World War I and some suggest that his concept of Thanatos, the death drive, was related to the experience of the war, particularly his son's death (Freud, 1920). Wilhelm Reich, outside of his psychotic wanderings, acutely foresaw the individual's psychological difficulty and susceptibility to mass psychology, particularly in a Facist society. Fromm attempted to wed his psychoanalytic with his Marxist influences to suggest optimal relationships between man and society. And Bettelheim, culling from his and others' experiences in the Nazi concentration camps, moved our thinking about the individual and society's institutions from a reactive, even victimized, stance, such as that portrayed by political philosophy, sociology, anthropology, and even by some psychoanalytic writers, to a *mentally* active position.

Psychoanalytic Perspectives on Institutions

We therefore have several schools in Western thought that, at least since Socrates's time, have addressed the same concerns. This chapter uses a psychoanalytic perspective to address the issues of the individual and his relationship to his institutions. I use vignettes from institutions (schools and mental hospitals) that society has designed to help individuals, because I am most acquainted with these. I will focus an various members of these institutions—those to be helped as well as the intended helpers—in order to illuminate the living struggle that we continue to face with and within our institutions, despite the centuries that separate us from Aristotle and Socrates. We may agree with Aristotle that happiness should be the same for the individual and society's institutions. We need to define, however, what we mean by happiness in a democratic society that needs to balance an individual's autonomy with one's integration with society and with oneself.

A More Personal Motivation

I would like the reader to have some of my personal motivations for addressing this subject. There are many ways to keep alive the experiences, the lessons of the Nazi era, particularly the oppression and dehumanization in the concentration camps. Fortunately, I have seen nothing that comes near matching that horror. Nevertheless, one of Bettelheim's ideas is that the Nazi era and its concentration camps were extreme examples of a totalitarian society, extensions of modern mass society. As such, we can discover and examine qualitatively similar phenomena in modern mass society and be grateful that they are not quantitatively as extreme.

When I think or read about the Nazi era, the experiences are so extreme that they appear alien to our everyday life. From Bettelheim's perspective, however, the Nazi era was the beginning of a new way to control man and society, the first chapter in a history of totalitarianism. Given that, I found numerous examples of how even in a nontotalitarian society we are prone to the tendencies of a mass society.

For this chapter, I will present three professional encounters. However, I would first like to recount two personal experiences that galvanized my resolve to write this chapter. These are separated by some ten years, yet bring home dramatically opposing views of the concentration camp experience: On the one hand, that the camp experience endures traumatically, relentlessly across generations; on the other hand, that it has no psychological residue.

In the late 1970s, there was a surge of interest in children of survivors (who, although now adults, were still referred to as "children"). This was carried by the popular press in addition to the usual professional articles that make a business of creating syndromes. The *Chicago Tribune* Weekend Section had a large photograph of a young man and his three-year-old child. I was dismayed by his remark quoted in the caption. His parents had been in Nazi Germany. He said that every day he felt sad for his daughter, for she would suffer because she was a *child* of a *child* of concentration camp survivors. I felt anger at that father and sorrow for his child because this father abrogated personal responsibility for perpetuating what he felt were his psychological sufferings because of his parents' horrible experience in the camps. For him, this transmission of misery was inevitable.

It was my next experience, however, ten years later, that came while I was thinking about this chapter and that helped me to crystallize my thoughts.

On a flight to a professional meeting, my seatmate, by happenstance, was a psychiatrist. While I tried to work, he chattered. He was in his late sixties and had a thick German accent and name. He spoke of himself and his work as if I should know him. Near the end of this predominantly one-sided conversation, he noticed from my reading material that I worked with infants. He turned to me and in a conspiratorial tone said that he knew of a prominent infant researcher who had demonstrated, yet was reluctant to publish, that infants' experiences in the Newborn Intensive Care Unit did not have adverse psychological affect upon the infants afterward. Pleased by this, he added with a wink, "Just goes to show you, it's just like the concentration camps: no objective, bad effects years later." His remark took my breath away. As to why, it took me some months to sort: his self-satisfied judgment that the darkening experience of the concentration camps that cast such shadows upon men's souls would have no lasting effects; his arrogance that such effects would not be "objective," that is, measurable *by him*; his opinion that one could equate the life-draining, life-taking concentration camp with the life-sustaining intensive care unit. Yet, I was impressed that he could ignore the extraordinary and basic differences between a concentration camp and an intensive care unit, in order to justify his caustic view of the world.

As I reflected on these personal experiences and associated professional experiences, I recognized how often I turn to Bettelheim's work in order to make sense of such discrepant views.

AUTONOMOUS VERSUS ALIENATED RESPONSES TO INSTITUTIONAL VICISSITUDES

Although there are major differences among the settings to be discussed, they all share a basic function, that is, caring for a dependent population. To the extent that they are mainstream organizations, they reflect our society's attitudes about these dependent populations: they are focal settings, a confluence of the individual, the institution, and society.

Now, I can turn to professional vignettes that touched me personally and brought into palpable relief the issues of autonomy and integration for individuals in an institution.

The Impact of Research on Children and Staff in a Psychiatric Hospital

As a visitor to an academic hospital, I was invited to sit in on a weekly community meeting of eight- to fourteen-year-old children hospitalized for psychiatric reasons. The unit chief had been called away unexpectedly. His research became the substance of this meeting.

This children's unit housed twenty children, who stayed for three to four months, but occasionally up to nine or twelve months. There was a tradition of psychological research. The *new* research involved giving a drug, then drawing blood from a recently admitted, acutely disturbed child six times in two days. This was repeated several weeks later. The hospital had to approve all research with humans, as required by law. Therefore, this research was sanctioned.

The aim of the research was to determine which dose of the medication was effective for diagnosing (not even treating) depressed children. Depressed children, however, were not the only ones who received it. For research reasons, every child admitted received this series of tests. In addition to taking the blood samples, the children were given a special diet and medication.

Now to the children's meeting.

This research had never been discussed at community meetings, although we learned that both staff and children had been preoccupied with it. Today, with a new visitor and their unit chief not present, the children talked. All were incensed. They may have been psychologically disturbed: they certainly were articulate.

The children complained that they had not consented to this research. Their parents had. Some children knew that their parents did not understand that this was research or did not understand its nature. Several of the older children had canvassed the adolescents in a nearby ward and learned that those patients had to give personal consent for research. Why should not the children also be asked for consent, they inquired?

As one young fellow put it, "They have our parents' permission, but they don't have our permission. We are human beings."

And another, "They don't tell us no results. They use us as guinea pigs, like monkeys, goats." Or again, "They just take our blood, not for ourselves (but) for others, for medical students." (I learned that the medical students often were called to draw the late-night blood samples, awakening the children to do so, oftentimes needing two or three staff people to restrain the child.)

More to the point, "We pay $450.00 a day. We shouldn't be used as guinea pigs."

Followed by, "They took my blood six times in two days. They messed up my arm." (He was referring to extensive bruising.)

And with finality, "If I don't get an answer, I'm going to call a lawyer, man."

I asked what they thought this test was for. Here, some of their answers were poignant in their attempts at understanding. Said one, "Dex test. It's to test our dexterity."

I asked "What's dexterity?"

He said, "To see if you're nervous, dexterity."

Again, I wondered aloud, "Why can't they just ask you if you're nervous?"

"I don't know."

A younger child explained, "It's to see if your blood flows the right way."

A nine-year-old boy who had been admitted and had blood taken two days earlier said simply, "They hold us down, and I don't want (them) to take my blood." (I learned from the nurses that this boy's bloodletting also had been traumatic for them.) One young girl, nearing discharge and trying to be kind to the researchers, (perhaps in order not to jeopardize her upcoming discharge), said to her peers: "They want to find out if you have a disease or not." When the children pressed about what kind of disease, she said she did not want to talk about it. From the children and nurses, I learned that this girl tended to be masochistically compliant.

In the formal post-community staff meeting and in informal meetings, I learned the following. The nursing staff, even those devoted to the unit chief, were distressed by this bloodletting. Blood was drawn before breakfast, at midday, and at 11:00 PM. This was stressful, particularly in the early morning and late night—difficult transitional times for disturbed children in any case, times that are complicated by nursing shift changes. One morning, for instance, the nine-year-old mentioned above was so frightened of needles, let alone of his recent admission, that four nurses were needed to pin him down, while the resident physician made several unsuccessful blood-drawing attempts over a half hour. Since all four nurses were in the blood-drawing room, only the unit secretary could watch the remaining fourteen children. Many began congregating outside the blood-drawing room, both attracted to and made anxious by the screams of pain and fear. The nurses, who usually tried to make the transition to breakfast smooth, if not pleasant, were upset at how frightened and wild the other children were becoming outside the treatment room door. In addition, the staff felt guilty and angry about holding down a panicked nine-year-old for research. Further, as we discussed, one nurse candidly admitted that she was angry at the child because his struggling and screaming made her feel like an ogre. She found herself holding him more vigorously, even punitively, because the boy was making her job harder.

This, of course, is too reminiscent of the SS soldiers' anger directed at Jews when the Jews struggled against being rushed to slaughter. The Jews struggling made the SS feel guilty about killing, and in their anger at the Jews for making them feel guilty, they treated them more horribly.

How did the physician and staff feel about this? The resident physician confided that she drew blood in order to get a good letter of recommendation from the unit chief. Thus far, her participating and learning consisted only of drawing blood at the bedtime hours. She found this last episode with the 9-year-old most distressing. She wanted to write about these children's reactions to bloodletting, trying to understand them from a "cognitive perspective." She seemed unaware that this "cognitive perspective" was her attempt to distance her feelings from her acts. About one year later, I met her again. She said that although she still wanted to write the paper, she felt that doing so might jeopardize her relationship with the unit chief, even though she no longer worked at the institution.

The social worker was responsible for asking all parents of prospective admissions to give informed consent for the research. Although she was obligated to read the detailed legalistic informed consent to them, she was severely upbraided by the unit chief when one parent refused to consent. She was not alone in feeling this conflict between the explicit legal, ethical, and clinical obligation to fully inform parents versus the implicit message that in order for the research to be valid, not a single child should be excluded from the study. On one occasion, the nursing staff overheard two research assistants threatening a child: If he did not leave his art class to participate in the research interview, he would lose "privileges." The nurses having heard this were upset, but said nothing. They feared for their jobs if they interfered. Yet, they felt guilty about their complicity. This is an example of what Bettelheim referred to as restrictive actions, that is, those that are not legally sanctioned, yet complied with out of fear of one's superiors and at odds with one's values. Even the unit secretary, a mainstay since the unit's opening years ago, volunteered that if she were a parent, she would refuse to consent to this research.

Now, if I have presented this persuasively as I heard it, you may feel as appalled as I did. Any reasonable person would see that this was wrong and not justifiable, or so I thought. But we need not remind ourselves that when the facts of the horrors at Auschwitz were presented to Eichmann in Jerusalem, Arendt (1963) reports that he calmly and reasonably saw these in a different light and was willing to clarify this for his audience.

Arendt crisply states how Eichmann's language veiled his thinking, the "clichés, stock phrases" that her quote referred to earlier. Bettelheim (1960), in the *The Informed Heart*, enumerates a psychological defense as used by the SS for self-justification. After all, most were not psychopathic killers. These defenses I will review below. But for now, I would relay my discussion with the unit chief and his attempts to justify his research studies.

The unit chief reminds us of Arendt's cautionary scene from *Eichmann in Jerusalem*: that today we will find evil in rather banal individuals. Arendt describes this banality as a "manifest shallowness . . . (without) deeper levels of roots or motives. The deeds were monstrous, but the doer . . . quite ordinary. . . . The only notable characteristic (was) thoughtlessness" (Arendt, 1963). Now, this psychiatrist was not monstrous. His deeds, however, were marked by the same thoughtlessness pervaded with psychological clichés and stock phrases. He seemed well-meaning. He considered his chemical research as an extension of his early psychological research, but more valid: it might help future children (and it certainly would his career).

He seemed mildly taken aback, if not distressed, that the children raised this matter of the research in community meeting in his absence, particularly with a visitor. He was sufficiently sophisticated to gather that they did so because they did not feel comfortable doing this in his presence. His basic theme, however, was if only this were explained better to the children and parents, they would not object; if only the nurses had prepared the children better for the blood drawing, they would not be as upset; and if only the resident physician had used a smaller-bore needle, a steadier hand, she would not have had such difficulties. In fact, this psychiatrist was sufficiently knowledgeable about psychodynamic ideas that he suggested that the difficulty the staff was having marshaling compliance from both children and parents was due not to the staff's lack of knowledge or incorrect descriptions of the research, rather to the staff's conflict-ridden feelings about the research.

The psychiatrist suggested that the staff did not have their hearts in the matter and this was conveyed to the children. The staff was "acting out," he insisted. In turn, the unit chief continued, the children were acting out. Now, here was his coup de grace in this intellectualized battlefield. The unit chief, in a firm, didactic manner, upbraided the staff for getting the children and parents to act out the staff's personal conflicts about this research! Those of us who treasured psychodynamic or psycho-analytic language and ideas will recognize here how the language has become the "clichés and stock phrases" that Arendt says can protect us against reality. Bettelheim demonstrated that technical language and euphemisms helped protect the SS from thinking of Jews as human.

As I discussed this meeting privately with the unit chief, he fell back on the following. *He* was the unit chief. *He* was doing what the institution was asking him to. Staff and children could express their feelings about this research (although this was for him an administrative annoyance), but that would have no bearing on whether or how this research was done. And so it continued.

For the next vignette, I want to turn to a different setting: public school classrooms for emotionally disturbed children in which the problems and the feelings they engendered smoldered for months or years.

The Teacher's Frame of Mind: Autonomy versus Alienation in Classrooms for Emotionally Disturbed Children

On my first day as a psychiatric consultant to a large public school system's program for emotionally disturbed children, I braced myself to learn the jargon assigned by Public Law 94-142 for handicapped children: behaviorally disordered, emotionally disturbed, learning disabled, and educable mentally retarded. When I left the central downtown office to visit classrooms, I expected to find alienated youngsters and the occasional "burnt out" adult. But I was not prepared for what I did witness: teachers overwhelmed with alienation, anomie, and resentment. As I began to navigate through the fog of apathy, my attention shifted to the few teachers who were able to create a therapeutic environment. What distinguished them from their colleagues and enabled them to foster autonomy and hope, even in the most trying circumstances?

SETTING. The special education program for emotionally disturbed (ED) children was started in the 1970s under congressional mandate. By 1980, in the large city where I consulted, there were approximately fifty classrooms for emotionally disturbed children. The classes were quan-titatively well staffed: each classroom had a teacher and a teacher's aide for every five to six children. In addition, approximately six master teachers and an equal number of social workers were assigned to the program. Although funded for a consultant psychiatrist, for several years the pro-gram made do without.

By legal mandate, classrooms for these children were "mainstreamed" into various public schools. Prior to this, the classrooms had been segregated. As an extension of the Supreme Court's *Brown* decision, the separate-but-equal classrooms were found to be unconstitutional. In some cases, this "mainstreaming" was to the dismay of the local principal, others were accommodating. Resistant principals were concerned that these children would disrupt their peers in the regular classrooms. These principals showed resistance in the ways mentioned below.

Children were assigned to programs for the emotionally disturbed if they showed difficulties that reflected internal discord, such as severe sadness or withdrawal. Those children with more "antisocial tendencies" were assigned to a different program, that for behavioral disorders (BD); some teachers referred to these as the "BAD" kids. There was some crossover of both children and teachers between these programs.

When I began consulting, the entire school system faced a severe fiscal crisis. Teachers, unpaid for several weeks, were uncertain of their positions. Some were laid-off. Some were switched from one classroom, or even one job description, to another. Some who wanted to teach emotionally disturbed were transferred out because they lacked seniority. In some cases, the replacements were teachers with less interest in teaching the emotionally disturbed but with more seniority.

Teachers described chronic concerns that existed independently and preceded the financial problems. Some ED classrooms, at the principal's insistence, were placed in basements, converted bathrooms, or, in one case, a teacher's lounge that retained some of its original functions— teachers from other parts of the school would stop in and out to get their lunch or coffee during class time. Supplies were short, sometimes because they were bootlegged by other departments. Finally, the system was a political hostage to battles among black, Hispanic, and blue-collar white politicians.

Most of the classrooms were physically dismal with broken windows, torn shades, peeling paint, and bare walls. Some classrooms offered an appearance of external order: rules and regulations printed carefully on the blackboard, desks evenly in line. But such neat outward appearance did not preclude alienation.

One teacher had all the children face the front of the room while she sat in the back. The pupils were not permitted to turn around if they wanted to get her attention. They would raise their hands and she would decide to call them or not. They were not allowed to hand completed work to the teacher but deposited them in an envelope hanging on her desk. These teachers described their classrooms as "structured"; to an outsider it seemed that this rigidity exacerbated the disturbed child's preexisting alienation of inner feelings and thoughts from expressed thoughts and behavior.

ANOMIE: THE CLASSROOM OF SCREENS.   This teacher, like many others, was trying to manage a classroom with difficult children in an impersonal system. I met him in an informal session with several other teachers in the ED classrooms.

The principal of this school was unusual; he invited several ED classrooms under his supervision and encouraged primary-grade teachers to help those children who were showing early emotional difficulties. However, this particular teacher, Mr. L., had not chosen an ED classroom. He was certified in special education and had elected to teach in the BD classroom. Those children were delinquent and thus were judged administratively not to have emotional problems. When there were significant layoffs, Mr. L. opted to be transferred to an ED classroom. He had sufficient seniority to claim that position, but not enough to stake out his preferred BD classroom. With pugnacious pride, he claimed ignorance about teaching emotionally disturbed children.

I explained my interest in visiting his classroom some day. Mr. L., a massive man teaching nine- and ten-year-old children, had no objection to my visiting his classroom that day at my convenience. The children, he said, were accustomed to people walking into the classroom unannounced. Although I offered to defer my visit, he invited me to stop in.

The classroom was in good physical shape. The building was relatively new. There were five or six boys in the room, but only two or three were visible from the teacher's front desk. The others were obscured by freestanding barriers Mr. L. raised.[1] I thought I saw two boys at one desk behind a barrier by the back window. Mr. L. said that one was helping the other with arithmetic. We went to look in on them. Both were at one desk. One youngster still wore his coat and hood in this warm classroom; his head was on his desk buried in his folded arms. After some questions, he looked up, revealing the scalp stitches that he had hidden under his hood. He said he had cut his head after a fall from a roof the previous day and did not want people to see the wound. From the classroom's barriers, we could speculate that this boy felt that his teacher did not care to see the wound either.

The other boy was telling stories of mutilations he had seen in his life to the first child. He jumped anxiously from desk to window as he excitedly related his own injuries in life. The math book lay unopened on the desk.

Unfortunately, this vignette is not atypical (for some teachers, it may be too reminiscent). The teacher was not unfeeling, although he appeared more embarrassed before me than distressed by this child, who, he said, frequently sat in the school with his head buried.

There are many factors operating in a public school system that foster such a dismal scene: an overburdened, financially strapped, politicized, and (at that time) leaderless school system; societal antipathy to emotional disorders; parental abrogation of the responsibility for their children; a beleaguered teacher with his own family responsibilities who wants to retain his job even if it were in a classroom not of his own choosing. All of these factors contribute to some degree to the final scenario of two children emotionally lost behind a barrier. However, this denouement is not inevitable.

THE AUTONOMOUS CLASSROOM.   In the following classrooms the teachers were able to foster a therapeutic environment and impart to their students a sense of self-direction and independence.

The "Bricoleur."[2] Mr. M.'s high school classroom is strikingly different from Mr. L.'s. Although in a rather old building, the room is large, light, and airy. The space is subdivided into different functional areas within visual contact of each other: a library, a desk area, a carpeted lounge, a makeshift kitchen, a place for animals, and even a basketball hoop attached with wire to the airway vent. The walls are attractively decorated with artwork by the students and hung at different heights. When I entered, some students were working at their desks while the teacher, an aide, and other pupils ate lunch. The lounge, with two sofas and a patchwork carpet, is comfortable and welcoming.

Although the visual and tactile content of the room are appealing, the story of how the room was furnished is even more so. The students and teacher had decorated and furnished it at minimal or no expense. When the teacher saw secondhand sofas discarded in a nearby suburb, he and his students borrowed the school truck and brought them back. Because the legs were too tall, they sawed them off. To carpet the lounge area, the teacher approached carpet companies for scraps, gave them receipts for tax write-offs, and with the students sewed the scraps together.

When he found himself chronically short of art supplies to decorate the room, Mr. M. helped the students organize a brunch for the art teachers. Subsequently, the art teachers donated the art scraps instead of discarding them. When he needed more bookshelves, Mr. M. had one student build shelves into what became their "library." The "locked storage closets" were old school lockers that he salvaged from the back alley and had repainted in bright primary colors. When he wanted his students to use the swimming pool, he volunteered to be the school basketball coach in return for the pool time.

Perhaps I can best characterize the process in terms that are meaningful to the emotionally disturbed youngster. The teacher's message to the students is that it is possible to salvage and rehabilitate physical objects and, implicitly, the emotional parts of themselves that others felt should be discarded. Like the *bricoleur* (artist/craftsman), this teacher took discarded fragments and put them together imaginatively to create new meaning, new value.

The "Bricoleur's" Assistant. The effect of this teacher's approach is reflected in the case of a young man the teacher asked me to see. Mr. M.'s concern was that the young man, who otherwise enjoyed being in his class, was absent from school periodically to refurbish a dilapidated, abandoned building near his home. His teacher was also concerned that the boy catch up on his math. This seventeen-year-old, whom I shall call Joe, had been expelled from another high school for blatant, frequent drug use and truancy. To be expelled on such grounds was no minor accomplishment; the former school was notorious for and inured to drug traffic. He was quite hardened and skeptical of schools and teachers.

Joe's father had died recently. Since that time, he was in frequent conflict with his mother. He used the house he was rehabilitating to get away from her when he felt they might come to blows.

When I entered the class, I found Joe sitting with his back to me, hunched over his math book. He was expecting me. His hands reflected hard, physical labor: dirt was ground under the fingernails and into the crevasses of his knuckles. Otherwise, he was clean, although his clothes were threadbare. When I asked about his renovated house, he brightened and told me how he had refurbished it imaginatively, had bought furniture, and protected his new home-away-from-home. He had studied the history of that old neighborhood. All of the houses on this block, he told me, looked as if the first floor were the basement, because they were built before there were sewer systems. When the city put in sewers (he knew these dates), they had to raise the street level, so that the first floor was below and the second floor at street level.

This house and the one nearby had been abandoned by absentee landlords. "His" house had been torched. He plasterboarded each room whenever he had the money for materials. The kitchen stove did not work, so he replaced it with a Franklin-type stove from the basement for both heating and cooking. Because of vandalism, he had learned which locks were vandal-resistant and protected the front door with these. He was trying to contact the landlord so that some day he might buy the house. Although his teacher was realistically worried about the dangers of Joe's neighborhood, I suggested that he not discourage the boy's efforts. As for arithmetic, I recommended that he work out scale models of his new home.

In rehabilitating an abandoned building, this young man had identified successfully with his teacher and in so doing had developed a sense of self-direction and responsible freedom.

DISCOVERING "CHARLIE BROWN."   The next teacher asked me to visit her classroom of eight- to ten-year-olds. She wanted me to meet a child who periodically spoke as if he were the cartoon character Charlie Brown. While he did all of his academic work well, often with obsessive detail, he would whisper dialogues between Charlie Brown and other "Peanuts" characters. During his work or classroom activity, he might burst into laughter.

Before entering the classroom, I met his teacher as she was breakfasting with the children. Unlike some other teachers who stood chatting with each other, she did not leave the children to talk with me until she could find another teacher to watch them. As she told me about the Charlie Brown character, she asked reluctantly whether she should "extinguish this behavior." I asked her what she thought about this. She seemed ambivalent. Her teacher's education had taught her to "extinguish undesirable behavior." Yet intuitively, she knew that Charlie Brown was a precious creation of this boy's inner life that should not be snuffed out.

As we talked, she realized that the Charlie Brown tale could open up a line of communication with this child's inner self. She became curious about which character she played in his work of Charlie Brown. By participating in this child's world in a nonintrusive manner, she recognized that she might be able to understand the meaning of his laughter.

The classroom space was the one briefly noted above: a cramped, partly converted teacher's lounge. Teachers walked in and out to store and retrieve their lunches or snacks. Yet, the room was busily quiet and the children seemed comfortable at my "intrusion." The teacher's attitude overcame the physical limits of the classroom and the potential disruptions by visitors. As I left, this woman described her successes in her three years teaching these emotionally disturbed children. As importantly, she admitted how much the children contributed to her own personal development.

The teacher understood intuitively that the children's symptoms were creative acts which she could value and treasure. In some cases her reactions to the symptoms taught her about herself. Her attitude of learning from the child the meaning of the symptom—valuing rather than eliminating the symptom—fostered the child's self-esteem. The teacher's efforts to learn with the child about his or her inner life leads the child to feel that there is something valuable about himself or herself.

ANTIQUES IN THE JUNK SHOP.   Mr. S. was one of the six master teachers who supervised approximately eight to ten ED classrooms in one area. He, like the other master teachers, met regularly with classroom ED teachers to discuss pedagogical techniques in problem children.

The classroom teachers had varied reactions to these supervisors. Some felt that the master teachers were only dabblers in teaching who had no real expertise at "roll-up-your-sleeves" teaching of disturbed children. Many considered them unwanted intrusions from downtown who would criticize and, possibly, jeopardize the classroom teachers' position. Consequently, the master teachers were often challenged with concrete and, occasionally, impossible tasks such as "get this crazy kid out of my classroom."

Mr. S., however, was popular among his group of teachers and their children, probably because when he came to visit, he offered to teach antiquing—one of his loves. He could detail the differences among Southwest American Indian, early twentieth-century rugs, distinguishing between a "Two-Gray-Hills" from an "Eye Dazzler." On one occasion, he might describe the plant sources of the dyes used and their manufacture, or he would describe a new find, like the Early Prairie-Style chair, discovered in a junk store, now standing in his living room. Mr. S. could explain how the Prairie Style influenced Frank Lloyd Wrights's architecture in the city or a nearby suburb.

The youngsters were enchanted by the idea that this man could roam the local junk stores and spot antiques among the debris. Mr. S.'s interest in antiques evolved out of his work as a counselor in a renowned residential treatment center for emotionally disturbed children, which had lovely antiques as well as contemporary art throughout the living quarters. In fact, once a child was admitted, he or she could help design an emblem for the tall, custommade headboard of his or her bed.

After several years, Mr. S. noticed that he had a favorite antique table. As he found himself fingering the grain and admiring the color and texture, he realized that he wanted to learn more about it and so became engrossed in the history of early twentieth-century design. Subsequently, he became a teacher in the public school system and brought his love of antiques into the classroom. In working as a master teacher, like Johnny Appleseed, he sowed his interest wherever he visited.

I found myself, like the teachers and children, entranced with his descriptions. The emotional message for these disturbed children was like that of the *bricoleur*: one could find something aesthetically valuable in the ruins of the past. He was neither afraid nor confused by the past, as are many disturbed children who live the past as a recurrent nightmarish present. Furthermore, he imparted to the children the idea that one must take great care of restoring an antique—too rigorous a job could destroy its value. In fact, a good cleaning may be all that it needs. On the other hand, an antique might look quite good and yet be quite fragile, too fragile a chair to sit in.

The *bricoleur* finds debris and reassembles it in such a way that we see our world with new aesthetic meaning: the antiquarian discovers valuables from the past, takes care not to modify them significantly, and studies how to integrate them with other antiques and contemporary pieces. These metaphors are valuable to the emotionally disturbed child, for this is how personality reintegration takes place, as Bettelheim wrote in *Home for the Heart* (1974). One does not buy or create a completely new personality de novo. Rather, one needs to assess the elements of the personality, disassemble some, rehabilitate others, and rebuild that structure. Dante knew this when, dissatisfied with his life in his middle age, he understood he had to descend to the Inferno, to Hell, to his beginnings, to reevaluate and reconstruct the foundation of his being. There he needed to engage a guide, Virgil, the poet of reason.

A FRAME OF MIND. In a sprawling urban public school system, besieged with difficulties, the possible causes of alienation appear endless. The recent fiscal crisis associated with cutbacks in federal aid are an obvious scapegoat. Yet, as teachers described it, the same malady of anomie had existed before that fiscal crunch. Another source of problems is the difficulty of helping children who are subject to a grim array of sociocultural pressures, notably poverty, neglect, and, in some cases, abusive parents. Understandably, many of these children were mistrustful of teachers and the school system in general. There are other sources of alienation that spring from the dynamics of the classroom itself. Many teachers identify with and exhibit symptoms similar to those of their disturbed students, a psychological phenomenon described by Erving Goffman (1961) and Bruno Bettelheim (1974). Clearly, these factors contribute to alienation.

How do some teachers, like modern-day Virgils, guide their youthful Dantes through the Inferno of life's vicissitudes?

I suggest that the differentiating variable is the human resource often overlooked in the politicized debates over education: the frame of mind that recognizes value and possibility in society's castoffs. A caring, vibrant teaching approach stems from this perception. Congress can legislate PL 94-142 classrooms for handicapped children, a small student–teacher ratio, teachers' credentials for special education, and other external factors, but they cannot legislate a frame of mind.

I couch my comments in a note of caution. We know from extreme situations, such as the concentration camp, that an external environment can have profound effects on an individual's integration. I do not want to suggest that I believe in some form of social Darwinism in which those teachers who create an atmosphere of autonomy in our classrooms are necessarily hardier than their colleagues and that the surrounding external impingements should not be changed. Nevertheless, those teachers who give up in despair and place complete blame on a truly disorganized school system succumb to one of the dangers of living in a mass society: the loss of their individuality.

In summary, the general characteristic of teachers who could foster an autonomous atmosphere in their classroom was their capacity to circumscribe an area, an observational frame of reference, over which they had some potential control. The three teachers in these vignettes implicitly, or on some occasions explicitly, communicated the following to their children. First, they had high regard for what comes from the child. Second, they fostered an atmosphere of hopefulness. Third, that atmosphere was nonjudgmental, while maintaining a clear idea of physical safety in the classroom. Fourth, they showed their regard for the value of history. Fifth, by valuing history, they communicated to the child a view that psychological remediation depended on using the building blocks of his current personality in order to build a new personality.

Education of the Soul: Selling an Institution's Soul—When Psychotherapy Becomes Secondary to Profit

Now, I would like to turn from a system beset by chronic difficulties and devoted to education of the mind to an acute crisis in a psychiatric hospital, an institution allegedly committed to education of the soul.

In this next vignette, I focus on therapists' reactions to learning that their long-standing, well-established mental hospital was to be sold to a private, for-profit organization. Therapists set the stage for the interpersonal milieu. I identify their various reactions over several months when they learned that the purported purpose of the institution—treatment of emotionally disturbed patients—became secondary to a new purpose—making money.[3]

Unlike other facilities, this psychiatric hospital had made money for many years. It was prestigious, its beds were filled, and it attracted a coterie of devoted faculty who worked long hours for modest pay. Despite its near-urban location, the hospital had a lovely setting of many acres. Because some psychiatric stays are relatively lengthy, most faculty, the patients, and their families considered this setting a necessary asset.

However, the psychiatric hospital became associated with several general medical hospitals, sharing a joint board of trustees. Its modest profits propped up these facilities. In recent years, with greater medical competition and decreased government funding, the associated medical facilities hemorrhaged millions of dollars.

Hence, the board's decision to sell the exquisite grounds to a private corporation that would cover the landscaped area with shopping plazas, office buildings, and luxury apartments. Psychiatric buildings would remain, although managed by a private for-profit hospital corporation, for whom the faculty would now work.

LAYING THE GROUND WORK. The board of trustees attempted to use what Bettelheim referred to as restrictive actions, those not legally proscribed, to press the physicians of their own volition to follow the board's wishes. Before announcing the sale, the board confidentially asked the clinical director to appoint an ad hoc committee of prominent faculty to report on the minimum amount of land the psychiatric facility needed to function. The faculty heard rumors. The final report was leaked. To the faculty's dismay, the director and committee, thought to be committed to the therapeutic value of these grounds, recommended to the board that only a small rim of bushes and lawn was needed: after all, the hospital's major therapeutic asset was its faculty. Now what faculty member would care to argue against the latter!

Only after this report was made public did the board schedule a joint meeting with the faculty and the purchasing corporation to say that the board was accepting this ad hoc committee's recommendations.

Another device the board used was infantilization. When the board became aware that a core of physicians were opposed to the sale, the board invited what they thought were the ringleaders to a small meeting. At the meeting, the ringleaders were each given a personalized package of colored pencils and a map of the grounds. They were told that each color represented a degree of importance, blue being most important and red being least important, with intermediate colors. On their personalized map of the hospital grounds, sectors were divided up. The chairman of the board then asked the senior physicians to use their colored pencils to help the board decide what could be sold. The senior faculty busily went to work on their coloring books. It was only after this meeting that they could reflect angrily on how infantilized they felt as they, like kindergartners, had abrogated their autonomy to this authority figure.

THE CLINICAL DIRECTOR AND FACULTY'S REACTION.[4] The faculty had been deeply committed to the clinical director. Their reaction, in part, needs to be understood in terms of the director's public reaction. The general categories of faculty reaction were those who openly resisted the sale, those who openly supported it (a small number), and the majority who either quietly resisted or who fearfully demurred yet opposed the sale.

The clinical director had a reputation among the faculty as being forthright and powerful. He spoke tersely and candidly. He was more respected than liked. With the sale, his manner changed. In the first public meeting of the faculty, trustees, and developer, the director spoke mincingly, carefully selecting his words. He sounded like the worst kind of bureaucrat. As the chairman of the board of trustees and the developer stood in front of the auditorium, the clinical director stood at the side, next to—and almost hidden—by one of the columns. This was an unusual position for this proud man, in an institution where rank was graphically portrayed by who sat closest to front and center.

In private faculty meetings, his careful stance was mitigated by an almost conspiratorial tone. He leaked news from board meetings about future maneuvers, then warned the faculty that if anyone repeated what he said outside the meeting, he would publicly deny what he had just said. He suggested countermoves that might delay the board, while denying that he was encouraging any faculty member to oppose the board. He states that he would oppose any punitive act by the board against a faculty member, citing academic freedom. Then he warned that nonfaculty staff could be fired for such action. Nontenured faculty (the majority) felt uncertain about his protection.

The clinical director recounted and lamented previous directors' unsuccessful attempts to oppose the board on lesser matters. His approach was to try to salvage as much as was salvageable: to minimize the losses. This is reminiscent in quality, although certainly not in degree, of the ghetto leaders, the *Judenrat*, who would mollify the populace as cattle car loads were being set to the camps. Some, like Rumkowski, the King of Lodz, sincerely saw themselves as protectors, not collaborators. For the hospital faculty, this was a shocking transformation.

FACULTY REACTION. The faculty reacted in various ways that were not easily explainable by demographic characteristics. Some tenured faculty openly resisted the prospective plans, but many were quiet or acceded. Other nontenured faculty either resisted or acceded. Those faculty who were psychodynamically oriented, that is, committed to the impact of human and environmental influences on the psychological rehabilitation of the patient, might be expected to resist such a change. But many of these individuals did not. On the other hand, some faculty who were biologically oriented, that is, as one said, believing in "only what comes out the end of a needle," openly resisted the prospective sale.

But as mentioned above, there were four major categories of reaction: some openly and actively resisted the sale; a large number were quiet activists; many were quietly, even fearfully, uninvolved; and a minority supported the sale. To demonstrate some of the diversity of the individuals in each one of these groups, I will describe specific individuals.

The Active Resisters. The paragon for active resisters was one woman faculty member who was relatively senior. At the first public meeting with the board of governors, after listening quietly to much of the discussion, this woman arose and articulately, poetically, clearly, and unambivalently described the prospective plans as a rape of the land and the destruction of the therapeutic environment that was necessary for the psychological rehabilitation of these patients. After that opening salvo and despite colleagues' concerns about her status at the institution, she disclaimed fear for her position and continued actively organizing resistance to the prospective sale. Interestingly, she also was very protective of the clinical director, saying that she was concerned that he could be fired since he had an administrative position. Psychoanalytically oriented and an environmental activist, this woman believed strongly that the human and physical milieu were critical to the psychological rehabilitation of severely disturbed patients who often needed stays for many months or even years. She was able to organize not only other vociferous activists, but also to enlist the support of quieter activists.

Another open activist was a relatively young, although tenured, faculty member who was biologically oriented. When asked why he resisted the sale, he explained that as a Jew who had lost relatives to the Nazi concentration camps, he wanted to be able to tell his children he stood up openly when he was faced with making a moral decision about protecting an environment that he felt was needed for a patients' well-being.

A third activist surprised many faculty. She was an elderly woman who had grown up in the neighborhood and had been a junior faculty member for many years. Previously, faculty had thought of her as rather doddering, possibly even senile. In fact, she was quite articulate and effective in organizing resistance to the prospective plan. Her reason was rather straightforward: she had grown up in the neighborhood and had a personal attachment to the grounds, continued to live on the grounds, and was willing to remain at the institution, even though she had been passed over for many promotions. Her attachment, after all, was a very personal one to individual trees, the pond, and paths on the grounds.

The Quiet Activists. A larger number of faculty fell into the category of quiet activists. They tended to be those who were nontenured. They became involved by contributing money or even attending private meetings, but rarely spoke up at public faculty meetings. One young man, typical of this group, had been one of the rising stars in the faculty and had received accolades for his clinical, administrative, and research work. He became tentatively involved in the resistance, contributing money, researching the history of the grounds in order to support its historical value, and attending meetings at private homes. He did not publicize his involvement, although he did not deny that he was involved if asked directly.

The institutional reaction to him appeared insidious at the time, although it seems clearer in retrospect. For the first time since he had arrived, his immediate superior (who claimed quietly to support resistance to the grounds sale) became critical of his work, even though this same superior had previously promoted him for awards. He was denied tenure and was passed up for promotion. Shortly thereafter, this fellow left the institution to continue a very successful career elsewhere.

A second person in this category was a young tenured faculty member who contributed substantial amounts of money and buttonholed others at meetings or in the hallway to try to find out what the status of the resistance was and whether additional money or community support were needed. Nevertheless, he never openly spoke up at faculty meetings and was concerned that he might harm his status at the institution if he did so.

The Fearfully Uninvolved. Many faculty fell under this category and seemed to be those who were young and not tenured. Interestingly, a good number of them left the faculty shortly after this episode and left academia for more lucrative private practice settings. When interviewed, none of the three I will cite here made a conscious connection between this episode and their decisions to leave behind the modest academic salary for a money-making career.

The first faculty member was someone who, although young, had followed a very rigorous, lengthy academic career and was psychodynamically oriented. In addition to being an environmentalist and ornithologist, he had been living on the grounds. He was well-born and committed to the very specific and narrow kind of psychodynamically oriented work that could be found in only a few hospitals around the country such as this one.

His immediate reaction to the sale was a fearful one, but it was the kind of fear that Dostoyevski describes in *Notes from Underground* of the mouse that runs to his hole, hiding and shuddering, at the same time regretting that he did not have the gumption to strike back. In private conversations, he rationalized that he could have no impact on these prospective plans. He did not admit to concerns about an adverse impact upon his career, should he openly confront the board.

He decided shortly thereafter to abandon what had been his lifelong dream of professional work and to enter a very lucrative private practice. He did so with a vengeance. Leaving his very modest salary, he bought a house that was far beyond his means, opened two offices, and involved himself in serious indebtedness, buying someone's private practice and charging rather steep fees in an already competitive area. During all this, he described a sense of impoverishment (to his academic colleagues) as well as his determination never to work for an institution again. Even when he said the latter, he resisted suggestions that there was a connection between his sudden and radical change in his professional career and the recent episode at the institution.

The second faculty member had a similar reaction, although a different background. This woman was biologically oriented, but enjoyed working in an academic environment and living on the grounds. When the plans were announced, she refused to be involved in active opposition, even though her husband, who was not a faculty member, became an open activist. This woman asked her husband to stop being involved for fear that her academic career would be harmed, despite the medical director's lukewarm assurances. Nevertheless, shortly thereafter, she accepted a position and became a very successful partner in a private medical corporation. She left what she claimed to be her desire: to remain within an academic setting committed to education and research.

The third faculty member was relatively new, having left private practice to return to psychiatric research. He was independently wealthy, yet when approached to contribute funds, said that he was really quite short of funds at the time because he had recently bought some new suits. Although strongly psychodynamically oriented and invested in environmental aesthetics, he reacted apathetically to the prospective plans, denying that it affected him at all. Within a few months, he left for a lucrative, nonteaching job at a private for-profit corporation, saying that he felt it was important for his lifestyle to make more money.

The Sellouts. There were only a handful of faculty members in the category of those who supported the board of trustees. They were viewed by other faculty members as sellouts. I will cite one as an example. This faculty member had been at the institution for many years, even living on the grounds. He was tenured and was seen as a company man. He had been known prior to that as one who dwelled in the shadow of intellectual greats. Shortly after the board of trustees made their announcement, he not only supported them in public faculty meetings but also called several newspapers which quoted him as saying that the lovely environment of the grounds was not healthy for psychiatric patients! Instead, those patients should be exposed to the rough-and-tumble environment of urban life so that they would be better prepared for discharge. Although one could make such an argument, this was certainly at odds with what he and his colleagues had been saying and practicing for decades.

DÉNOUEMENT

I have selected three different settings to study the individual's relationship with his institution during periods of crisis: an in-patient child psychiatry unit, special education classrooms, and a large mental hospital for adults.

I began this chapter with Aristotle's (1962) rhetorical question whether happiness is the same for the individual and the state. He answers that it is the same. The vignettes suggest that happiness can be the same, but not necessarily so. We need to clarify what we mean by happiness. To some degree, this changes with eras and with cultures. Psychoanalytic and psychodynamic thinking, with its indebtedness to intellectual heirs (Nietzsche (1968, 1985), Weber (1948, 1949), Hobbes (1968), Locke (1968), and others), and recent experiences in mass society (such as the Nazi concentration camps) add new dimensions to how we think of the balance between an individual's and society's happiness. Bettelheim (1979) suggests that the concordance of opposites, a philosophical concept, becomes the task for the individual living in a mass society, as he attempts to balance autonomy and integration.[5]

In order to clarify the contribution of psychodynamic thinkers, particularly Bettelheim's perspective on the individual and society, I would like to juxtapose it to other intellectual perspectives that tend to view the individual in more universal terms and as a more atomistic, heteronomous member of society and its institutions, particularly Max Weber and Erving Goffman from a sociological prospective and Michel Foucault from a historical prospective.

Weber (1948, 1949), using a more diachronic framework, predicted a relentless, deadening rationalization and bureaucratization of society and its institutions, suffocating the liveliness of human diversity. Foucault (1973), also following a temporal perspective (or, to use his phrase, "a genealogical dimension"), portrays society's "problematization" of previously normative aspects of being (desire, sexuality, madness, or punishment). Goffman (1961), using a more synchronic framework, portrays the individual against the institution and individuals struggling pathetically to accommodate to a total institution, that is, one that handles "many human needs by one bureaucratic organization of whole blocks of people" (Goffman, 1961, p. 6).

With all three thinkers, we find a sense of inevitability with little focus on the individual's freedom of choice about his inner world. Rather, at best there is some middling accommodations to the institution's dehumanizing influence. Goffman's examples are nominal accommodations to an institution at the cost of loss of autonomy and paradoxically of integrity.

This pessimistic view of institutions leaves us with a society peopled with individuals who, like Nietzsche's "last man," find equilibrium in uncreative conformity and mild hedonism. This is the type of man in whom Hannah Arendt discovered the banality of evil. Is this inevitable?

From Weber (1948), we sense the power, the enormity of a society or an institution, but little sense of what the individual can do. From Goffman, particularly in *Asylums* (1961), we have the details of a total institution's oppressive weight and individuals' sad machinations to accommodate to that. From Foucault (1973), we sense how good it was among the Greeks and how, subsequently, society has made problems of normal, libidinal feelings. From Nietzsche (1985) we have an evocative presentation of the individual's existential dilemma and the individual's options to become a "last man" or to become a superman, not weakened by Judeo-Christian teachings. None of these are satisfactory or palatable. But let us consider these in more detail.

A Socio-Logie

The purview of sociology has been the relationships among an individual, his society, and its institutions. This was recognized by the founders of sociology: Comte's (Levine, 1986) distinction between the individual's intellect versus the organization of knowledge and rational systems; Toennies's (1971) pairing of rational will versus its manifestation in the constitutional forums and judicial agencies of *Gesellschaft*. Ironically, throughout sociological writing, as recently as Parsons (Levine, 1986), the recognition of this dilemma is often put in such abstract emotionally distancing terms, as if to compound the sociological observation of the individual alienated from increasingly rationalized institutions. The sociologist's words alienate. There are few exceptions, notably Levine's (1986) study of ambiguity or Simmel's (1971) portrayal of ambiguous concepts in relatively simple words.

It was Weber, an interpretative sociologist, who adopted sociology even as he abjured its practitioners, who come closer, I believe, to setting the modern dilemma in "feeling-near" words. Modern man is faced with bondage to inanimate machinery (the factory system) and bondage to animate machinery (the bureaucracies). Paradoxically, as we develop greater rationalization of our institutions (economic, political, legal, medical, psychiatric), we face impingement upon personal freedom.[6]

Weber's (1948) sensitivity to cultural differences or balances in institutional structures brings him closer to the cultural anthropologists than most sociologists (Boon, 1985). In this sense, Weber's work lies closer to the heart of a *socio-logie*, a mode of studying what early anthropologists such as Boas (1911/1965) thought would be contained in a true anthropology. But what choices does Weber's stark portrayal of the individual's dilemma in modern mass society leave the individual reader?

As we read, we feel the progressive deadening, apparently insuperable, movement that bureaucratic rationalization of society's institutions hold in store for the individual. In public hospitals, we hear this in the stock phrase, "This isn't in my job description," as a registered nurse, for instance, refuses to bathe a patient, looking for a licensed nurse, who in turn looks for a nurse's aide. The stark view of man in modern society does not bring us much hope or sense of direction, nor, to my knowledge, does it focus on the individual's responsibility or sense of action, although some recent sociologists attempt this (Levine, 1986).[7]

Total Institutions

The institutional settings in this chapter are those designed to serve a dependent social class. The mental hospital is a total institution in Goffman's terms. Its target members, mental patients, are absolutely dependent on the institution for all aspects of the daily care—food, shelter, and vocation/avocational activities. The institution is charged with some moral aims—to help patients function better in society. (In too few institutions, the major aim is also to feel better rather than only function better.)

The school system, although strictly speaking not a total institution, is designed for a highly dependent population—our children—and therefore carries more weight in their lives than would a comparable institution designed for adults (universities or workplaces). Children are legally obligated to attend schools with few (religious) exceptions. Furthermore, the school's charge from society is to inculcate societal values, a charge that we do not put on our universities or workplaces in Western society. In the example I cite, special (ED) classrooms for children who are designated as deficient or defective, the children are more dependent or in need of greater help than their peers in regular classrooms. This brings the ED setting closer to a total institution.

Goffman's work remains the most incisive sociological study of the mental institution. *Asylums* (1961) does not read as impersonally, as abstractly as many of the preceding sociologists' works. Perhaps this reflects the very personal manner by which Goffman carried out his research. By posing as a mental health technician,[8] rather than the Ph.D. researcher he was, Goffman was sufficiently close to the patients to learn the social structure among them and between them and staff. Perhaps as a patient he might have learned more from the patients, but certainly less from the staff.

The thrust of Goffman's work is that the mental institution is more like other total institutions (the army, the monastery, the prison) than not. More specifically for this chapter, the mental institution, with its too complex bureaucratic organization, puts the patient in a position of busily figuring out the external bureaucratic structure, rather than reflecting on his or her inner structure. Bettelheim captured this sad paradox—the patient, too disturbed to function in a complex world outside the hospital, is placed in a hospital world that is often more complex.

As valuable as Goffman's work is to our understanding of the mental institution,[9] his sociologic perspective leaves us with a portrait of individuals buffeted, if not overwhelmed, by an impersonal institution, one allegedly (ironically) designed for the individual's well-being and needs. Although Goffman's study is an important first step, it leads us back to our initial question. How does an individual maintain a sense of autonomy in modern mass society's institutions? The answer is complicated by knowing that these institutions are filled with individuals with different roles—patients, physicians, nurses, aides, people who clean, who serve food, or emotionally disturbed children, their teachers, and principals.

We shift from what is to what ought to be, as we move from sociology to Arendt's political philosophy, a discipline also preoccupied with the relationship between the individual and his society.[10]

"What is versus what ought to be" may be an artificial distinction, for even an early political philosopher such as Aristotle studied and cataloged the political systems and their associated institutions (such as the home) before suggesting what ought to be. Certainly in the *Republic*, a blueprint for what ought to be, Plato based his "oughts" on the shortcomings of existing republics. Hannah Arendt follows this tradition. Her work, *Thinking* (1971), was inspired, perhaps driven, by two preoccupations. The first, and of interest to this chapter, was what existed—the unusual, blandly malignant evil of the Nazi era recounted in Eichmann's trial. The second was the paradox that the *vita contempliva* was traditionally considered passive as opposed to the *vita activa*, when, in fact, philosophers and other thinkers often described themselves as most active when contemplating. But this is of secondary concern for this chapter.

From such a basic and evidently personally wrenching experience as the Eichmann trial, Arendt discovered a new form of evil: one that was banal and related to a society so suffused with technological thinking that it imbued its bureaucrats, such as Eichmann, with the ability to think of humans as so many pieces of material to be processed. Claude Lanzman's (1985) powerful interviews with the SS in his movie, *Shoah*, demonstrated how these men continue to think of their work as technocrats, processing people as if they were material. Bettelheim recounts the power of this impersonal language to permit the doer to perform horrible acts impersonally. Arendt hypothesizes that a lack of a basic form of thinking may be at the root of such evil. She speaks of thought that is invested in the process of thinking, much like Socrates's aporetic arguments, rather than the thought that is primarily end- or content-directed. The latter is the thought needed to make hammers, run football games, design administrative flow charts, or murder Jews efficiently.

Let us look at this more closely. Like Arendt, I ask that we not leave such apparently high-flown ideas, such as thinking about thinking, to professional philosophers. Like Socrates, we should take our concerns to the public square.

The Process of Teaching and Healing

I suggest that the institutions described in this chapter—mental hospitals and schools—share at least one basic quality. When we are doing things right, we are invested in not only the end result (getting patients healthier, students smarter), but also in the pleasure of the process of such thinking. When these institutions are invaded by those who value end-result thinking, such as those who buy hospitals, bottom-line men, this threatens the fabric of those institutions. Teachers, physicians, and the like, when they do work well, find excitement in the process by which a patient discovers a moment of enlightenment or when a child pleasurably and yet effortfully reworks a task, without diminishing the value of the end result. This is similar to a mother's pleasure in watching her ten-month-old work at getting up on his knees and hands to crawl. Most certainly, a mother celebrates the final product—crawling. However, part of what sustains her through the months and years of work is the lively process. If mothers, teachers, and doctors were only interested in the bottom line, like businessmen or manufacturers, they would simply wait for the annual report, looking into the manufacturing process only if they see a decline of productivity.

In fact, we note that even in the United States, a society successfully devoted to how to make money, education has remained outside of the money-making sphere. Even private schools, where the wealthy can send their children, are not private in the sense of a private corporation—that is, devoted to generating income for a group of investors. Is this not a sign of societal recognition that profit-taking and education are fundamentally incompatible? I do not mean for this to be a diatribe against making money; there is much to be said for it. I ask only that we recognize that within our society there are institutions whose basic character would be adversely affected if that became their primary aim.

In this sense, I follow Weber's demonstration that different institutions within the same society have different characteristics. He did not apply this to education or mental health institutions; rather, he applied this in comparing tolerance–intolerance attitudes across different cultures with regard to religion and language. In any case, today this proscription of the profit motive is being breached in the two institutions discussed, psychiatric (corporate medical) and education (day-care centers), much to the detriment of their recipients and care givers.

The three vignettes demonstrate how complex it is for us to balance the nature of happiness for the individual, society, and its institutions in Western thought. (This may be less of a difficulty in some Oriental thought.) Psychoanalytic and psychodynamic thinkers, like Bettelheim, help us understand the individual's inner life, not only how it can be reactive, but also how it can be moved into action. There has been some distortion of psychoanalytic thinking that the individual's hedonistic needs are impinged upon by society and should be placed above society's needs. It is certainly true that psychoanalytic thinking suggests that there may be conflict between an individual's need and society's. Freud (1930) suggests that that may be the price of civilization. However, Erikson (1950, 1968), Bettelheim, and others have elaborated that this unavoidable conflict is a price well worth paying. In contrast, L. Takeo Doi (1982) suggests that in Japanese society the malaise may not be the individual against society, but the individual who cannot feel dependent upon society and its members. What can we now do with this enriched understanding of the individual from psychoanalytic thinking as well as a rather rich understanding of society from other fields?

The Third Step to Insight and Autonomy

For a paradigm of how to approach the problem, let us listen to Bettelheim's suggestion about the three steps in successful psychoanalysis, remaining aware that one cannot simply draw conclusions from the consulting room to life outside it. In a successful analysis, the first step the patient often takes is reciting what evils have been done unto him by others (mother, father, siblings, and so forth). For the second step, the patient says "Look what has become of me because of what evils have been done unto me." In unsuccessful analyses or in parlor discussions of analysis, these are the only two steps taken and taken repeatedly: look what has been done to me by these people and look what has become of me because of that.

Bettelheim suggests that there is an important third step for a successful analysis, that is, one that fosters the individual's autonomy. "Look at what I have contributed to the outcome of my inner life." That contribution may be minimal compared to what was done to the individual, but that contribution is potentially within his control. He may have little effect over what was done to him in the past, perhaps more effect upon what has become of him, but certainly much effect upon how he has contributed to what he is and how he maintains what he has become.

I suggest that we can extend this to the individual within the institutions and particularly so with a democratic society, where the individual's contribution has potentially more impact. It is easier to see what a society or institution has done to an individual. It is more complex to see the second step, that is, what becomes of the individual, because it is influenced by the third step, what the individual contributed to his misery. For instance, we can look at the victims in the most extreme institution, the concentration camp. Although there are general ways in which they reacted similarly (this is one of the bases for Bettelheim's book, *The Informed Heart*, as well as the basis for outcome studies of those who survived the camps), there was some individuality; that is, a personal contribution maintained the reactions. To take the most polar reactions, there are those who became *Musselman*, who let themselves whither to death in the latrine, and those who became saboteurs of the ovens in Auschwitz. There were many in between those two reactions. The difference in outcome is in part, in small part, perhaps, but in part, something that comes from the individual and is available to him to maintain at least a sense of inner autonomy in the case of extreme environments and of manifest autonomy in a democratic society.

We can view the three vignettes in this chapter from this perspective. Our task is to tease out what are potentially autonomous contributions. We need to do this for ourselves if we are parents, teachers, physicians, or psychotherapists, and we need to facilitate this in our dependent charges. Just as we define a sense of autonomy, we can also maintain some sense of integration within ourselves as well as with the institution. In extreme cases, we need to rupture the integration with the institution and, if possible, to reform the latter. Doing so, we can begin to achieve the harmony among the individual, the institution, and society that Aristotle believed results in happiness.

NOTES

1. To underline how much Mr. L. was psychologically invested in these barriers, I would remind you that it took great effort and ingenuity to get stock supplies of paper and books in the school system. To get mobile walls, it must have taken near-heroic means.
2. The "*bricoleur*," as used by Levi-Strauss (1966), is one who finds fragments or objects and combines them in ways that help us see the world from a new perspective.
3. To maintain confidentiality about the institution and the individuals, I have changed the facts about the sale, providing a composite picture from several completed, threatened, or averted sales. In addition, the faculty members' titles and personal characteristics, such as gender and age, have been changed. Their reactions, however, will be reported as they occurred. As I describe different categories of the clinician's reactions, what underlies them is a common crisis of conscience as they recognized that the overt statements by the board of trustees undermined the assumed aim of the institution: treating and learning about the mentally ill.
4. Observational reactions are based on reports by faculty who were present at the institution as well as on interviews with many of the faculty involved.
5. Integration is a good term precisely because it is ambiguous. It can refer to an individual's sense of integration within himself (Erikson 1968). It can also refer to the individual's sense of integration with society. Perhaps earlier psycho-analytic thinkers overemphasized autonomy over and against integration with society. By autonomy we mean simply psychological self-government. Even this term contains ambiguity. For an individual can be autonomous at the expense of society's interest. He can also be autonomous while incorporating both society's general interests as well as maintaining a state of critical thinking about society's and his own interests. We ascribe to the latter idea.
6. The one exception at first glance may be the legal system, which has protected external freedom for the majority of mankind. If we look closely at this, however, as one prescribes and proscribes behavior through legal (that is, externally sanctioned) means, one diminishes the need for (internal) autono-mous decision except whether to follow a law or not. This concept is captured in Piaget's (1932) idea of the progressive movement from heteronomy to autonomy and, of course, more fully in Kohlberg's (1967) life work in this area. This is not to say that we should abjure the legal system in some recidivist manner. Only that we should recognize that with every advance in society, we need to take into account what personal price we may pay for it or what shift in personal responsibilities it may entail.

7. Weber's brilliant analysis followed and may have reflected a personal experience in his life: his father's death and Weber's subsequent lengthy and profound depression. This does not diminish his powerful insights.
8. Technician is an abysmal term in itself, depersonalizing what should be a very personal task—caring for another's feelings and body. Perhaps this term well embodies Weber's concept of bondage to animate machinery that is bureaucracy.
9. Stanton and Schwartz (1954) and Strauss and co-worker's (1964) studies also are significant contributions that nevertheless share the shortcoming I find in Goffman's sociological perspective.
10. I select Hannah Arendt because she shares with Bettelheim the influence of the Nazi experience. For a recent review of political philosophy, particularly insofar as it has to do with education, see Allan Bloom's (1987) *The Closing of the American Mind.*

References

Arendt, H. (1963). *Eichmann in Jerusalem*. New York: Vintage Books.
Arendt, H. (1978). *The Life of the Mind: Judging*. New York: Harcourt Brace Jovanovich.
Arendt, H. (1971). *The Life of the Mind: Thinking*. New York: Harcourt Brace Jovanovich.
Aries, P. (1962). *Centuries of Childhood*. New York: Vintage Books.
Aristotle (1962). *The Politics* (T. A. Sinclair, trans.). New York: Penguin.
Bettelheim, B. (1960). *The Informed Heart: Autonomy in a Mass Age*. New York: Free Press.
Bloom, A. (1987). *The Closing of the American Mind*. New York: Simon and Schuster.
Boas, F. (1911/1965). *The Mind of Primitive Man*. New York: Free Press.
Boon, J. (1985). *Other Tribes, Other Scribes*. New York: Cambridge University Press.
Doi, L. Takeo. (1982). *The Anatomy of Dependence* (Bester, trans.). Tokyo: Kodansha Press.
Erikson, E. (1950). *Childhood and Society*. New York: Norton.
Erikson, E. (1968). *Identity, Youth, and Crisis*. New York: Norton.
Foucault, M. (1973). *Madness and Civilization*. New York: Vintage Books.
Freud, S. (1920). Beyond the Pleasure Principle. In J. Strachey (ed. and trans.), *The Standard Edition of the Complete Psychological Works of Sigmund Freud*, Vol. 18. London: Hogarth Press.
Freud, S. (1930). *Civilization and Its Discontents*. London: Hogarth Press.
Goffman, E. (1961). *Asylums*. New York: Anchor Books.
Kohlberg, L. (1967). Moral education, religious education and the public schools: A developmental view. In Sizen, T. (ed.), *Religion and Public Education*. Boston: Houghton Mifflin.
Lanzman, C. (1985). *Shoah*. New York: Pantheon.
Levine, D. N. (1986). *The Flight from Ambiguity: Essays in Social and Cultural Theory*. Chicago: University of Chicago Press.
Levi-Strauss, C. (1966). *The Savage Mind*. Chicago: University of Chicago Press.
Nietzsche, F. (1985). *Thus Spoke Zarathustra*. New York: Penguin.
Nietzsche, F., Weber, M., Hobbes, and Locke, J. (1968). *Economy and Society: An Outline of Interpretive Sociology*. New York: Bedminster Press.
Piaget, J. (1932). *The Moral Judgement of the Child*. New York: Free Press.
Simmel, G. (1971). *On Individuality and Social Forms* (Donald N. Levine, ed.) Chicago: University of Chicago Press.
Stanton, A. and Schwartz, M. S. (1954). *The Mental Hospital*. New York: Basic Books.

Strauss, A., Schatzman, L., Bucher, R., Ehrlich, D., and Sabshin, M. (1964). *Psychiatric Ideologies and Institutions*. New York: Free Press.

Toennies, F. (1971). *On Sociology: Pure Applied and Empirical*. (W. J. Cahnman and R. Heberle, eds.). Chicago: University of Chicago Press.

Weber, M. (1948). *From Max Weber: Essays in Sociology* (H. H. Gerth and C. Wright Mills, trans.). London: Routledge and Kegan Paul.

Weber, M. (1949). *Methodology of the Social Sciences* (E. Shils and A. Finch, trans.). Glencoe, IL: Free Press.

2

Psychoanalysis and the Classroom

Intent and Meaning in Learning and Teaching

BERTRAM J. COHLER
and ROBERT M. GALATZER-LEVY

EDUCATION REMAINS A FRONTIER FOR PSYCHOANALYSIS. Cohler and Galatzer-Levy explore and extend the boundaries of this frontier. They articulate that any curriculum has both objective and subjective elements: a course on the origins of the universe may, for some, entail questions about one's own origins; a course on the American Civil War may, for some, evoke feelings about one's family's uncivil wars, such as divorce. Psychoanalysis, to the extent that it is the study of subjectivity—our wishes and intents, both in or out of awareness—enlightens us about education.

In addition to curriculum, the classroom can be considered as an intermediate space, as Winnicott uses this term: an area between two persons in which something is mutually created, an area of play, of illusion, and creativity. As such, both persons bring feelings, needs, and wishes to this intermediate space, influencing each other and the thing created, in this case knowledge. Both student and teacher bring a life history that colors the

BERTRAM J. COHLER • Committee on Human Development, University of Chicago, Chicago, Illinois 60637.   ROBERT M. GALATZER-LEVY • The Institute for Psychoanalysis, 180 N. Michigan Avenue, Chicago, Illinois 60601.

Educating the Emotions: Bruno Bettelheim and Psychoanalytic Development, edited by Nathan M. Szajnberg. Plenum Press, New York, 1992.

present, as well as daily experiences (a fractious battle with mom or spouse, a disturbing dream).

Finally, there is the student–teacher relationship that psychoanalysis can illuminate. For a teacher, does the student's expectations or accomplishments threaten self-esteem; does admiration threaten, resulting in demurral, arrogance, or withdrawal; does the student not admire sufficiently, in the teacher's eye; is there competition or intergenerational envy?

Cohler and Galatzer-Levy point out how even the timing of a curriculum can be psychoanalytically more sound. In a first-year college social science sequence, the readings and subjects were reorganized so that the autumn quarter focused on issues of work and economy, by winter to symbol and meaning, and by spring to meaning and person. This recognized the developmental step from adolescence to young adulthood and the need to permit time for a student to trust his teacher and peers enough to address the more personal issues found in readings such as Durkheim's *Suicide*, Freud's *Interpretation of Dreams*, or O'Neill's *Long Day's Journey into Night*. Cohler and Galatzer-Levy suggest general psychoanalytic principles that apply from elementary to postsecondary education, then concentrate on specific principles for the latter.

Yet Cohler and Galatzer-Levy take an intriguing passage in their discourse on education. They begin with a critical self-reflective review of what and how psychoanalysis has learned about itself—how it has educated itself about itself. This is most fitting for a discipline initiated by Freud's critical self-reflection.

Cohler and Galatzer-Levy recast starkly, in bas-relief, the tension between the mechanistic, abstract metapsychology (what they call experience-distant) versus the more personal, subjective realm of what occurs between analyst and analysand (what they call experience-near). After adroitly reviewing the metapsychology, including how the English translation of Freud exacerbated our misunderstanding of psychoanalysis, Cohler and Galatzer-Levy say that, ironically, psychoanalysis had neglected the study of experience-near attributes (shame, embarrassment, will, hope) for which psychoanalysis is uniquely constructed. These are joint constructions of meaning between psychoanalyst and patient. By refocusing on persons and lives, we can learn how individuals develop a sense of coherence, continuity, and personal integrity.

This is a rich, complex way to approach psychoanalytic contributions to education: by following psychoanalysis's vicissitudes as the discipline learns about itself. (Frattaroli carries this further in his chapter on orthodoxy and heresy.) Cohler and Galatzer-Levy remind us that what happens in a good psychoanalysis is the development of a more flexible, coherent, believable narrative of one's life. These adjectives can also be applied to good learning and knowledge. Cohler and Galatzer-Levy close by suggesting that by attending to the subjective curriculum, the meanings constructed in a classroom, the dynamics within and between student and teacher, we can foster the sense of vitality and spontaneity that "leads to the capacity for engagement in the classroom."

INTRODUCTION

Significant intellectual and clinical advances across the past two decades within psychoanalysis suggest new means for studying the contribution of psychoanalysis in understanding the student, the teacher, and life in classrooms. These advances include clarification of Freud's own intellectual contributions to the study of intention and action and increased awareness of psychoanalysis as a means for studying intersubjectivity and maintenance of personal integrity. Intentions manifest in thought and action often reflect variation in feelings of self-sufficiency and the capacity to manage tension states. Until the past few decades, psychoanalytic inquiry has focused primarily on issues that arise from intrinsic developmental conflicts between society's demands and certain early childhood wishes and the experience of loving and rivalrous feelings within the family. In recent years, developmental and clinical study has been extended to include wishes concerning the emergence and resolution of more archaic tensions, particularly efforts to maintain a sense of coherence and to experience solace at times of distress.

The classroom is an important arena for studying the significance of intersubjectivity and maintenance of personal integrity. Among the contributions of psychoanalysis to education, none is more important than its means for understanding the psychological significance of what is learned in school and the milieu most likely to foster learning. Observations reported across the past century, based on clinical psychoanalytic study, have shown that persons endow present experiences and relationships with particular meanings founded on the experiences of a lifetime. These meanings reflect the larger culture made personal through the process of growing up, based on a history of particular expectable relationships with others (Atwood and Stolorow, 1984; Stolorow, Brandchaft, and Atwood, 1987; Stern, 1985, 1989a). Among the unique contributions of clinical psychoanalytic intervention is the ability to portray wish and intent represented in meaning and to make explicit those meanings that are implicitly enacted within relationships. These meanings, constructed across a lifetime, are enacted in the classroom, just as in other aspects of life, and may be studied through encounters between students and teachers.

Everything that happens in school is endowed with meanings for both teacher and student; however, these meanings cannot be discerned through the experience-distant mode of observation characteristic of much contemporary educational research. Rather, these meanings emerge in the context of an experience-near method of observation, similar to the psychoanalytic setting itself, focusing on those jointly constructed meanings resulting from the interplay of the differently organized experiences of both teacher and students. The advantages of this psychoanalytic method of study have been documented in the work of psychoanalytically educated anthropologists. Recent reports by Crapanzano (1980) and others (Kracke, 1981) have portrayed the relationship between informant and ethnographer in a manner that is similar to that which can be used to study of life in classrooms.

CHANGING PERSPECTIVES ON THE STUDY OF PSYCHOANALYSIS AND EDUCATION

The history of the relationship between psychoanalysis and education parallels the application of psychoanalysis within the humanities and the human sciences. This change may be attributed to several factors, including: increased historical study which has clarified the role of Freud's own neuroscience study across the formative years of psychoanalysis; reconsideration of the contributions of ego psychology within psychoanalysis, particularly with the advent of renewed interest in study of intersubjectivity and self; reevaluation of approaches portraying personality development in terms of a neatly ordered, easily predictable, linear or epigenetic model; and, finally, critical study of the translation of the *Standard Edition* itself, which has led to renewed appreciation of Freud as a theorist of wish and intent, as well as of function and mechanism. This study, in turn, fostered extension of the clinical perspective within psychoanalysis to the study of culture and the humanities.

From Mechanism to Person in Psychoanalytic Inquiry

Freud's concept of the unconscious provided a new means for understanding wish and intent, which replaced functionalist theories of consciousness based on the physiological study of sensation and perception. However, as Klein (1976) observed, Freud's effort to supplant Wundt's mechanistic explanation of attention resulted in yet another mechanistic model. Freud's model of attention has the same problems as Wundt's earlier model, Galatzer-Levy and Cohler (1990) suggest that Freud's adherence to this scientism principally reflected his intellectual worldview, the product of an education during a time of prestige accorded to the newly popularized demonstration laboratory science of the late nineteenth century. This scientism has little relevance to Freud's pioneering study of wish and intent.

THE BIOLOGY OF THE MIND AND PSYCHOLOGICAL DEVELOPMENT.   Much of Freud's intellectual program early in his career has been reviewed by his colleague Bernfeld (1941, 1949, 1951), and Jones (1953), Gay (1988), by Sulloway (1979). What emerges from this study, as well as from Freud's letters to Fliess (Masson, 1984), his "Project for a Scientific Psychology" (Freud, 1895), his essay on Leonardo DaVinci (Freud, 1910), and his autobiography (1925), together with his essays "Beyond the Pleasure Principle" (Freud, 1920a) and "A Outline of Psychoanalysis" (Freud, 1940), is an effort to apply concepts learned in his scientific study, across roughly two decades from 1873–1891, to the course of psychological development (Cohler, 1987). This application focuses on the analogy between laboratory findings and the course of human development. While Freud acknowledges (1905) the valuable contributions that may be realized from developmental study, he was loathe to undertake such systematic observation, commenting to Fliess that "the women would never let him in the nursery" (1897/1985, p. 192). However, his acuity for such observation (Freud, 1920a) is shown in his study of his grandson's mastery of the concept of object permanence as later formulated by Piaget (1967, Piaget and Inhelder, 1969).

Freud's comparative laboratory study of the eighth (acoustic) nerve as it enters the medulla oblongata from the spinal cord provided support for Hackel's (1868) concept of the fundamental biogenetic law—that ontogeny recapitulates phylogeny. This biological model was consistent with archeological exploration taking place during Freud's youth, particularly Schliemann's mid-nineteenth-century excavation of Troy, which suggested that later civilizations overlay more primitive ones that provided the foundation for later attainments (Steele and Jacobsen, 1979). As Freud (1910) observed in his essay on Leonardo:

> impressive analogies from biology have prepared us to find that the individual's mental development repeats the course of human development in an abbreviated form; and the conclusions which psychoanalytic research into the child's mind has reached concerning the high value set on the genitals in infancy will therefore not strike us as improbable. (p. 97)

Other aspects of development were explained in a similar way. For example, in his discussion of the concepts of fixation and regression, extending the work of the English neurologist J. H. Jackson (1884) Freud (1951–17)

notes the analogy between his comparative developmental neurobiological studies and the dual concepts of fixation and regression in which some
aspects of development have remained behind at earlier stages (Jackson,
1969).[1]

The genetic point of view, long held to be the defining perspective in
psychoanalysis (Freud, 1913; Hartmann and Kris, 1945), has been questioned in terms of assumptions made about development as an epigenetic
phenomena depending on the concept of critical or sensitive period. The
significance of the critical period concept has been reconsidered both in
terms of personality development (Clarke and Clarke, 1976; Kagan, 1980)
and also in terms of the deterministic portrayal of developmental process
apart from interaction with the context in which development takes place
(Winnicott, 1953; Vygotsky, 1978). Finally, study of development has
shifted from concern with external forces impinging on socialization to the
manner in which children come to construct stories, including those
regarding the course of life. Clinical psychoanalytic perspectives have
suggested that the impact of both expectable and eruptive life changes is
mediated by continuing, recollected accounts of the presently remembered
past, rather than the time–space significance attributed to past events
(Novey, 1968; Schafer, 1980, 1981, 1983).

Detailed study of the first two decades of Freud's scientific career has
revealed the extent to which essential postulates regarding the determinants of personality development were largely an extension of developmental neurobiology. The genetic point of view, claimed both by Freud
(1913) and by Hartmann and Kris (1945) as intrinsic to psychoanalysis, is
more a representation of Freud's scientific worldview derived from study
of Hughlings Jackson, Darwin, Haeckel, and others than to a finding
emerging from application of the clinical psychoanalytic method to study
of lives over time (Bernfeld, 1941; Stengel, 1963; Sulloway, 1979; Ritvo,
1990). Much the same paradox is presented by the so-called ego psychology emerging from Freud's restatement of his model of the mind (Freud,
1923), which Rapaport (1951, 1960/1967) portrays as propositions describing
the relations among the macrostructures (ego, id, superego) of the structural theory.

Ego Psychology and Mental Apparatus

Ego psychology focuses on the metapsychology, or model of the mind
beyond consciousness, which preoccupied Freud across much of his
career. Freud coined the term "metapsychology" after Aristotle's *Metaphysics*, which he had read some two decades earlier with his teacher
Brentano (Bernfeld, 1951) (who also first inspired Freud to study the

concept of intentionality; see Rapaport, 1951, p. 427). In the February 13, 1896 letter to Fliess (Masson, 1984, p. 172), Freud reports that he is "continually occupied with psychology—really metapsychology . . . I hope to be well supplied with scientific interests unto the end of my life." Two years later, Freud (1898/1985, pp. 301–302) writes to Fliess, "It seems to me that the theory of wish fulfillment has brought only the psychological solution and not the biological—or, rather, the metapsychical one. (I am going to ask you seriously, by the way, whether I may use the name metapsychology for my psychology that leads behind consciousness.)" In fact, already in the previous year, Freud had sketched a model of mental functions explaining the phenomenon of attention in his "project for neurologists" following a visit with Fliess. Appearing in revised form, this project provided the foundation for Chapter 8 of *The Interpretation of Dreams*, where Freud described this model in a revised form.

Major revisions of the metapsychology were made across the succeeding decades, resulting in the shift from a topographic model of consciousness (Freud, 1911, 1915) to a structural one (Freud, 1923, 1932–1933). Common to both models is the effort to explain thought as a motivated activity determined by psychological forces outside of awareness. This shift from a topographic to a structural point of view in psychoanalysis in understanding how persons are protected from awareness of conflict led to increased understanding of self-punishing actions (Arlow and Brenner, 1964). Clearly, both Freud's (1926) discussion of anxiety and efforts to ward off the impact of psychological conflict, and Anna Freud's (1936/1966) elaboration of this model, fostered increased concern with issues of conflict and defense. Much of this perspective has been ably summarized in Nunberg's classic (1931) paper and his (1932/1955) text and, in a more cautious manner, Fenichel's (1945) summary.

Rapaport (1951a, 1951b, 1967), Hartmann (1939/1958, 1964) and his collaborators (Hartmann, Kris, and Lowenstein, 1964) elaborated the implications of this perspective. The contributions of Hartmann and his colleagues were principally theoretical, focusing largely on Freud's genetic point of view, issuing from his biology of instinctual development first portrayed in the essays on sexuality (Freud, 1905/1953). Hartmann's (1939/1958, 1939/1964) essays on ego process and reality extended Anna Freud's discussion of ego and defense. Ego psychology decisively influenced the future course of psychoanalysis, showing that ego and id alike issued out of common neural energy. Primary autonomy of the ego from the id could be assumed since the ego was no longer viewed as emerging out of the id and necessarily destined to serve the id.

Over the succeeding decades, Hartmann further explored the consequences of this assumption, elaborating the functions of the ego, clarifying the relationship of the ego and such other psychological structures as the self, and elaborating the relationship of developmental biological phenomena. The goal of this inquiry, so well discussed by Hartmann, Kris, and Lowenstein (1964), was the construction of psychoanalysis as a general psychology. This inquiry extends well beyond Freud's initial concern with the explanation of conflict into a general theory of motivation, emotion, and learning based on the elaboration of the concept of drive across psychological development. Directly relevant for the study of learning and education, Hartmann had argued that such basic ego functions as memory and attention could be relatively conflict free. However, these functions could be drawn into the service of conflict, serving to gratify powerful forces emanating from the id. The success of education depended on the ability of the ego to remain relatively free of such conflict.

Rapaport suggests that ego psychology has proceeded through four phases: (1) "pre-psychoanalytic" study of the means used to ward off memories and certain painful experiences in reality; (2) study of repression and the mental topography; (3) interest in psychic conflict and defense, marked by elaboration of the structural model along the lines of the 1923 essay on *The Ego and the Id*, and the essay on anxiety and defense (Freud, 1923); and (4) concern with the relative autonomy of ego functions in managing relations with reality. This fourth phase is marked by publication of Hartmann's (1939/1958) essay *Ego Psychology and the Problem of Adaptation*, including the concept of adaptation to the "average expectable environment." Rapaport's (1951b/1959) English translation of Hartmann's landmark essay made it possible for a broad readership to become familiar with this critically important restatement of psychoanalytic theory.

Rapaport and his associates portrayed a fifth, penultimate phase of ego psychology, systematically studying Freud's conceptual model, first elaborated in the project and enlarged through study of the determinants of consciousness, the relationship among mental microstructures, and the relationship of ego process and reality. Psychology became the vehicle for this systematic study of ego functions. Experimental psychology was well versed in methods for the study of memory, attention, judgment, and other cognitive functions. Rapaport showed that these experimental methods could be applied to ideas that Freud had sketched from the time of the project through his posthumous *An Outline of Psychoanalysis* (1940). The intellectual foundations for this ambitious research program have been particularly clearly elaborated in Rapaport's (1951/1967) essay on the conceptual model of psychoanalysis, providing a comprehensive model of thinking that integrates affect and cognition.

Across more than two decades of systematic study, principally by a group of experimental psychologists also well versed in theoretical and clinical psychoanalysis, Rapaport and his colleagues undertook systematic studies of awareness outside of consciousness (Klein, 1970) and emergence of cognitive control over wish and drive (Gardner, *et al.*, 1959, 1960). Much of this work was published in the monograph series *Psychological Issues* and contributed to a significant reformulation of central assumptions within psychoanalysis. Ego psychology also eagerly embraced findings emerging from increasingly sophisticated developmental study of cognition in infancy and early childhood, relying upon Piaget's work as the foundation for much of this study (Wolff, 1960, 1966; Anthony, 1976; Greenspan, 1975; 1979).

One of the unsolved paradoxes of psychoanalysis concerned Freud's dual concern with a general psychology (metapsychology), founded in biology, reflecting his scientific worldview (Galatzer-Levy and Cohler, 1990), and a theory of meaning, based on experience-near study of wish and intent (Kohut, 1959/1978; Klein, 1976). While the theory of meaning has had most direct impact upon the arts and letters across the twentieth century, psychoanalysis as a general psychology has attracted the greatest scientific interest. Indeed, as Klein (1976) has observed, psychoanalytic research has focused on the metapsychology, virtually to the exclusion of systematic study of such significant clinical constructs as the use of repression, or emergence and resolution of the transference across the course of analysis. Freud himself was acutely aware of both the promise and problems inherent in the construction of a general theory of motivation. Indeed, citing Goethe, as he frequently did at times when he found himself at the limits of his understanding, he observed:

> If we are asked by what methods and means [the instinct is brought into the harmony of the ego] we can only say: "we must call the witch to our help after all"—the witch metapsychology. Without metapsychological speculation and theorizing—I had almost said "phantasying"—we shall not get another step forward. (Freud, 1937, p. 225)

The "hex" of metapsychology continues to plague psychoanalysis. Increasingly sophisticated study of ego processes and ingenious experimentation has fostered enhanced understanding of factors shaping attention, judgment, memory, and other cognitive processes, but has added little understanding to the role of wish and intent in lives over time.

In a series of cogent, carefully argued essays, Klein (1976) reviewed the contributions of metapsychology, including its most recent reincarnation as ego psychology. Klein suggested that all of the ego functions carefully delineated by Rapaport, Hartmann, and their colleagues could be more parsimoniously understood as basic psychological processes, long the province of experimental psychology, and most appropriately studied using traditional laboratory procedures. Reviewing the current status of ego psychology, Klein concluded that it was little more than a catalog of functions and mechanisms in no way different from the mechanistic psychology that Freud initially eschewed.[2] Further, assumptions of a now-discredited drive psychology (Wallerstein, 1977) are hidden within implicit assumptions prevalent in ego psychology. Klein suggests that ego psychology straddles concepts of explanation and mechanism, and fails to provide an adequate basis for a psychoanalytic theory of motivation:

> Freud's metapsychology is not distinctively psychoanalytic. Moreover, it reduces human behavior to a conceptual domain which requires a kind of observational datum different from that available in the analytic situation . . . metapsychology throws overboard the fundamental intent of the psychoanalytic enterprise-that of unlocking meanings. (Klein, 1976, p. 49)

Gill (1976) has made the same point regarding metapsychology, showing the extent to which Freud's metapsychology is neither science nor psychology. Indeed, reflecting "unbridled speculation" (p. 102), Gill maintains that metapsychology has no place within psychoanalysis as a psychology of intention. As Klein (1976) has noted:

> It was the genius of Freud that brought [problems of meaning] back squarely into the psychologists' concern; he developed a taxonomy and a code of deciphering the meanings of personal relationships in their conscious and unconscious aspects. Psychoanalysis imputes meaning to behavior by showing the significance of myth in our live, those inner phantoms of fantasy which render objects significant, and which lead us to establish and react to relationships. (p. 53)

Klein refers to this contribution of psychoanalysis to experience-near study of wish and intent as the "clinical" theory, and contrasts this clinical theory with metapsychology or psychoanalysis as a general psychology. Klein (1976) observed that ego psychology is little more than poor experimental psychology. Further, Klein maintained that the central contribution of psychoanalysis resides in the study of meanings as they emerge in the psychoanalytic encounter. The psychoanalytic situation provides unique data about enactments based on meaning that are beyond awareness and the means people use to protect themselves against awareness of unacceptable wishes (Edelson, 1984, 1989).

Holzman (1985) and Wallerstein (1986, 1987) have been particularly strident in their critique of Klein's distinction between the clinical theory, which they understand to refer to "curative" aspects of the psychoanalytic process itself, and the scientific (ego psychological) view of psychoanalysis as a general psychology with broad explanatory power in the study of human behavior. These critics disregard Klein's detailed critique of the fundamental assumptions underlying ego psychology and, more generally, psychoanalysis as a "general psychology," which has also been emphasized by other critics of psychoanalysis as a scientific worldview (Gill, 1976; Klein, 1976; Ricouer, 1977; Schafer, 1976, 1983). Critics of Klein's distinction between these two types of theory in psychoanalysis misunderstand the concept of "clinical" as used by Klein in his portrayal of the clinical theory within psychoanalysis and disregard his detailed critique of the concept of theory as used within both ego psychology and psychoanalysis more generally. Klein and others have questioned the value of psychoanalysis understood as a general psychology (Gill, 1976; Klein, 1976; Ricouer, 1977; Schafer, 1976, 1983). Klein (1976) has observed that not only is ego psychology little more than general experimental psychology, but also that the premier contribution of psychoanalysis concerns study of meanings as enacted in the relationship between analysand and analyst. These enactments, together with the means used by persons in order to protect themselves against enhanced awareness, are accessible to systematic study (Edelson, 1984).

It is ironic that so much consideration has been given to functions and mechanisms that by definition are not accessible using that empathic or experience-near mode of study which is unique to psychoanalysis (Kohut, 1959/1978, 1971). Psychoanalysis has largely neglected the study of important, experience-near attributes such as embarrassment or shame and will or hope, together with means used to protect oneself from feelings of distress. Constructs such as selective and sustained attention are more appropriately studied within experimental psychology. Relying on the study of enactments taking place within the psychoanalytic situation, psychoanalysis provides a unique means for studying *joint construction of meanings*, or intersubjectivity, central to understanding psychological development and social life.

Intersubjectivity and the Intellectual Mission of Psychoanalysis

Increased appreciation of the particular intellectual contributions provided by psychoanalytic study, evident in several critiques of theory and method of study in psychoanalysis (Gill, 1976; Klein, 1976; Ricoeur, 1977; Schafer, 1976, 1983), may be attributed to a number of factors. Several decades devoted to applying Freud's metapsychology, or scientific worldview, have led to few significant findings. Within the larger culture, particularly literary criticism and philosophy, the "hermeneutic turn" has led to a renewed interest in meaning, its construction, and its communication. Psychoanalysts interested in meanings and motives found natural allies and intellectual support for their endeavors to formulate their thinking outside the traditions of positivistic science. Significant revisions in the complex superstructure of ego psychology (Holt, 1967) have failed to make underlying assumptions amenable to empirical study. Critics such as Fisher and Greenberg (1977), Grunbaum (1984), and even Spence (1982) have noted the problems in understanding psychoanalysis from a natural science perspective. This problem in translating psychoanalysis as a general psychology into testable terms has been accompanied by concern more generally regarding the contributions of the ego psychology tradition, emphasizing function and mechanism, in terms of the study of wish and intent as expressed within lives over time.

CLINICAL PSYCHOANALYTIC THEORY AND STUDY OF EDUCATION.   While clarifying the place of metapsychology within psychoanalysis, there has been renewed interest in the clinical theory and the experiential world within psychoanalysis. This shift may be observed in the current interest in the concept of "self" within psychoanalysis. Most recently associated with the work of Kohut and his associates (Kohut, 1971, 1977, 1984; Kohut and Wolf, 1978; Wolf, 1988), this particular approach to the study of a sense of personal integrity is but one of several approaches within psychoanalysis regarding concern with persons and lives rather than with functions and mechanisms (Winnicott, 1953, 1960b; Khan, 1963; Klein, 1976).

Bettelheim (1983) has observed that much of the problem with psychoanalysis, including the earlier shift away from study of experience, is founded in the translation itself, including Strachey and Jones's preference for the experience-distant Latinate term "ego" rather than the more introspective and experience-near term "I" as the best translation of the German term "Ich." While Kernberg (1982) supports the editors of the *Standard Edition*, others have argued that "self" may be a better translation for this term than ego (Hartmann, 1950; Laplanche and Pontalis, 1973; Gedo, 1979; Kernberg, 1982; Richards, 1982a; Meissner, 1986). Strachey, in the *Standard Edition* (Strachey, 1961, p. 8; 1955, pps. 7–8), notes that the term "Ich" sometimes refers to self in an effort to distinguish Freud's different uses of the term. Schafer's (1976, 1980, 1983) concept of the active self may be more consistent with Freud's thinking than the terms employed in the *Standard Edition*.

Problems apparent in the translation of such terms as "ego" and "id" reflect lack of clarity regarding the contribution of experientially relevant concepts within psychoanalysis. The term "self" is perhaps the most readily confused of these concepts and may be too easily viewed as psychosocial or interpersonal constructs (Meissner, 1981). Understood more generally within psychoanalysis as experienced coherence, continuity, or personal integrity (Klein, 1976; Gedo, 1981; Kaplan and Stechler,

1981; Bach, 1987; Wolf, 1988; Pine, 1989), the psychoanalytic construct of self refers to an intrapersonal or subjective state or agency leading to enhanced sense of personal spontaneity and wholeness (Winnicott, 1960b).

Concern with differentiation between the realms of the interpersonal and the intrapsychic or intrapersonal was central in the efforts of Hartmann (1950) and Jacobson (1964) to clarify the concept of self. Together with Van Spiviell (1981) and Richards (1982a), these pioneering theoreticians view the self as including the ego, the sense of being the subject (versus the object) of experience, the bodily self, and sense of being a whole individual person. Even recognizing these efforts, Meissner (1986) remains uneasy with Hartmann's (1950) equation of "self" and "person," and views "person" as a social rather than intrapsychologic term. Further, as both Meissner (1986) and Gedo (1979, 1981) have observed, Jacobson's (1964) view of the self-concept fosters an inconsistent understanding of the self. Jacobson (1964) views the self as an intrapsychic function resulting from experiences or representation of others (as contrasted with actual experiences with others) (Sandler and Rosenblatt, 1962). Jacobson also maintains that the self constitutes both a structure in the ego, serving as the repository of experience of an active sense of personal integration and coherence (Klein, 1976), and a structure containing the ego.

Perhaps the greatest concern with the concept of self in psychoanalysis has been evident in the contributions of Kohut and his collaborators (Kohut, 1971, 1977, 1984; Basch 1981, 1983a, b; Goldberg, 1982, 1988; Kohut and Wolf, 1978; Wolf, 1988; Tolpin and Kohut, 1990). In a series of clinical and theoretical papers these clinical investigators have explored the role of the experience of others for the emergence of personal vitality and capacity for soothing tensions. Similar in many respects to the discussions of Winnicott (1953, 1960b), Khan (1964), and Giovacchini (1979, 1986), Kohut and his associates have coined the term "self psychology" for a clinical and developmental theory stressing intertwined poles of grandiosity, idealizations, and appreciation of talents and skills.

Central to this clinical–developmental theory is the assumption of the infant's experience of vitality from earliest infancy. Sense of agency and effectance (White, 1963) from earliest childhood facilitates emergence of coherence and continuity within space and time, and reflects a complex developmental process, beginning with the parent's image of the infant's physical and historical coherence, and continuing in the infant's experience of ever more organized and differentiated positions in life, through the child's discovery of an essential psychological self associated with, but different from body, to subsequent variation in the experience of personal integrity or coherence within ever increasing contexts of self within society.

The formulation of self emerging from self psychology is of a person embedded in a complex matrix of meanings, including the capacity for self-soothing and appropriate use of others as a source of comfort, formed by the experience of others as more or less able to provide solace during critical times of psychological distress. The "good enough" parent provides a context in which the young child is first able to experience soothing of tensions that facilitates emergence of a sense of self as vital and effective (Cohler, 1980). Too often, self is defined largely in terms of psychopathology, or absence or impairment in a sense of wholeness and well-being (Wolf, 1988). Particularly in the work of Kohut and his associates, such self states as grandiosity, fragmentation, emptiness, or a sense of being overburdened or overstimulated, all become ways of understanding self in terms of its impairment (Gedo, 1977, Gedo and Goldberg, 1973). It is important to understand the implications of self psychology for the development of self beyond those instances in which the child experiences the care-giving environment as failing to support tension regulation, leading to significant impairment in the child's own capacity for regulation.

Clinical inquiry within this tradition, together with normative developmental study (Sander, 1962, 1964, 1969, 1975; Stern, 1985, 1989a), suggests that limitations in the capacity for experiencing self-soothing is first attributed by the child to her or his own actions; only later is the child able to differentiate between his or her own initiative and the actions of others on the child's behalf. This perspective on the development of self contrasts with that of Mahler and her colleagues (Mahler, et al., 1975), stressing development from an unrelated, "autistic" state through a confusional symbiosis in which the baby now experiences mother and self as one toward enhanced psychological autonomy. Kohut (1971) has observed that Mahler's method of study and formulation of the development of self represents an experience-distant perspective from without the baby's emerging subjectivity (Stern, 1985), rather than the experience-near perspective characteristic of psychoanalysis. Careful reading of Mahler's work reveals the absence of empirical data for an autistic or symbiotic phase while the observations she provides in support of later phases are highly theory-determined and require the existence of the earlier phases to have the meaning which she attributes to them.[3]

Further, as Kohut and his associates have observed, the separation—individuation approach to psychological development pioneered by Mahler and her colleagues (Mahler, et al., 1976) emphasizes individualism rather than enhanced relatedness as the outcome of personality development across the years of early childhood. This lonely individualism contrasts with the reality of the continuing psychological use of others as a source of affirmation and support across the course of life (Cohler, 1983;

Cohler and Stott, 1987). Beginning with earliest infancy and continuing across the course of life, we turn to others for comfort and support during times of distress. Variations in the ability to experience solace and to realize continuing, sustaining comfort reflects variations in the vitality and sense of coherence of self. Persons seek ties with others that provide solace in times of crisis and vitality at times of depletion (Winnicott, 1953, 1960b; Khan, 1964; Kohut, 1977; Giovacchini, 1979, 1986; Stern, 1985).[4]

Perspectives such as those formulated by Kohut and his colleagues, Klein, Stechler, Kaplan, Winnicott, Khan, Andre Green, and others, all point in the direction of a new understanding of the development of subjectivity based on experience-near or empathic modes of observation. This perspective focuses on the concept of person rather than function and mechanism and is concerned with the process by which we come to experience the world as coherent and congruent over long periods of time, even as confronted by unexpected adversity. Experience-near issues such as agency or activity, attribution of particular meanings to experience, and use of time in particular ways, replaces more experience-distant and mechanistic concern with presumed functions and mechanisms that are more the province of experimental psychology than a human science concerned with origins and significance of wish and intents enacted with others over long durations.

EMPATHY AND INTERSUBJECTIVITY.   Freud's metapsychology, and the effort at construction of a general psychology on which it is based, reflects Freud's scientific worldview (Gill, 1976; Klein, 1976; Galatzer-Levy and Cohler, 1990). Findings claimed to issue out of this scientific worldview may be accounted for largely in terms of experimental psychology (Klein, 1976): psychoanalytic explanations do not add further significance to these findings beyond those provided by experimental and developmental psychology. Indeed, these normative contributions reflect a contradiction between experience-distant and experience-near perspectives (Kohut, 1959, 1971). The experience-distant perspective is based on observation apart from the meaning of the relationship between observer and observed, while the experience-near perspective focuses on the joint construction of meaning.[5]

This experience-near realm has been portrayed by Trevarthan (1980), Atwood and Stolorow (1984), and Stern (1985) as intersubjectivity. Atwood and Stolorow observe that inclusion of the different worlds of observer and observed within a common frame of reference provides a unique opportunity for psychoanalytic study of social life and provides a bridge between the intrapersonal and the interpersonal. Following Trevarthan and Hubley (1978) and Trevarthan (1989), Stern (1985, 1989b) further notes that the effort to share experiences regarding events and things (shown by joint attention and shared intention and "interaffectivity") reflects an essential task of development, leading to emergence of the capacity for relatedness over the first year of life. Realization of enhanced intersubjectivity not only facilitates completion of psychological development, but also is essential as the foundation of empathy, the capacity for social understanding as reflected both in normative study and the psychoanalytic process.

Based both on developmental study and clinical observation, Stern (1985, 1989a) posits that the child's "subjective experience of the observable event" (1985, p. 119) results from the unique life experiences of each partner in the relationship. Starting at birth, and experiencing a short-lived episode of assistance with regulation and attunement, by the second half of the first year of life, caretaker and child have fashioned a relationship based on reciprocally shared intents and feelings. Attunement permits the baby to match his or her own state with that of others, providing the foundation both for the subsequent capacity to use care provided by others and to offer this care to another.

Stern's study of the development of intersubjectivity is consistent with Winnicott's (1953, 1960a,b) observation that children create an intermediate, transitional space between self and caretaker that over time increases the child's capacity for self-regulation. Stern's study is also consistent with the formulations of psychological development posited by Kohut and his colleagues, suggesting that infants experience the caretaker's regulation of their inner states in the same manner in which they experience self-regulation (Cohler, 1980). Stern describes a matrix of reciprocity enhancing self-regulation, concerned less with the child–caretaker tie than with the child's *experience* of the relationship and its connection with the capacity for self-regulation, vitality, and creativity (Winnicott, 1953; Sander, 1975; Klein, 1976; Stechler and Kaplan, 1980).

Kohut (1959, 1971, 1977, 1984) maintains that psychoanalysis represents a mode of study using the method of empathy, or vicarious introspection, which may be contrasted with the experience-distant mode of experimental laboratory study. In the experience-near mode the observer uses his or her own psychological processes in understanding the other from *within* the field of observation which constitutes observer and observed, while in the experience-distant mode this method is ruled out as inappropriate in favor of a perspective from without this relationship. As Kohut (1988) has suggested, the issue is not whether these observations are subsequently transformed into counted data but the perspective of the observer.

INTERSUBJECTIVITY AND THE PROBLEM OF THE TRANSLATION.   Kohut's formulation of the distinction between experience-near and experience-distant defines the nature of that discourse which we regard as distinctively psychoanalytic. Accepting this perspective for understanding the nature of psychoanalytic contributions has been enhanced by psychoanalytically informed developmental study (such as Sander, 1962, 1964, 1969, 1975), Stern's epochal discussion of the course of development, clarification of the nature of psychoanalytic contributions (Gill, 1976; Klein, 1976), and recent study of how Freud's work has been translated from German into English. As Ricoeur (1971) has emphasized, translations represent particular interpretations of a text and do not occupy a privileged status apart from other interpretations of a text.

Translations do not require a status different from any other critical study of texts. Intellectual developments lead emerging generations of scholars to view translations in terms quite different from those adequate for a previous generation. This is particularly a problem with Freud scholarship. Without question, Freud's major concern was with the construction of a "scientistic" psychoanalysis (Sulloway, 1979; Galatzer-Levy and Cohler, 1990; Ritvo, 1990). Along the way, particularly in such work as the collaboratively authored *Studies in Hysteria* (1893–1895) and *The Interpretation of Dreams* (1900), Freud also posited the study of wish and intent as a human science in which the expression of wishes provides an understanding of symbol formation in culture.

To date, these "two theories" of psychoanalysis (science versus interpretive study) have not been successfully integrated (Klein, 1976): the Strachey–Jones translation of Freud's work emphasized the scientistic approach. Recent critiques (Bettelheim, 1983; Orston, 1985a, b, 1988) have posed important questions regarding the completeness of this earlier translation. Understood from this perspective, it is not surprising that scholars have questioned the nature of the Strachey–Jones translation of the *Standard Edition*. If emerging concern with issues of intersubjectivity and self within psychoanalysis and psychoanalytic developmental psychology is understood as a reflection of postmodern social science (Homans, 1989; Toulmin, 1990), then it is important to study Freud's work from within an experience-near realm of wish, intent, and self. This contrasts with the approach adopted in the *Standard Edition*, which emphasizes study of psychic function and mechanism.

Understood as a human science, psychoanalysis rests on the concept of intersubjectivity and of the person's active construal of context in terms of wish and intent. It is ironic that this experience-near mode of observation, which has had such an impact on arts and letters, from the humanities to anthropology and education, should be so readily confused with an experience-distant perspective focused on structure, functions, and mechanisms. Confusion regarding the essential contribution of Freud's work may stem as much from the translation of his work into English as to the attribution of what is actually his scientific worldview into the content of his contribution (Gill, 1976; Klein, 1976). This problem of the translation has already been noted in discussion of the concepts of self and ego within psychoanalysis. Bettelheim (1983) has shown that translation of the German word "Ich" as "I" rather than as "ego" makes a profound difference in the understanding of Freud's (1923) structural theory. One translation makes the structural theory experience-near and concerned with owned actions and feelings (Schafer, 1976, 1983), while the other translation turns experience into an attribute experientially different from self. One translation portrays wish and intent in terms of intersubjectivity, while the other translation poses study of wish and intent in terms of functions and mechanisms that cannot be studied from a distinctively psychoanalytic perspective.

Ornston (1985a, b, 1988) quotes Anna Freud saying that her father preferred the plain language version of his terms to Latinate or Greek terms. However, Jones and Strachey opted for technical terms with more limited but precise meaning. Jones, in particular, preferred those Latin or Greek terms that provided greater distance from the emotional impact of the subject matter of sexuality and the neuroses than the vernacular. Indeed, Jones deliberately set about to create an experience-distant reading of Freud with little reference to experience-near content (Ornston, 1982, 1988; Pines, 1988; Steiner, 1988). For example, Ornston (1985a,b) has discussed Freud's construct of "besetzung," investment or interest, as a particular example of the problems of translation. Strachey and Jones (Ornston, 1988) constructed a glossary for the translation of particular words and phrases in order to render them consistent in their use (thereby making Freud more consistent in English than he ever intended to be in German). The confusing triad of cathexis, countercathexis, and hypercathexis was constructed by Jones and Strachey to deal with possible inconsistencies between process and end state and does not appear in the original German text. Freud's work might have had even greater impact on both arts and letters and education if the translation had been more accessible and if it had more completely reflected the immediate relevance of his work for understanding the human condition.[6]

Psychoanalysis and Subjectivity: The Narrative Turn

Freud's important contributions to the study of subjectivity emerged parallel to his scientistic concerns, reflecting the worldview of his time. Appreciation of the significance of meanings and intents emerged quite clearly in Freud's clinical papers, particularly the collaborative volume with Breuer on hysteria (Breuer and Freud, 1893–1895). Freud observes in this account that hysterics suffer primarily from reminiscence. The body cooperates in the symbolic expression of wishes linked to past memories and seeking renewed satisfaction in the present. The paralyses and other afflictions of the patients whom Freud observed could be understood through a study of meanings that persons attributed to these symptoms. Symptoms characteristic of hysterical paralyses and other conversion of anxiety into physical event symbolically reflected psychological conflict whose meaning could be understood using the method of free association (Breuer and Freud, 1895). The symptom joins the discourse between analyst and analysand and becomes part of the story or narrative of illness and affliction (Schafer, 1980, 1981; Slavney and McHugh, 1984; Kleinman, 1988).

Subsequently, Freud (1900) elaborated this model, suggesting that these wishes of which persons were mostly unaware, emerging in disguised form, originated in the context of the family circle during early childhood. The content of these wishes focused on sexual satisfaction, principally with the parent of the opposite gender but, regressively, the same-gendered parent as well. These wishes have intensity or force demanding satisfaction and are countered by prohibitions based on social convention requiring disguise in order to pass censorship in a socially acceptable form and achieve at least partial satisfaction. A compromise is struck between driven wish and the restrictions of social convention, leading to at least partial satisfaction of the wish through transfer on to some aspect of daily reality taking advantage of the mechanisms of condensation and displacement. Condensation permits fusion of several images into one overdetermined content, while displacement permits images distant in time or place to occur together.[7]

The "narrative turn" in psychoanalysis has placed study of the past into new perspective and is part of an experience-near developmental "turn" within both psychoanalysis and child development. This replaces Freud's mechanistic genetic psychology based on assumptions founded on his developmental neurobiological study (Freud, 1910; Sulloway, 1979). Focus on self as constructed from the experience of "living with" others (Winnicott, 1960a,b; Kohut, 1977), and as able to integrate diverse aspects of experience into a reasonably coherent life story, even as early as the second year of life, provides a very different perspective on the study of development from that preoccupying psychoanalysis across the past few decades.[8] The narrative turn has been possible, in large part, as a result of the reconsideration of the concept of development within psychoanalysis.

Increased appreciation of the genetic point of view as an expression of Freud's own concern in maintaining the consistency of his prepsychoanalytic study suggests that concepts of fixation and regression should be viewed as metaphor. Bernfeld (1951; Bernfeld and Bernfeld, 1944) has traced the impact of Freud's developmental neurobiology study on his later fascination with the course of psychological development. Freud observed in the study of Leonardo (1910) that "[i]mpressive analogies from biology have prepared us to find that the course of the individual's mental development repeats the course of human development in an abbreviated form" (p. 97). Freud's reference is to Hackel's (1868) "fundamental biogenetic law" and the assumption that ontogeny recapitulates phylogeny. Clearly influenced by his reading of Darwin and the British neurologist James Hughlings Jackson (Stengel, 1963; Sulloway, 1979; Ritvo, 1990), Freud studied the histology of cells in the spinal cord of a number of species on the evolutionary ladder.

Freud's detailed discussion of this earlier study in the *Introductory Lectures on Psychoanalysis* (1915–1917) is in the context of an analogy between these findings from evolutionary biology and the concept of fixation in our own instinctual life. Nowhere else is Freud so explicit regarding the use of this prepsychoanalytic study as the foundation for the genetic point of view developed more explicitly in the 1919 and 1921 revisions of *The Three Essays on Sexuality* and by Abraham (1924), Hartmann and Kris (1945), and Erikson (1950/1963). Just as the very concept of the libido has been challenged within psychoanalysis itself (Galatzer-Levy, 1976; Swanson, 1977; Gill, 1977; Wallerstein, 1977), the associated concepts of fixation and regression are increasingly understood in metaphoric terms (Schafer, 1983). Indeed, recent study of autobiographical memory (Rubin, 1986) supports observations originally made by Schachtel (1947), Novey (1968), Ricoeur (1971, 1977), and Schafer (1981, 1983) that the only account of development that is significant is that which emerges in the collaboration of analyst and analysand as they jointly construct a story of the course of life that fosters enhanced sense of coherence and integrity and leads to increased sense of personal vitality, over that which the analysand brings to the analytic process.

Ricoeur (1977) and Schafer (1980, 1981, 1983) both maintain that clinical psychoanalysis consists of the construction of a new story that is more flexible than that which the analysand brings to the analysis, and one that is both more coherent and also less rigid than the analysand's initial account. This narrative perspective is consistent with important intellectual shifts within criticism itself (Booth, 1961/1983; Mitchell, 1980, 1982). Indeed, Freud's own effort to construct a scientistic theory of development reflects his concern with finding an account of his own intellectual development rendering coherent an apparent incongruity between earlier histological study and later clinical psychoanalytic concern with intent and meaning. As Schafer (1980) has observed, the telling of a story about oneself is a narrative action of a particular kind. Further, as Schafer (1978, 1980) emphasizes, the process of telling the story to another is a doubly narrative activity, including the story of the relationship itself as influenced by the changing nature of the analysand's presently told life story.

This view of narrative and the psychoanalytic process has important implications both for understanding the course of personality change within clinical psychoanalysis as well as for portraying the course of development. The "narrative turn" reflects increasing concern with issues of meaning and intent elaborated in Klein's (1976) discussion of the significance of personal integrity and the self. Together with new understandings emerging from study of the course of child development (Winnicott, 1960; Stern, 1985, 1989a; Trevarthan, 1989), appreciation of the concept of self and sense of coherence points to the significance of personal vitality as evidence of coherence or integrity experienced in lives over time. This "narrative turn" makes possible increased understanding of the role of wish and intent revised across a lifetime in the construction of meanings emerging in relations with others, including such diverse aspects of action as going to school and making meaning out of what is learned. This capacity to make meanings includes the psychological meaning or significance for both students and faculty for the curriculum itself, as well as the intersubjectivity inherent in this relationship: student and teacher each endow their relationship with particular meanings based on their respective life histories.

PSYCHOANALYSIS, SUBJECTIVITY, AND EDUCATION

Little of the intellectual ferment within psychoanalysis has been reflected in the study of psychoanalytic contributions to education. Indeed, viewed as a formal intervention in development fostering new learning across the course of life, education may be the least well understood of all the areas of applied psychoanalytic inquiry (Cohler, 1989). However, both because of the close connection between developmental and educational study and also because of the significance of education as the single most important source of interventions likely to positively influence the lives of young people (Freud, 1913), there is an understandable affinity between psychoanalysis and the study of learning (Ekstein, 1989a). Freud's own concern with issues of learning and attention provided the foundation of the topographic point of view (Rapaport and Gill, 1959; Gill, 1963).

It was inevitable that Freud would view both nursery and classroom as ideal sources for confirmation of his theory. Indeed, writing in the introduction to Aichorn's presentation of his work with troubled youth, Freud (1925) observed that:

> None of the applications of psychoanalysis has excited so much interest and aroused so many hopes, and none, consequently, has attracted so many capable workers as its use in the theory and practice of education. . . . Analysis has shown how the sick child lives on, almost unchanged, in the sick man as well as in the dreamer and the artist. . . . It is not surprising, therefore, that an expectation should have arisen that psychoanalytic work with children would benefit the work of education, whose aim it is to guide and assist children upon their forward path and to shield them from going astray. (p. 273)

This initial enthusiasm for the classroom as a psychoanalytic laboratory was reflected in the volumes on "Psychoanalysis and Pedagogy (Education)," published in Vienna before the World War II, which were the inspiration for the series on *The Psychoanalytic Study of the Child*, published in the United States from 1945 to the present time. The expectation was that observation of the child's life in the classroom might inform psychoanalysis regarding the course of child development while also providing the optimal climate for intervention.[9] Rather than demanding that the classroom be both laboratory and consultation room, perhaps psychoanalysis can best contribute to education from the psychoanalytic method as an experience-near means for observing meanings and intents and for explicating wishes implicit in social action. Psychoanalysis provides a unique means for understanding the significance of the curriculum for learning from early elementary grades through professional education and also for appreciating the complex relationship among students and faculty.

Largely because psychoanalysis has focused on personality development across the first years of life, reflected in Freud's interest in the classroom as a laboratory for observing the personality development of young children, there has been less study of psychoanalysis and higher education than of psychoanalysis and education through the elementary grades. More recently, with extension of interest within psychoanalysis to study of the life course, including both adolescence and adulthood through oldest age (Erikson, 1981; Greenspan and Pollock, 1980; Nemiroff and Colarusso, 1990), concern with life in classrooms across secondary school and post secondary education has become increasingly relevant in attaining increased understanding of lives over time.

While the college classroom has been beyond the purview and interest of psychoanalysis, psychoanalytic study of higher education is critical in attaining increased understanding of the transition between adolescence and young adulthood, including those factors that facilitate successful realization of the developmental tasks of young adulthood. With increasing emphasis in our own society on education as a lifelong process, there is particularly great need to understand the distinctive psychology of adults as students and to address the particular problems that arise as students continue with schooling (Heath, 1968). Adult students are particularly concerned about the danger of "infantilization" on the part of bureaucratic administrators and teachers that interferes with learning. Psychoanalytically informed understanding of life in classrooms must extend beyond the nursery years to postsecondary and even professional education and must focus on both issues of curriculum and the relationship between students themselves and students and instructors (Katz, 1962, 1968, 1976; Ekstein, 1988b).

Psychoanalysis and the Curriculum

Freud had argued in the presentation of the topographic model, particularly in Chapter 7 of *The Interpretation of Dreams* (1900), the essay on "Formulations on the Two Principles of Mental Functioning" (1911), and the essay on "The Unconscious" (1915) that study of the sense organs of consciousness was not sufficient to explain the phenomenon of becoming conscious. It was necessary to reconsider the very question of consciousness and to argue for the existence of another force that determines becoming conscious. The concept of the unconscious, the repository of the nuclear wish, evident by its impact on thought and action by the third to fifth year of life, provided a means for explaining consciousness. In the well-known portrayal of the mental topography, Freud posits that consciousness, or the phenomenon of attending to internal and external reality, is determined by wishes issuing from the nuclear (oedipal) wish and that, in a suitably disguised manner, this wish is transferred across the repression barrier forming the contents of the system preconscious. The system consciousness becomes "interested" in noticing some content of the preconscious, or thought, as relevant to the satisfaction of a need. In the revised structural model of "The Ego and the Id" (1923) and "The New Introductory Lectures" (1932), the extent to which conflict determines mode of perception is emphasized to an ever greater extent: the ego searches the real world on behalf of providing satisfaction for the id.

THE SUBJECTIVE CURRICULUM.   This model of the determinants of thinking suggests that all secondary process, or formal, logical thought, is determined by need or wish (Cohler, 1972a). The model is consistent with the clinical theory in which Freud maintains that persons understand experience in terms of wish and intent. Understanding of the actions of others and of what interests us may be understood both in terms of satisfaction of wish or intent and also in terms of contributions to enhanced sense of personal integrity. This perspective on learning and education, distinctive from the psychoanalytic perspective, has been portrayed by Richard Jones (1968) as the "subjective curriculum." Jones maintains that parallel to the so-called objective curriculum, or what is presumed to be learned in school, there is a subjective curriculum that, if properly employed, may actually enhance learning.

Jones's observations regarding the curriculum stem from his participation in Bruner's project for a junior high school social studies curriculum. Jones was asked to consult with the project when it became clear that students were not profiting from a carefully constructed curriculum, part of the *Man, a Course of Study*, designed by Jerome Bruner and others. Jones found that the material was so personally threatening that students protected themselves from it. The classroom teacher focused almost exclusively on the objective curriculum. Empathic observation of student responses led Jones to recognize the intense and personally painful content reflected in lessons such as that showing Eskimo families leaving their elders behind to die when harsh winter conditions made it difficult to feed a large family. Jones realized that many students reacted powerfully to issues of care for dependent and helpless family members. In the absence of an opportunity for discussing these feelings, students were forced to block out particularly personally painful and frightening scenes. This observation led to efforts to talk about the meaning of the filmstrip for the students, after which it was possible to reflect on the intellectual significance of the lesson.

Focus on the personal or subjective experience of the curriculum should not be regarded as a substitute or replacement for the formal curriculum; concern with issues of meaning (the subjective curriculum) enhances the power of what is learned in school by removing potential resistance to learning new and possibly threatening material. Prior to the discussion of students' own responses to observing the filmstrips in Bruner's social studies curriculum, classroom discussion of the material was tentative and superficial. Following acknowledgment of the subjective meanings inherent in the filmstrips, students were able to become much more engaged in the discussion of the material. Jones's point is that recognition of meanings emplotted in the formal curriculum enhances rather than interferes with learning the formal curriculum.

Recognizing the subjective curriculum may make it possible to teach the more troubled student who is not as easily reached by traditional materials. For example, a youngster who was seriously injured by a passing auto when he was quite young, with lasting impact upon both intellectual functioning and adjustment, had developed a preoccupation with issues of knighthood and armor. This student was particularly fascinated by the legend of King Arthur. His teacher recognized that the youngster's fascination with protective armor expressed his concern with his own physical and personal frailty. An entire curriculum was developed around the theme of knighthood. Story problems in arithmetic were phrased in terms of knighthood, history focused on the Middle Ages, science began with alchemy, and English literature and composition dealt almost exclusively with stories of the time of King Arthur. This focus on the subjective curriculum was accompanied by intensive psychotherapy and educational therapy (also using material from the Middle Ages). The result of this pioneering educational experiment was that this student was able to make up five years of school in two, and by the third year of the "experiment" was nearly at grade level (7th grade).

Anne Roe (1956) has pointed to the importance of matching personal history and career interests. Her work on personality characteristics and planning for vocation implicitly recognizes the concept of the subjective curriculum. In a similar manner, student selection of undergraduate concentration program may be dictated by the subjective meaning of this choice. An undergraduate student from a southern community had relatives on both sides of his family fighting for both the North and the South in the Civil War. Following his parents' divorce when he was in high school, this student developed a passionate interest in the Civil War and, particularly, the origins of the conflict in the preceding decades. The student selected a concentration program in American history and wrote a senior paper on Henry Clay, which was described by one instructor as publishable in a scholarly journal. This student went on to a distinguished career in American history; he reported that his personal psychoanalysis further clarified the personal significance of his intellectual interests.

SUBJECTIVE CURRICULUM AND BOTH PERSONAL AND INTELLECTUAL DEVELOPMENT. Jones argues that issues of both developmental and educational timing must be considered in planning the curriculum. A major point in his critique of Bruner's curriculum is that it demanded a level of abstract thinking that could not be attained by the junior high school students for whom the curriculum was designed. Based on Piaget's genetic epistemology, there has been much consideration of this issue across the past two decades, particularly as educators studied Piaget's work for clues regarding match between curricular concepts and classroom demands in "headstart" programs (Kamii and Radin, 1966). Just as there is little to be gained from asking students to master concepts that are presently beyond their cognitive capacity, there is little to be gained from expecting students to deal with concepts that are both meaningful and personally painful apart from discussion with teachers and classmates.[10]

The issue of timing of the introduction of curricular topics posing potentially personal threat has seldom been discussed. Across the academic year, accompanying students' changing experience of self, other, and schooling, meanings are attributed to classroom and instruction that often escape notice by those who plan curricula. For example, there is presently much concern regarding education in the area of substance abuse. An affectively charged topic, instruction in this area requires both confidence in the instructor and trust of one's fellow students. September, when the year is just getting underway and when students do not yet know the instructor or their fellow students, appears to be a particularly poor time of the year to engage in discussion of this topic.

This issue of subjective curriculum and timing across the academic year has been addressed in planning the general education social science sequence in the college of the University of Chicago. In past years, it was common to teach Durkheim's (1897) book *Suicide* and Freud's case studies and *Interpretation of Dreams* (1900) to first-year college students in the autumn quarter. Common sense alone would suggest that students just beginning their career in a residential college, often away from home for the first time, struggling with the new-found freedom and responsibility provided by college life, may find it difficult to engage topics so personally relevant. Further, students must gain some degree of comfort with their instructor and fellow students in order to comfortably discuss the emotionally "loaded" topics explicit in the work of both Durkheim and Freud. Even the subject of religion, and Durkheim's (1912) demonstration that religious worship is ultimately the worship of society itself, may pose painful conflict for students from families in which religious commitment is a major aspect of daily life. As difficult as this topic is for students when introduced in the winter quarter of the course, it would be virtually impossible for students just beginning college to confront such personally threatening topics.

If the goal is to have students master the curriculum, it may be better to discuss these possibly threatening topics later in the academic year, when students feel more comfortable with their place in the classroom and the college, than to deal with these topics immediately at the beginning of the fall term. Relying upon the concept of the subjective curriculum, the entire course was redesigned: the autumn quarter now begins with the issue of work and economy, the winter quarter takes up the issue of symbol and meaning, while the spring focuses on concepts of meaning and person. Since issues of vocation and career are central in the lives of students, albeit less painful to discuss, it is particularly appropriate that the year begin with this issue, which is of such a concern and yet which is not too affectively laden for students to discuss. The work of Karl Marx and Max Weber, together with historical studies such as those of Le Geoff (1980) on the emergence of time in the West as central in defining the workday or Thompson (1967) on time and work discipline in the Industrial Revolution, are important in helping students to deal with issues of work and management of time in their own lives.

Having worked together across the academic year, generally with the same fellow students and the same instructor, by the spring quarter students have realized enough self-confidence and have sufficient experience at the college to be able to talk about issues regarding sexuality posed by the study of Freud's work. The goal in each instance is not to "pander" to student interests, or even to regard students as emotionally fragile and in need of protection. Just as in *Man, a Course of Study*, the goal is to teach the curriculum and to have students profit from having studied this material. Developmental and instructional timing is critical in realizing these curricular goals.

Efforts to force students to question themselves and society may produce overwhelming feelings of confusion and uncertainty. This is certainly not to say that controversy should be avoided, or that we should abandon the goal of enhanced understanding and personal freedom uniquely possible through education, but rather that the significance of the subjective curriculum must be explicitly acknowledged so that these challenges are not so overwhelming as to produce disorganization or, more likely, defensive operations that may preclude real learning. The significance of the subjective curriculum for learning must be explicitly acknowledged so that accompanying challenges will not be so overwhelming that they foster a sense of personal disorganization or, alternatively, disengaging from instruction in an effort to protect oneself from these uncomfortable feelings. Writing about the captivating power of Sophocles's tragedy, *Oedipus Rex*, in a rare discussion of the emotional significance of the curriculum, Freud (1900) argued that the continuing power of this classical drama for our own time is founded in the conflict that it portrays. However, without recognition of the power of this message, intense feelings are elicited that interfere in the appreciation of this tragedy.

A student reading *The Interpretation of Dreams* gained increased understanding of a problem in his own life: he was always attracted to women who were unavailable, either because they were about to graduate from college and leave town or because they were going out with a friend or roommate. He had lost a number of close friendships by becoming involved in relationships that, by common understanding, were "off-limits" to him. Working on an assigned paper discussing a recent dream, this student became aware of some of the reasons for this attraction, which ultimately was not satisfying. As a consequence, he has been shifting his romantic interests in a direction that might offer the prospect of more satisfying intimacy. Another student, an avid sailor, became aware of feelings of resentment regarding an intrusive father who had been inappropriately involved in his older brother's achievements in world-class tennis. Reading Freud's *Interpretation of Dreams*, he realized that his interest in sailing emerged, at least in part, because that was an activity that his father could hardly observe and in which his father could not take an active part. This student was able to talk about his disappointments regarding his father, particularly regarding his father's efforts to relive, through his sons, his own mid-life career and personal crisis after early social and business success.

About one in three marriages end in divorce, most often preceded by conflicts between parents that have greater impact on children than the actual divorce (Hetherington and Camara, 1984). Particularly among upper-middle-class families, divorce is most likely to take place early in the marriage, prior to parenthood, or at about the time children leave home for college. O'Neill's drama *Long Day's Journey into Night*, portraying interpersonal conflicts within the family circle, elicits powerful feelings among students reading this work. Student essays regarding this play attest to its powerful capacity to evoke memories regarding similar dilemmas within the students' own families.

One student who found the play particularly compelling was still shaken by his parents' announcement of their impending marital separation the night before his departure for college. His essay about the play proved important in resolving intense feelings regarding his parents long-standing marital conflict. The fact that the O'Neill play is able to stimulate such powerful feelings should not rule it out of the curriculum. Indeed, the power of the text argues for its inclusion in classes in the humanities and social sciences. Failure to attend to meanings implicit in this work, and to make them explicit in discussions with students, may lead students to protect themselves against the full power of the drama and to keep the play at a safe distance without having to confront its personal significance.

Jones's reform of Bruner's junior high school science curriculum enhanced understanding of the goals that Bruner had attempted to realize in *Man, a Course of Study*. In a similar way, discussion of personally significant texts increases student appreciation of these texts. A student from a wealthy, politically connected family became fascinated with Thomas Mann's *Buddenbrooks*. He readily recognized the salience of

Mann's novel for his own life, using the novel as a means for increased understanding of the problems faced by his own family. Ultimately, he was able to reconcile long-standing differences with his father through study of this text. Another student, grieving the sudden death of a parent shortly after beginning college, found solace through a seminar on Plato's *Phaedo*, a dialogue focusing on the question of the immortality of the soul.

Psychoanalysis and the Student–Teacher Relationship

Jones did not ask why senior, well-regarded, classroom teachers showed a break in empathy in the failure to recognize the personal significance of the filmstrips used in *Man, A Course of Study*. Teachers may become more concerned with the objective curriculum than with the subjective curriculum; little is known about the reason why teachers may be unable to use the latter in the classroom, from elementary school to the university. Katz and Sanford (1962) note the increased impact that could be realized by the curriculum if instructors were able to attend more directly to their student's feelings about what they learn. Sometimes the curriculum affects the instructor in ways that parallel its effect on students. Temporary lapses in the instructor's capacity to respond empathically to student concerns regarding the curriculum should be understood as markers of likely areas of student anxiety requiring particular effort if the instructor is to engage the student with the full force of the text (Adelson, 1962).

TEACHING AND THE SUBJECTIVE CURRICULUM. Texts such as Freud's case studies, much of modern drama, or certain ethnographic accounts are particularly likely to pose problems in the instructor's capacity to respond empathically to student concerns. In a university general education course focusing on cultural construction of gender, one of the course staff pronounced an ethnographic account of ritual homoerotic activity in New Guinea as "disgusting and revolting." Clearly, this account elicited parallel concerns that made if difficult for this course staff member to make the implicit meanings contained within the text explicit within the context of the continuing discussion of what it means to be a man or woman in society. Had the instructor had the capacity to do so, perhaps with the aid of a colleague, he might have turned the experience to good purpose. Recognizing a judgmental stance, uncharacteristic of a scholarly approach to ethnography, he would have been moved to inquire into the reasons for his reaction. In doing so he would not only have understood himself and the ethnographic material better but also would have been better able to understand and address the students' emotional response to the same material.

Freud's writings, work of such novelists as Dostoyevski, Faulkner, and Virginia Woolf, all require the instructor's close attention to conflicts stimulated by the text among teacher and student alike. Freud's contributions to the study of person and culture are particularly challenging texts to read and to teach. Reading about psychoanalysis demands that students confront concerns that they may have previously evaded. Essay assignments, such as having students write a paper on their own dream (or that of a friend or roommate), using Freud's concept of the dream work, parallel to Freud's discussion of the specimen dream in Chapter 2 of *The Interpretation of Dreams* (1900), leads students to appreciate the significance of conflicts in their own life of which they had previously not been aware. Since these texts may reciprocally be painful for both student and instructor, the problem of making explicit the meanings implicit in Freud's discussion of wish becomes particularly difficult. The instructor may not be sufficiently comfortable with his or her own intentions to be able to teach the book effectively. Indeed, much of the controversy regarding Freud's contribution may derive from the powerful feelings that are elicited and are difficult for all of us to acknowledge (Busch, 1989).

The Classroom as "Intermediate Space"

Teacher and student each contribute to the construction of meanings within that "intermediate space" (Winnicott, 1953) which is the classroom. Just as in all relationships, each participant enters into this discussion with particular wishes, fears, and experiences across a lifetime. A teacher growing up in circumstances of poverty may find it difficult to teach in an affluent suburb. An instructor unsure of her or his own scholarly abilities may find it difficult to be supportive of the fledgling scholarly efforts of college students. Bettelheim (1969) has observed that, as child and teacher meet each morning, they enter a world in which even experiences of the present day influence life in the classroom. The child may have had an argument with his parents about clothes selected for school, breakfast, or other details of the daily round. The teacher may have had an argument with spouse or children, or may already have had a heated discussion with those ubiquitous school administrators whose sole task, at least as perceived by teachers, seems to lie in creating obstacles to effective teaching. Meeting in the classroom, teacher and student jointly construct shared meanings based on separate and shared life experiences. If the child should feel quarrelsome as a result of events prior to coming to school or the teacher should feel particularly impatient as a result of his or her own life experiences of the morning, the conditions are prepared for conflict between them (Bettelheim, 1969).

THE PERSONAL IMPACT OF STUDENT ON INSTRUCTOR. This psychoanalytic perspective on life in the classroom may be observed from preschool education through postsecondary education into professional and adult education (Salzberger-Wittenberg, Henry, and Osborne, 1983). There is an understandable reluctance to view higher education in the same terms as the elementary school classroom. Certainly, the nature of the discourse differs dramatically in postsecondary education. Further, particularly in the nation's elite liberal arts colleges and collegiate divisions of research universities, instructors understand their own participation in the classroom in quite different terms than in the elementary school. Indeed, the instructor in the college or university classroom identifies with scholarly study or research to a greater extent than with teaching. All too often, teaching is viewed as a burden or obligation that makes it possible to continue with one's own scholarly study.

Students also assume a greater seriousness of purpose and fascination with the subject matter, which may be less characteristic of precollegiate study. Students particularly relish the opportunity to work with scholars who are active contributors to scholarship and to bask in the glow of the faculty member's enjoyment of scholarly study and recognition for scholarly accomplishments (Adelson, 1962; Basch, 1989). However, faculty themselves may not be comfortable with this admiration and may flee from the classroom and from feelings of grandiosity or from discomfort with a perceived discrepancy between perceived goals and accomplishments that may be stimulated by student admiration. Regardless of "real world" attainments, faculty grandiosity may be so great that even Nobel prize accomplishments may be minimized when contrasted with imagined success and desired attainments.

Beneath superficial differences between the roles of elementary or secondary school teacher and university professor, many of the same classroom dynamics may be observed in each situation. As Ekstein (1989b) and Salzberger-Wittenberg, Henry, and Osborne (1983) have shown, students and faculty endow the classroom situation with meanings reflecting the life experiences of each. Indeed, the very seriousness of purpose that distinguishes the collegiate classroom may merely highlight issues less significant in primary or even secondary education. Concerns with self and who one is (Erikson, 1959) may become especially a matter of concern at the collegiate level. The relationship between student and instructor may also become a concern as students seek faculty supervision for reading and writing about particular texts. Self-esteem, concern with issues of competition, and concern with issues of identity all are brought into particularly sharp focus during late adolescence and early adulthood. The complex interplay between student, faculty, and curriculum often become entangled in ways difficult to distinguish.

For faculty as well, many of the issues of concern in precollegiate education are heightened in collegiate and university teaching. For example, student expectations regarding accomplishments of faculty may threaten the self-esteem of those faculty who question the nature of their own contributions. Other faculty may feel threatened by student accomplishments or feel enhanced competitiveness with students whose research may call their own contributions into question or who may succeed in resolving an issue whose solution has eluded them. The very competence of the advanced undergraduate student or the graduate student may be experienced as a threat by faculty mentors. Instead of taking advantage of this competence as an opportunity to increase their own understanding of their scholarly discipline, these faculty may feel threatened or competitive with their students. Particularly in the sciences, where knowledge is cumulative, the possibility that the student will find a "fatal flaw" in an experiment conducted by a mentor or will provide a more parsimonious explanation of a phenomenon poses particular problems for faculty, often reflected in a final dissertation oral examination in which the candidate is forced to defend his work in ways that are beyond what is reasonable to expect. These meetings for the defense of the dissertation may become burdened by the additional meaning evoked by intergenerational envy.[11]

Concerned with issues of intellectual productivity, professional evaluations, and, at times, feelings of inability to live up to their image of themselves as scholars, faculty may be so preoccupied with issues of evaluation and productivity that they fail to respond empathically to students. Research university faculty experiencing conflict between teaching and scholarly work and liberal arts faculty often feeling overwhelmed by student expectations may find it difficult to maintain an empathic stance. Obviously, students look to faculty for guidance in understanding the curriculum. Less obviously, students seek assurance from faculty about their talents and skills, which supports continued learning. Letting oneself be used by students, attempting to maintain self-esteem when confronted by challenging situations, is an important element of what Levinson (1977, 1980, 1986) calls "mentoring," the care and concern expressed by more senior for more junior members of an organization.

In his portrayal of career development, Levinson describes how in organizations as diverse as universities and businesses, people in established positions commonly support the development of those beginning careers. Successful men in follow-up studies of mental health of college men at mid-life were more explicitly concerned with mentorship and mentoring (Vaillant, 1977, 1978, 1981; Vaillant and Milofsky, 1980). Studying career attainments of college undergraduates, Thistlewaite (1959, 1962) has shown that mentorship, defined as devoted faculty concern for student careers, is a better predictor of whether students will obtain a doctorate than such school characteristics as quality of laboratory facilities or library size. In the natural sciences, the instructor's collegial manner and expectation of particular intellectual rigor and, in the social sciences and humanities, concern for student welfare, enthusiastic teaching, and fostering controversial discussion, all are associated with student's completing doctorates.

The mentor may be particularly important in fostering a student's determination for success in spite of adversity or in giving the student "the courage to try" (Bernstein, 1989). In Vygotsky's (1934) discussion of the "zone of proximal development," the skillful teacher is able to give the student courage to work on a problem of particular difficulty, perhaps one even at the growing edge of his academic competencies, and to stick by the student during times of difficulty in realizing new learning. As Bernstein observes, in every effort to learn new material, there are those "dark moments" when the concept is particularly confusing or when the answer eludes the student's best efforts at understanding. A valued mentor can assist a student with low self-esteem to evaluate her or his own talents and skills more accurately and arrive at an appreciation of self more in line with the reality of previous attainments and potential for the future. In this manner, the mentor is able to facilitate new learning and to give students the courage to try.

Despite evidence that faculty mentors are important for student growth, college teachers often find it hard to tolerate student admiration. Student idealizations provide important psychological support, permitting them to feel they can achieve great things through association with admired teachers. Kohut (1971) observed that analysands' idealizations of psychoanalysts arouse anxieties in the analyst who feel their own grandiosity overstimulated by such veneration. As a result analysts tend to interfere with these admiring attitudes to the detriment of the analytic work. Similarly, faculty often feel unequal to students' admiration. A common response is to demur; another is to be arrogant, masking doubts of being worthy of admiration. Many faculty withdraw from teaching or avoid contact with students rather than having to deal with the emotional strain of student idealizations.

On the other hand some instructors are disappointed when students do not admire them enough or assume their values. They seek in students a mirror for their own interests and attainments and become disappointed when they are unable to obtain this mirror from students who fail to adopt their own interests and concerns in just the manner that they had initially sought. For example, an instructor who tries to foster rebellion against adult authority may be disappointed when students fail to adopt his cause as their own. Instructors who were activists in the 1960s and 1970s commonly feel discouraged that most contemporary students are uninterested in the issues that so moved them in their youth. Women instructors who have worked actively for feminist causes may feel dispirited when young women of another generation appear to be less identified with the feminist cause or may be more concerned with issues of marriage and family formation than with career.

Still other faculty responds competitively to student successes, withdrawing support, trying to outdo the students or demeaning student achievements. It is difficult to distinguish between the advisor's effort to encourage the highest level of performance and expectations that may be unreasonable: student progress, especially at advanced levels, may be delayed by perfectionistic demands used as a disguise for feelings of envy and competition. (Far less common deliberate destruction of potential competitors and thinly rationalized exploitation of student research labors also occurs.)

Some instructors successfully manage threats to self-esteem, the overstimulation of student idealization, and issues of competition. They often become great teachers. However, when faculty anxieties interfere with helping students with similar issues, vicious circles of escalating anxiety are common. Where grading is by a "curve," with some students inevitably getting average or lower grades, issues of competition and self-worth are particularly intense, such as in the nature sciences or classes related to professional school admission or career placement. Institutional and personal characteristics are interrelated—some institutions are deeply concerned with the human side of learning while others foster competition and so enhance a sense of personal inadequacy.

A tragicomic incident illustrates how far students and faculty can move from an emotional collaboration in the service of learning. When medical school admission was enormously competitive and comparative anatomy was thought essential to admissions, the following event occurred at a college where many undergraduates competed fiercely and faculty promoted competition: The professor of comparative anatomy's office was "torched" at the end of a semester. It was widely assumed that the perpetrator was a student who wanted to erase an unfortunate semester. However, he was foiled—the professor announced to the school newspaper the next day that he had kept a second set of class records at his home *in anticipation* of exactly the event that had occurred.

Faculty helps shape student self-esteem. However, most college teachers do not consider this provision of support to be an important part of their work. Of the three dimensions of the "job description" of college professors (Knapp, 1962)—scholarship, instruction, and character development—the first two are common in discussions of faculty quality while the third is rarely addressed. Consistent with Weber's views (1904–1905) in *The Protestant Ethic,* Knapp suggests that the secularization of the American college in the last half of the nineteenth century, creation of public universities, impersonal natural science instruction through lecture and demonstration, and concern to separate church and state led most nondenominational American postsecondary institutions to systematically avoid issues of faculty contributions to moral development.

The emergence of the academic professions shifted the faculties' primary identifications from educators (especially in a broad sense that includes moral development) to members of disciplines. Promotion and tenure came to be determined primarily by disciplinary contributions (Caplow and McGee, 1958). Geographic mobility became an important part of academic career development. Always moving to institutions with the most social and academic prestige, faculty grew more concerned with professional success than with student's lives. At the same time, concerned with getting the most prestige for the dollar, administrators offered research facilities, reduced teaching "loads," and academic leaves as recruitment incentives. Contact with students was believed to, and often did, interfere with academic prestige.

There need not be tension between faculty careers as research scholars within a discipline and student needs for faculty devotion to effective teaching and availability as role models and counselors. Scholarship, at least in the sense of deep interest in the field, and teaching are inseparable. Effective instruction requires both knowledge and understanding of the emotional process of learning. Concern for student wellbeing and empathic responses to fledgling scholarly efforts are critical to teaching, enhancing learning across the course of life (Wolf, 1989). Effective university education should engage students in a lifelong process of learning that can be sustained despite dangers that efforts will not live up to internal and external standards (Elson, 1989), the fears of success that are commoner in women, or the fears of failure that are commoner in men (Horner, 1972). This can be achieved only when students have an opportunity to expose themselves to teachers who provide the emotional support for learning.

Conclusion

Psychoanalysis is the study of subjectivity, including both wish and intent of which persons are aware and those which are kept out of awareness due to their socially or personally potentially reprehensible nature. A part of Freud's genius was to recognize that these wishes can be symbolically represented with partial satisfaction out of awareness. Such disguise meets standards of acceptable thoughts without disrupting the experience of personal congruence. These wishes begin with early childhood and may be observed across the course of life. At first, concern is with sense of comfort and caring realized from a caretaker experienced as providing tension relief and solace. Across the nursery years, at least within our own culture, the child's complex wishes regarding the imagined parents of early childhood, including sexual and rivalrous feelings, add further to the construction of subjectivity.

Understood together as factors contributing to a continuing sense of vitality and spontaneity, resolution of these issues posed across early childhood leads to a capacity for engagement in learning in the classroom, from the time of earliest formal instruction through adult education, and determines the content of the subjective world of experience (Ekstein and Motto, 1969). Parallel with what is formally learned, students attribute personally relevant meanings to all aspects of schooling, from the emotional climate of the classroom to characteristics of the teacher and fellow students and subject matter which is being taught. Traditionally, it was assumed that attention to the subjective curriculum would interfere with educational objectives. However, rather than distracting students from presumed proper concern with the formal curriculum, focus on the subjective curriculum enhances educational objectives. This concern with the personal meaning of what is learned in school permits students to discuss fears and wishes, and creates a classroom optimally attuned to learning. As a consequence, students feel increasingly comfortable, integrated, and able to remain engaged in curriculum and instruction.

Concern with the relationship between student and instructor is also of critical importance for understanding life in classrooms. Just as students attribute meanings based on experiences of a lifetime to the curriculum, meanings are also attributed to the instructor. At a commonsense level, a student who rebels against the imposition of "arbitrary" authority will find it difficult to learn in school. Recognition of the variety of wishes enacted in the relationship between student and instructor increases the student's ability to understand and to resolve factors such as competitiveness, resentment, or personal attraction that might interfere in this relationship. Greater attention must be extended to the reciprocal role of student and instructor within the classroom.

The instructor's own wishes and concerns are played out in the classroom in a manner parallel to those of students. The instructor who believes it is necessary to be particularly challenging to young men attending class may be enacting anew issues of authority and control stemming from early childhood. The instructor who is unable to allow him- or herself to be appropriately admired and emulated by students may be burdened and unable to live up to this praise or may be stimulated by such admiration to the point of feeling overwhelmed and disorganized. Optimally, instructors enjoy the intellectual challenges posed by students in the service of shared learning and are able to accept and appreciate student idealizations as a result of appropriately recognizing the value of their own scholarly achievements and their contributions in enriching the lives and careers of their students.

NOTES

1. Even as central a concept in psychoanalysis as the nuclear neurosis, later (Freud, 1910) referred to as the "Oedipus complex," was derived from sources other than observation of development (Sadow, et al., 1968; Gedo, 1976; Anzieu, 1986; Krull, 1986). Freud applied both neurobiological and archeological models (including his particular reading of Sophocles's tragedy of Oedipus Rex as a story of the evolution of culture) in his effort to understand the complexity of his grief surrounding his father's death in 1896 (Freud, 1900; Rudnytsky, 1987). It is significant for the history of psychoanalysis that this most fundamental hypothesis was derived from Freud's own self-inquiry, and that it has seldom been studied among women in a manner parallel to the study of men or used in the systematic study of personality development among preschool-aged boys and girls. Indeed, although there has been some anecdotal information regarding genitality and gender in the preschool years (Galenson and Roiphe, 1976; Parens, et al., 1976), there has been little systematic study regarding the origins, course, and resolution of the nuclear conflict.
2. Much the same criticism may be made of the application of ego-psychology to the study of psychological development, as portrayed by Anna Freud (1965) in her discussion of developmental lines.
3. Part of this difficulty arises because of Mahler's assumption, following Freud (1905) that pathological states represent the emergence in more mature individuals of earlier forms of psychological functioning. Although not formulated by Freud in this way, it is generally assumed in psychoanalytic discussions that the more severe the pathology, the earlier the normal developmental state to which it corresponds. This assumption provides an extraordinary window for studying early development and was central to Freud's construction of normal early development from psychoanalytic work with adults. It is on the basis of this assumption (as well as Freud's assertions) that Mahler posited a normal autistic phase that she believed was the point to which individuals with autistic psychosis regress. She by no means is unique in making and using this assumption. Freud and Kohut, among many others, use the same assumption in describing early development. The assumption, however, is erroneous.

Although regression to earlier forms of function is a common aspect of many psychopathological states, it is not universal nor is the role played by factors other than regression so clear that even where regression is a central factor is psychopathology is its particular contribution sufficiently clear to permit accurate reconstruction of earlier psychological function on the basis of psychopathology alone.

4. Kohut refers to these others experienced as part of self in terms of the concept of "self-object" ties, while Stern (1985, 1989a) portrays a similar concept of the emerging psychological use of others as "evoked companions" and Galatzer-Levy and Cohler (1990) prefer the term "evoked other" or "essential other" as a means for describing continued psychological use of others (as well as realization of tangible support and assistance) across the course of life.

5. Although the independence of the observed reality from the meaning of the relationship of observed and observer is the received vision of investigation in the physical sciences that is taken as normative by many psychoanalytic researchers, this notion has gradually narrowed its domain since the turn of the century when special relativity and quantum theory began to demonstrate that "reality" was contingent on the observer. But even strong versions of the interrelation of observer and observed that characterize the dominant trend in quantum mechanical thought do not include a notion of shared, mutually created, or negotiated meaning between observer and observed that is characteristic of the investigative methods of experience near observation.

6. Jones and Strachey were able to convince Freud of the value in using a scientific language for Freud's innovative psychoanalytic terms and the metaphors on which they were so often based. Freud continued to endorse a scientific stance regarding psychoanalytic formulations from *On Aphasia* (1891) and "Project for a Scientific Psychology" (1895), through his very last major work, the posthumously published "An Outline of Psychoanalysis" (1940). Across the course of his career, it was the metapsychology, a term for the psychology "beyond consciousness" (Freud, 1897), which was of greatest interest to him. Freud pledged to Fliess that he would devote himself single-mindedly to this purportedly scientific study modeled metaphorically on Aristotle's metaphysics (which Freud had read with Brentano at university in 1874). At the same time, he complained about the "witch" of metapsychology that preoccupied his thoughts, but which could not be resolved (Freud, 1937b).

Sulloway (1979) has documented the impact of late nineteenth-century natural science methods and findings upon Freud's intellectual development. While Klein (1976) and Galatzer-Levy and Cohler (1990) have observed that Freud's endorsement of a natural science understanding of wish and intent was principally a reflection of the scientific worldview in which he had been educated, he remained committed to this scientistic project; Bettelheim (1983) appears to disregard Freud's expressed sentiments supporting an experience-distant and scientistic worldview as the foundation of his work. Consistent with Freud's scientific preoccupation, Steiner (1988) provides the following quote from *Beyond the Pleasure Principle* (which does not appear in the translation): "The shortcomings of our description would probably disappear if for the psychological terms we could substitute physiological or chemical ones. These too constitute a metaphorical language, but one familiar to us for a much longer time and perhaps also simpler." (p. 187)

This quote from *Beyond the Pleasure Principle* reflects the Freud of the "Project" (1895) and the "Outline" (1939), endorsing the worldview initially formulated by Helmholtz and Brucke, and repeated across the half-century of Freud's psychoanalytic studies. This is the Freud who Bettelheim (1983) overlooks in his otherwise important reading of Freud's contributions to the study of subjectivity, and which Orston finds difficult to reconcile with an account which, in the original German edition, is both less internally consistent but also more compassionate regarding the human condition and more lively than the standardized translation of this work. This experience-near reading of Freud's work has the advantage of linking what appear to be mechanistic formulations in such works as *The Ego and the Id* with the clinical theory, reconciling at least some of the apparently unresolved confusion regarding the place of the metapsychology in the emergence of the clinical theory.

7. Dreams, neurotic symptoms, purportedly unintended actions or speech, slips of the tongue, artistic productions, and enactments within the therapeutic setting, all reflect compromises between wish and the demands of social convention. As Rapaport (1960) has shown in the model of thinking based on Freud's topography, the conflict between a wish possessing force seeking satisfaction and the opposing demands of social reality leads to continued compromise formations in which the academic curriculum becomes yet another area in which this conflict is enacted. From the child's fledgling efforts to learn to read and write to the advanced study of the doctoral student, interest in a particular curriculum may be understood as a displacement from the underlying conflict; the search for the riddle of the universe is but another means for understanding the mystery of the parental bedroom of early childhood. Indeed, Freud's own preoccupation with the Riddle of the Sphinx in Sophocles's play (Rudnytsky, 1987) reflects this same conflict. His self-analysis following his father's death in October 1896 seems to have somewhat reduced the intensity of this concern.

8. Realization of the significance of narrative or story for the emplotting of experience has placed new emphasis on developmental study of the child's construction of a story as an important means for understanding the child's emerging narrative of her or his own life. Talk that children engage in regarding self and others leads to particular conceptions of self and the relationship of self and others (Miller *et al.*, 1990). As Vygotsky earlier had shown (1978), talking is reality; particular narratives that persons do talk about become a reality for them as social speech becomes personal dialogue central to the formation of self (Stern, 1985, 1989b). Further, capacity for memory of the past emerges with language; 2-year-olds both remember the past and are able to talk about these memories. For example, detailed study of the accounts

provided by young children of their own past prior to the present interview, reported by Miller and Sperry (1988), suggested not only that these children could provide verbal accounts but also that accounts were primarily negative! Most often chosen by children were accounts emphasizing frightening events or fantasies that were clearly distinguished from these events. For reasons distinctive to our own culture, memories of the past appear to be largely negative.

9. Several schools continue with this model, most notably the Hannah Perkins School in Cleveland, and the Orthogenic School in Chicago.

10. Bettelheim (1969) has observed that use of the school as a medium for communication of social values and problems regarding these social problems both burdens the school in ways which interfere in the educational mission and pose particular demands for the classroom teacher to confront student concerns regarding issues of sexuality and life and death that may be beyond the competence of any teacher. (At the present time, this is a major issue impeding the effectiveness of educational programs concerning such sensitive social issues as substance abuse or AIDS.)

11. Faculty envy of students, which is commonly enacted to an astonishing extent, is often rationalized as monitoring standards and has many sources. Faculty members may recognize students as more able than themselves. In certain fields such as dance and mathematics, the younger person's age is an overwhelming realistic advantage. Scholars who endured financial hardship to pursue academic careers may feel that the better financial position of today's students mean that they have not "paid their dues." Resentment about real and imagined wrongs as well as fears and anxiety about aging can all find outlets in destructive hostility toward students.

REFERENCES

Abraham, K. (1924/1953). A short study on the development of the libido, viewed in the light of mental disorders. *Selected Papers on Psychoanalysis*, pp. 418–501. New York: Basic Books.

Adelson, J. (1962). The teacher as a model. In N. Sanford (ed.), *The American College: A Psychological and Social Interpretation of the Higher Learning*, pp. 396–417. New York: John Wiley and Sons.

Anthony, E. J. (1976). How children cope in families with a psychotic child. In E. Rexford, L. Sander, and T. Shapiro (eds.), *Infant Psychiatry: A New Synthesis*, pp. 239–250. New Haven: Yale University Press.

Anzieu, D. (1986). *Freud's Self Analysis* (P. Graham, trans.). London: Hogarth Press.

Applegarth, A. (1977). Psychic energy reconsidered: A critique. *Journal of the American Psychoanalytic Association* 25:599–602.

Arlow, J., and Brenner, C. (1964). *Psychoanalytic Concepts and the Structural Theory*. New York: International Universities Press (*Journal of the American Psychoanalytic Association* Monograph Series Number 3).

Atwood, G., and Stolorow, R. (1984). *Structures of Subjectivity: Explorations in Psychoanalytic Phenomenology*. Hillsdale, NJ: The Analytic Press.

Anzieu, O. (1986). *Freud's Self Analysis* (Tr. P. Graham). London: Hogarth Press.

Basch, M. F. (1981) Selfobject disorders and theory: A historical perspective. *Journal of the American Psychoanalytic Association* 29:337–352.

Basch, M. (1983a). The concept of "self": An operational definition. In B. Lee and G. Noam (eds.), *Developmental Approaches to the Self*, pp. 7–58. New York: Plenum.

Basch, M. (1983b). Some theoretical and methodological implications of self psychology. In A. Goldberg (ed.), *The Future of Psychoanalysis*, pp. 431–442. New York: International Universities Press.

Basch, M. (1989). The teacher, the transference, and development. In K. Field, B. Cohler, and G. Wool (eds.). *Learning and Education: Psychoanalytic Perspectives*, pp. 771–788. Madison, CT: International Universities Press.

Bernfeld, S. (1941). Freud's earliest theories on the school of Helmholtz, *Psychoanalytic Quarterly* 13:341–362.

Bernfeld, S. (1949). Freud's scientific beginning. *Imago* 6:163–196.

Bernfeld, S. (1951). Sigmund Freud, M.D., 1882–1885. *International Journal of Psychoanalysis* 32:204–217.

Bernfeld, S., and Bernfeld, S. C. (1944). Freud's earliest childhood. *Bulletin of the Menninger Clinic*, 8:107–115.

Bernstein, H. (1989). The courage to try—Self-esteem and learning. In K. Field, B. Cohler, and G. Wool (eds.), *Learning and Education: Psychoanalytic Perspectives*, pp. 143–158. Madison, CT: International Universities Press.

Bettelheim, B. (1969). Psychoanalysis and education, *The School Review* (*American Journal of Education*), 77:73–86.

Bettelheim, B. (1983). *Freud and Man's Soul*. New York: Knopf.

Bettelheim, B. (1990). *Freud's Vienna and Other Essays*, pp. 39–57. New York: Knopf.

Booth, W. (1961/1983). *The Rhetoric of Fiction* (2nd ed.). Chicago: University of Chicago Press.

Caplow, T., McGee, R. (1958). The Academic Marketplace. New York: Basic Books.

Clarke, A. M., Clarke, A. D. B. (1976). (Eds.). Early Experience: Myth and Evidence. New York: The Free Press.

Cohler, B. (1972a). Psychoanalysis, adaptation, and education: I. Reality and its appraisal. *Psychological Reports* 30:695–718.

Cohler, B. (1972b). Psychoanalysis, adaptation, and education: II. Development of thinking. *Psychological Reports* 30:719–740.

Cohler, B. (1980). Developmental perspectives on the psychology of the self in childhood. In: A. Goldberg, ed., *Advances in Self Psychology*, pp. 69–116, New York: International Universities Press.

Cohler, B. (1983). Autonomy and interdependence in the family of adulthood: A psychological perspective. *The Gerontologist* 23:33–39.

Cohler, B. (1987). Approaches to the study of development in psychiatric education. In S. Weissman and R. Thurnblad (eds.), *The Role of Psychoanalysis in Psychiatric Education: Past, Present and Future*, pp. 225–270. New York: International Universities Press.

Cohler, B. (1989). Psychoanalysis and education. III. Motive, meaning, and self. In K. Field, B. Cohler, and G. Wool (eds.), *Learning and Education: Psychoanalytic Perspectives*, pp. 11–84. Madison, CT: International Universities Press.

Cohler, B., and Stott, F. (1987). Separation, interdependence, and social relations across the second half of life. In J. Bloom-Feshbach and S. Bloom-Feshbach (eds.), *The Psychology of Separation and Loss*, pp. 165–204. San Francisco: Jossey-Bass.

Crapanzano, V. (1980). *Tuhami: Portrait of a Moroccan*. Chicago: The University of Chicago Press.

Durkheim, E. (1897/1951). *Suicide* (J. Spaulding, trans.). New York: Free Press/Macmillan.

Durkheim, E. (1912/1955). *The Elementary Forms of the Religious Life* (J. W. Swain, trans.). New York: Free Press/Macmillan.

Edelson, M. (1984). *Hypothesis and Evidence in Psychoanalysis*. Chicago, IL: University of Chicago Press.

Edelson, M. (1988). *Psychoanalysis: A Theory in Crisis*. Chicago: University of Chicago Press.

Ekstein, R. (1989a). From love for learning to love of learning. In K. Field, B. Cohler, and G. Wool (eds.). *Learning and Education: Psychoanalytic Perspectives*, pp. 85–89. Madison, CT: International Universities Press.

Ekstein, R. (1989b). From the love of learning to the love of teaching. In K. Field, B. Cohler, and G. Wool (eds.), *Learning and Education: Psychoanalytic Perspectives*, pp. 91–98. Madison, CT: International Universities Press.

Ekstein, R., and Motto, R. (1969). *From Learning to Love to Love of Learning*. New York: Brunner/Mazel.

Elson, M. (1989). The teacher as learner, the learner as teacher. In K. Field, B. Cohler, and G. Wool (eds.), *Learning and Education: Psychoanalytic Perspectives*, pp. 789–808. Madison, CT: International Universities Press.

Erikson, E. (1950/1963). *Childhood and Society* (rev. ed.). New York: Norton.

Erikson, E. (1959). *Young Man Luther*. New York: Norton.

Erikson, E. (1982). *The Life-Cycle Completed: A Review*. New York: Norton.

Fenichel, O. (1945). *The Psychoanalytic Theory of the Neurosis*. New York: Norton.

Fisher, S., and Greenberg, R. (1977). *The Scientific Credibility of Freud's Theory and Therapy*. New York: Basic Books.

Fliess, R. (1942). The metapsychology of the analyst. *Psychoanalytic Quarterly* 11:211–227.

Freud, A. (1936/1966). *The Ego and the Mechanism of Defense*. (rev. ed.). New York: International Universities Press.

Freud, A. (1954). Psychoanalysis and education. *The Psychoanalytic Study of the Child* 9:9–15.

Freud, A. (1965). *Normality and Pathology in Childhood: Assessments of Development*. New York: International Universities Press.

Freud, A. (1976/1981). *Collected Papers*, Vol. 8, pp. 307–314. New York: International Universities Press.

Freud, S. (1891/1953). *On Aphasia: A Critical Study* (E. Stengel, trans.). New York: International Universities Press.

Freud, S. (1895/1966). Project for a scientific psychology. In J. Strachey (ed. and trans.), *The Standard Edition of the Complete Psychological Works of Sigmund Freud*, Vol. 1, pp. 295–387. London: Hogarth Press.

Freud, S. (1897/1985). Letter of February 13, 1896. In J. M. Masson (trans. and ed.). *The Complete Letters of Sigmund Freud to Wilhelm Fliess, 1887–1904*, pp. 277–278. Cambridge, MA: Harvard University Press.

Freud, S. (1898/1985). Letter to Wilhelm Fliess of March 10, 1898. In J. M. Masson (Ed.), *The Complete Letters of Sigmund Freud to Wilhelm Fliess*, pp. 301–302. Cambridge, MA: Belknap/Harvard University Press.

Freud, S. (1900/1958). The interpretation of dreams. In J. Strachey (ed. and trans.), *The Standard Edition of the Complete Psychological Works of Sigmund Freud*, Vols. 4–5. London: Hogarth Press.

Freud, S. (1905/1953). Three essays on the theory of sexuality. In J. Strachey (ed. and trans.), *The Standard Edition of the Complete Psychological Works of Sigmund Freud*, Vol. 7, pp. 130–243. London: Hogarth Press.

Freud, S. (1910/1957). Leonardo DaVinci and a Memory of his Childhood. In J. Strachey (ed. and trans.), *The Standard Edition of the Complete Psychological Works of Sigmund Freud*, Vol. 11, pp. 59–137. London: Hogarth Press.

Freud, S. (1911/1958). Formulations regarding the two principles of mental functioning. In J. Strachey (ed. and trans.), *The Standard Edition of the Complete Psychological Works of Sigmund Freud*, Vol. 12, pp. 215–226. London: Hogarth Press.

Freud, S. (1913). The claims of psychoanalysis to scientific interest. In J. Strachey (ed. and trans.), *The Standard Edition of the Complete Psychological Works of Sigmund Freud*, Vol. 13, pp. 165–192. London: Hogarth Press.

Freud, S. (1915/1957). The unconscious. In J. Strachey (ed. and trans.), *The Standard Edition of the Complete Psychological Works of Sigmund Freud*, Vol. 14, pp. 166–216. London: Hogarth Press.

Freud, S. (1915–1917/1961–1963). Introductory lectures on psychoanalysis. In J. Strachey (ed. and trans.), *The Standard Edition of the Complete Psychological Works of Sigmund Freud*, Vols. 15–16. London: Hogarth Press.

Freud, S. (1905/1953). *The Three Essays on Sexuality*, pp. 125–243. In J. Strachey (ed. and trans.), *The Standard Edition of the Complete Psychological Works of Sigmund Freud*, Vol. 7. London: Hogarth Press.

Freud, S. (1920a). Beyond the pleasure principle. In J. Strachey (ed. and trans.), *The Standard Edition of the Complete Psychological Works of Sigmund Freud*, Vol. 18, pp. 7–66. London: Hogarth Press.

Freud, S. (1920b). Group psychology and the analysis of the ego. In J. Strachey (ed. and trans.), *The Standard Edition of the Complete Psychological Works of Sigmund Freud*, Vol. 18, pp. 67–144. London: Hogarth Press.

Freud, S. (1923). The ego and the id. In J. Strachey (ed. and trans.), *The Standard Edition of the Complete Psychological Works of Sigmund Freud*, Vol. 9, pp. 12–59. London: Hogarth Press.

Freud, S. (1925). An autobiographical study. In J. Strachey (ed. and trans.), *The Standard Edition of the Complete Psychological Works of Sigmund Freud*, Vol. 18, 67–143. London: Hogarth Press.

Freud, S. (1926). Inhibitions, symptoms, and anxiety. In J. Strachey (ed. and trans.), *The Standard Edition of the Complete Psychological Works of Sigmund Freud*, Vol. 20, pp. 77–178. London: Hogarth Press.

Freud, S. (1932–1933). The new introductory lectures. In J. Strachey (ed. and trans.), *The Standard Edition of the Complete Psychological Works of Sigmund Freud*, Vol. 22, pp. 5–184. London: Hogarth Press.

Freud, S. (1937a). Constructions in analysis. In J. Strachey (ed. and trans.), *The Standard Edition of the Complete Psychological Works of Sigmund Freud*, Vol. 21, pp. 221–246. London: Hogarth Press.

Freud, S. (1937b). Analysis terminable and interminable. In J. Strachey (ed. and trans.), *The Standard Edition of the Complete Psychological Works of Sigmund Freud*, Vol. 23, pp. 209–254. London: Hogarth Press.

Freud, S. (1940). An outline of psychoanalysis. In J. Strachey (ed. and trans.), *The Standard Edition of the Complete Psychological Works of Sigmund Freud*, Vol. 23, pp. 144–208. London: Hogarth Press.

Galatzer-Levy, R. (1976). Psychic energy: A historical perspective. *The Annual of Psychoanalysis* 4:41–64. (New York: International Universities Press.)

Galatzer-Levy, R., and Cohler, B. (1990). The developmental psychology of the self and the changing worldview of psychoanalysis. *The Annual for Psychoanalysis* (in press 18, 1–44).

Galatzer-Levy, R., and Cohler, B. (1992). *The Essential Other*. New York: Basic Books (in press).

Galenson, E., Roiphe, H. (1976). Some suggested revisions concerning early female development. *Journal of the American Psychoanalytic Association*, 25(Supplement), 29–58.

Gardner, R., Holzman, P., Klein, G., Linton, H., and Spence, H. (1959). *Cognitive Control: A Study of Individual Consistencies in Cognitive Behavior*. New York: International Universities Press (*Psychological Issues* Monograph 4).

Gardner, R., Jackson, D., and Messick, S. (1960). *Personality Organization in Cognitive Controls and Intellectual Abilities*. New York: International Universities Press (*Psychological Issues* Monograph 8).

Gay, P. (1988). *Freud: A Life for Our Times*. New York: Norton.

Gedo, J. (1976). Freud's self-analysis and his scientific ideas. In J. Gedo and G. Pollock (eds.), *Freud: The Fusion of Science and Humanism, The Intellectual History of Psychoanalysis*, pp. 286–306. New York: International Universities Press. (*Psychological Issues* Monographs 34/35).

Gedo, J. (1977). Notes on the psychoanalytic management of archaic transference. *Journal of the American Psychoanalytic Association* 25:787–803.

Gedo, J. (1979). *Beyond Interpretation: Toward a Revised Theory of Psychoanalysis*. New York: International Universities Press.

Gedo, J. (1981). *Advances in Clinical Psychoanalysis*. New York: International Universities Press.

Gedo, J. and Goldberg, A. (1973). *Models of the Mind: A Psychoanalytic Theory*. Chicago: University of Chicago Press.

Gill, M. (1963). *Topography and Systems in Psychoanalytic Theory*. New York: International Universities Press (*Psychological Issues* Monograph 10).

Gill, M. (1976). Metapsychology is not psychology. In M. Gill and P. Holzman (eds.), *Psychology versus Metapsychology: Psychoanalytic Essays in Memory of George S. Klein*, pp. 71–105. New York: International Universities Press (*Psychological Issues* Monograph 36).

Gill, M. (1977). Psychic energy reconsidered. *Journal of the American Psychoanalytic Association* 25:581–597.

Giovacchini, P. (1979). *Treatment of Primitive Mental States*. New York: Jason Aronson.

Giovacchini, P. (1986). *Developmental Disorders: The Transitional Space in Mental Breakdown and Creative Integration*. Northvale, NJ: Jason Aronson.

Goldberg, A. (1982). The self of psychoanalysis. In B. Lee (with collaboration of K. Smith) (ed.), *Psychosocial Theories of the Self*, pp. 3–22. New York: Plenum.

Goldberg, A. (1988). Experience: Near, distant and absent. In A. Goldberg (ed.), *A Fresh Look at Psychoanalysis: The View from Self Psychology*, Hillsdale, NJ: The Analytic Press.

Greenspan, S. (1975). *A Consideration of Some Learning Variables in the Context of Psychoanalytic Theory: Towards a Psychoanalytic Learning Perspective*. New York: International Universities Press (*Psychological Issues* Monograph 33).

Greenspan, S. (1979). *Intelligence and Adaptation: An Integration of Psychoanalytic and Piagetian Developmental Psychology*. New York: International Universities Press (*Psychological Issues* Monograph 47/48).

Greenspan, S., and Pollock, G. (eds.) (1980). *The Course of Life*. (three vols.). Washington, DC: The United States Government Printing Office.

Grunbaum A. (1984). *The Foundations of Psychoanalysis: A Philosophic Critique*. Berkeley, CA: University of California Press.

Hackel, E. (1868). *Natural History of Creation* (Naturaliche Schopfungsgeschichte). Berlin: George Reimer.

Hartmann, H. (1939/1958). *Ego Psychology and the Problem of Adaptation* (D. Rapaport, trans.). New York: International Universities Press.

Hartmann, H. (1939/1964). Psychoanalysis and the concept of health. In H. Hartmann *Essays in Ego Psychology*, pp. 3–18. New York: International Universities Press.

Hartmann, H. (1950). *Essays on Ego Psychology*, pp. 113–141. New York: International Universities Press.

Hartmann, H., and Kris, E. (1945). The genetic approach in psychoanalysis. *The Psychoanalytic Study of the Child* 1:11–30.

Hartmann, H., Kris, E., and Lowenstein, R. (1964). *Papers on Psychoanalytic Psychology.* New York: International Universities Press (*Psychological Issues* Monograph 14).

Hartmann, H. (1964). *Essays on Ego Psychology: Selected Problems in Psychoanalytic Theory.* New York: International Universities Press.

Hartnett, R. (1976). Environments for advanced learning. In J. Katz and R. T. Hartnett (eds.), *Scholars in the Making: The Development of Graduate and Professional Students*, pp. 49–84. New York: Ballinger-Lippincott.

Heath, D. (1968). *Growing Up in College.* San Francisco: Jossey-Bass.

Hetherington, M., and Camara, K. (1984). Families in transition: The process of dissolution and reconstitution. In R. Parke (ed.), *The Family.* Chicago: The University of Chicago Press (*Review of Child Development Research* Monograph Number 7)

Holder, A. (1988). Reservations about the Standard Edition. In E. Timms and N. Segal (eds.), *Freud in Exile: Psychoanalysis and its Vicissitudes*, pp. 210–214. New Haven: Yale University Press.

Holt, R. (1967). *Motives and Thoughts: Psychoanalytic Essays in Honor of David Rapaport.* New York: International Universities Press (*Psychological Issues* Monograph 18/19).

Holzman, P. (1985). Psychoanalysis: Is the therapy destroying the science. *Journal of the American Psychoanalytic Association* 33:725–770.

Homans, P. (1989). *The Ability to Mourn: Disillusionment and the Social Origins of Psychoanalysis.* Chicago: University of Chicago Press.

Horner, M. (1972). Toward an understanding of achievement related conflicts in women. *Journal of Social Issues* 28:157–175.

Jackson, J. H. (1884/1958). Evolution and dissolution of the nervous system. In *Selected Writings*, Vol. 2, pp. 411–421. New York: Basic Books.

Jackson, S. (1969). The history of Freud's concepts of regression. *Journal of the American Psychoanalytic Association* 17:743–784.

Jacobson, E. (1964). *The Self and the Object World.* New York: International Universities Press.

Jones, E. (1953). *The Life and Work of Sigmund Freud* (3 Vols.). New York: Basic Books.

Jones, R. (1968). *Fantasy and Feeling in Education.* New York: New York University Press.

Kagan, J. (1980). Perspectives on continuity. In O. G. Brim, Jr., and J. Kagan (eds.), *Constancy and Change in Human Development*, pp. 26–74. Cambridge, MA: Harvard University Press.

Kamii, C., and Radin, N. (1966). *A Framework for a Pre-School Curriculum Based on Some Piagetian Concepts.* Ypsilanti, MI: Ypsilanti Public Schools.

Katz, J. (1962). Personality and interpersonal relations in the college classroom. In N. Sanford (ed.), *The American College: A Psychological and Social Interpretation of the Higher Learning*, pp. 365–395. New York: John Wiley and Sons.

Katz, J. (1968). *No Time for Youth: Growth and Constraint in College Students.* San Francisco: Jossey-Bass.

Katz, J. (1976). Development of the mind. In J. Katz and R. T. Hartnett (eds.), *Scholars in the Making: The Development of Graduate and Professional Students*, pp. 107–126. Cambridge, MA: Ballinger Publishing Company.

Katz, J., and Henry, M. (1988). *Turning Professors into Teachers: A New Approach to Faculty Development and Student Learning.* New York: American Council on Education and Macmillan Publishing Company.

Katz, J., and Sanford, N. (1962). The curriculum in the perspective of the theory of personality development. In N. Sanford (ed.), *The American College: A Psychological and Social Interpretation of the Higher Learning*, pp. 418–444. New York: John Wiley.

Kernberg, O. (1982). Self, ego, and drives. *Journal of the American Psychoanalytic Association* 30:893–917.

Khan, M. (1963/1974). The principle of cumulative trauma. In *The Privacy of the Self*, pp. 42–59. London: Hogarth Press.

Khan M. (1964/1974). Ego distortion, cumulative trauma and the role of reconstruction in the analytic situation. In *The Privacy of the Self*, pp. 59–68. London: Hogarth Press.

Klein, G. (1970). *Perception, Motives and Personality*. New York: Alfred A. Knopf.

Klein, G. (1976). *Psychoanalytic Theory: An Exploration of Essentials*. New York: International Universities Press.

Kleinman, A. (1988). *The Illness Narratives: Suffering, Healing, and The Human Condition*. New York: Basic Books.

Knapp, R. (1962). Changing functions of the college professor. In N. Sanford (ed.), *The American College: A Psychological and Social Interpretation of the Higher Learning*, pp. 290–311. New York: John Wiley.

Kohut, H. (1959/1978). Introspection, empathy and psychoanalysis: An examination of the relationship between mode of observation and theory. In P. Ornstein (ed.), *The Search for the Self: Selected Writings of Heinz Kohut, 1950–1978*, Vol. 1, pp. 205–232. New York: International Universities Press.

Kohut, H. (1971). *The Analysis of the Self: A Systematic Approach to the Psychoanalytic Treatment of Narcissistic Personality Disorders*. New York: International Universities Press (*Psychoanalytic Study of the Child Series*, Monograph 1).

Kohut, H. (1974/1978). Remarks about the formation of the self. Letter to a student regarding some principles of psychoanalytic research. In P. Ornstein (ed.), *The Search for the Self: Selected Writings of Heinz Kohut, 1950–1978*, Vol. 2, pp. 737–770. Madison Ct: International Universities Press.

Kohut, H. (1977). *The Restoration of the Self*. New York: International Universities Press.

Kohut, H. (1984). *How Does Psychoanalysis Cure*. Chicago: University of Chicago Press.

Kohut, H. (1985). Self psychology and the sciences of man. In C. Strozier (ed.), *Self Psychology and the Humanities: Reflections on a New Psychoanalytic Approach by Heinz Kohut*, pp. 73–94. New York: Norton.

Kohut, H., and Wolf, E. (1978). The disorders of the self and their treatment: An outline. *International Journal of Psychoanalysis* 59:413–425.

Kracke, W. (1981). Kagwahiv mourning: Dreams of a bereaved father. *Ethos* 9:258–275.

Krull, M. (1986). *Freud and His Father* (A. Pomerans, trans.). New York: Norton.

LaPlanche, J., and Pontalis, J. B. (1973). *The Language of Psychoanalysis*. New York: Norton.

LeGeoff, J. (1980). *Time, Work, and Culture in the Middle Ages* (A. Goldhammer, trans.). Chicago: University of Chicago Press.

Levinson, D. (1977). The mid-life transition. *Psychiatry* 40:99–112.

Levinson, D. (1980). Toward a conception of the adult life course. In N. Smelser and E. Erikson (eds.), *Themes of Love and Work in Adulthood*, pp. 265–290. Cambridge, MA: Harvard University Press.

Levinson, D. (1986). A conception of adult development. *American Psychologist* 41:3–13.

Levinson, D., Darrow, C., Klein, E., Levinson, M., and Mckee, B. (1978). *The Seasons of a Man's Life*. New York: Knopf.

Lozoff, M. (1976). Interpersonal relations and autonomy. In J. Katz and R. T. Hartnett (eds.), *Scholars in the Making: The Development of Graduate and Professional Students*, pp. 141–160. Cambridge, MA: Ballinger-Lippincott.

Mahler, M., Pine, F., and Bergman, A. (1975). *The Psychological Birth of the Human Infant*. New York: Basic Books.

Masson, J. (1984). *The Assault on Truth: Freud's Suppression of the Seduction Theory*. New York: Farrar, Straus, and Giroux.

Meissner, W. (1981). Notes on the psychoanalytic psychology of the self. *Psychoanalysis and Contemporary Thought* 1:233–248.

Meissner, W. (1986). Can psychoanalysis find its self? *Journal of the American Psychoanalytic Association* 34:379–400.

Miller, P., Potts, R., Fung, H., Hoogstra, L., and Mintz, J. (1990). Narrative practices and the social construction of self in childhood. *American Ethnologist* 17:292–311.

Miller, P., and Sperry, L. (1988). Early talk about the past: The origins of conversational stories of personal experience. *Journal of Child Language* 18:293–315.

Mitchell, J. T. M. (ed.) (1980). *On Narrative.* (*Critical Inquiry* 7:1). Chicago: University of Chicago Press.

Mitchell, J. T. M. (ed.) (1982). *The Politics of Interpretation.* (*Critical Inquiry* 9:1). Chicago: University of Chicago Press.

Nemiroff, R., Colarusso, C. (eds.) (1990). *New Dimensions in Adult Development.* New York: Basic Books.

Novey, S. (1968). *The Second Look: The Reconstruction of Personal History in Psychiatry and Psychoanalysis.* Baltimore, MD: The Johns Hopkins University Press.

Nunberg, H. (1931). The synthetic function of the ego. *International Journal of Psychoanalysis* 12:123–140.

Nunberg, H. (1932/1955). *Principles of Psychoanalysis: Their Application to the Neuroses* (M. and S. Kahr, trans.). New York: International Universities Press.

Ornston, D. (1982). Strachey's Influence: Preliminary Report, *International Journal of Psychoanalysis,* 63:409.

Ornston, D. G., Jr. (1985a). The invention of "cathexis" and Strachey's strategy. *International Review of Psychoanalysis,* 12:391–399.

Ornston, D. G., Jr. (1985b). Freud's conception is different from Strachey's. *Journal of the American Psychoanalytic Association* 33:379–413.

Ornston, D. G., Jr. (1988). How standard is the "standard edition." In E. Timms and N. Segal (eds.), *Freud in Exile: Psychoanalysis and its Vicissitudes,* pp. 196–209. New Haven: Yale University Press.

Parens, H., Pollock, L., Stern, J., and Kramer, S. (1976). On the girl's entry into the oedipus complex. *Journal of the American Psychoanalytic Association* 24(Supp):79–108.

Piaget, J. (1967/1971). *Biology and Knowledge: An Essay on the Relations between Organic Regulations and Cognitive Processes* (B. Walsh, trans.). Chicago: University of Chicago Press.

Piaget, J., and Inhelder, B. (1969). *The Psychology of the Child* (H. Waver, trans.). New York: Basic Books.

Pines, M. (1988). The question of revising the Standard Edition. In E. Timms and N. Segal (eds.), *Freud in Exile: Psychoanalysis and its Vicissitudes,* pp. 177–180. New Haven: Yale University Press.

Rapaport, D. (1950). On the psychoanalytic theory of thinking. *International Journal of Psychoanalysis* 31:161–170.

Rapaport, D. (1951). The conceptual model of psychoanalysis. In M. Gill (ed.), *The Collected Papers of David Rapaport,* pp. 405–431. New York: Basic Books.

Rapaport, D., and Gill, M. (1959). The points of view and assumptions of metapsychology. *International Journal of Psychoanalysis,* 40:209–255.

Rapaport, D. (1960/1967). On the psychoanalytic theory of motivation. In. M. Gill (Ed.) *The Collected Papers of David Rapaport.* New York: Basic Books, 853–915.

Rapaport, D. (1967). *Collected Papers* (M. Gill, ed.). New York: Basic Books.

Richards, A. (1982). The superordinate self in psychoanalytic theory and in the self psychologies. *Journal of the American Psychoanalytical Association,* 30:939–957.

Ricoeur, P. (1971). The model of the text: Meaningful action considered as a text. *Social Research* 38:559–562.

Ricoeur, P. (1977). The question of proof in Freud's psychoanalytic writings. *Journal of the American Psychoanalytic Association* 25:835–872.

Ritvo, L. (1990). *Darwin's Influence on Freud: A Tale of Two Sciences*. New Haven: Yale University Press.

Roe, A. (1956). *The Psychology of Occupations*. New York: John Wiley.

Rosenblatt, A. and Thickstun, J. (1970). A study of the concept of psychic energy. *International Journal of Psychoanalysis* 51:265–278.

Rosseau, E. (1762/1979). *Emile or On Education* (A. Bloom, trans.). New York: Basic Books.

Rubin, D. (1986). *Autobiographical Memory*. New York: Cambridge University Press.

Rudnytsky, P. (1987). *Freud and Oedipus*. New York: Columbia University Press.

Sadow, L., Gedo, J., Miller, J., Pollock, G., Sabshin, M., and Schlessinger, N. (1968/1976). The process of hypothesis change in three early psychoanalytic concepts. In J. Gedo and G. Pollock (eds.), *Freud: The Fusion of Science and Humanism—The Intellectual History of Psychoanalysis*. (*Psychological Issues*, 10: Monographs 34 and 35).

Salzberger-Wittenberg, I., Henry, G., and Osborne, E. (1983). *The Emotional Experience of Learning and Teaching*. London: Routledge and Kegan Paul.

Sander, L. (1962). Issues in early mother–child interaction. *Journal of the American Academy of Child Psychiatry* 2:141–166.

Sander, L. (1964). Adaptive relationships in early mother–child interaction. *Journal of the American Academy of Child Psychiatry*, 3:221–263.

Sander, L. (1969). Regulation and organization in the early infant caretaker system. In R. Robertson (ed.), *Brain and Early Behavior*. London: Academic Press.

Sander, L. (1975). Infant and caretaking environment: Investigation and conceptualization of adaptive behavior in a system of increasing complexity. In E. J. Anthony (ed.), *Explorations in Child Psychiatry*, pp. 129–166. New York: Plenum Press.

Sandler, J., and Rosenblatt, B. (1962). The concept of the representational world. *Psychoanalytic Study of the Child*, 17:128–145.

Schachtel, E. (1947). Memory and childhood amnesia. *Psychiatry* 10:1–26.

Schafer, R. (1976). *A New Language for Psychoanalysis*. New Haven, CT: Yale University Press.

Schafer, R. (1978). *Language and Insight*. New Haven, CT: Yale University Press.

Schafer, R. (1980). Narration in the psychoanalytic dialogue. *Critical Inquiry* 7:29–53.

Schafer, R. (1981). *Narrative Actions in Psychoanalysis*. Worcester, MA: Clark University Press (Vol. XIV of the Heinz Werner Lecture Series).

Schafer, R. (1983). *The Analytic Attitude*. New York: Basic Books.

Slavney, P., and McHugh, P. (1984). Life stories and meaningful connections: Reflections on a clinical method in psychiatry and medicine. *Perspectives in Biology and Medicine* 27: 279–288.

Spence, D. (1982). *Narrative Truth and Historical Truth: Meaning and Interpretation in Psychoanalysis*. New York: Norton.

Spruiell, V. (1981) The self and the ego. *Psychoanalytic Quarterly* 50:319–344.

Stechler, G., and Kaplan, S. (1980). The development of the self. *Psychoanalytic Study of the Self* 35:85–105.

Steele, R., Jacobsen, P. (1979). From past to present: Freudian archeology, *International Review of Psychoanalysis*, 6:349.

Steiner, R. (1988). "Die Weltmachtstellung des Britischen Reichs": Notes on the term "Standard" in the first translations of Freud. In E. Timms and N. Segal (eds.), *Freud in Exile: Psychoanalysis and its Vicissitudes*, pp. 181–195. New Haven: Yale University Press.

Stengel, E. (1963). Hughlings Jackson's influence in psychiatry. *British Journal of Psychiatry* 109:348–355.

Stern, D. (1985). *The Interpersonal World of the Infant*. New York: Basic Books.

Stern, D. (1989a). The representation of relational patterns: Developmental considerations. In I. A. Sameroff and R. Emde (eds.), *Relationship Disturbances in Early Childhood: A Developmental Approach*, pp. 52–68. New York: Basic Books.

Stern, D. (1989b). Developmental prerequisites for the sense of a narrated self. In A. Cooper, O. Kernberg, and E. Person (Eds.), *Psychoanalysis: Toward the Second Century*, pp. 168–180. New Haven, CT: Yale University Press.

Stolorow, R., Brandchaft, B., and Atwood, G. (1987). *Psychoanalytic Treatment: An Intersubjective Approach*. Hillsdale, NJ: The Analytic Press.

Stott, F. (1989). Making meaning together: Motivation for learning to write. In K. Field, B. Cohler, and G. Wool (eds.), *Learning and Education: Psychoanalytic Perspectives*, pp. 329–354. Madison, CT: International Universities Press.

Strachey, J., et al. (1961a). Editor's annotation: Civilization and its discontents. In J. Strachey (ed. and trans.), *The Standard Edition of the Complete Psychological Works of Sigmund Freud*, Vol. 21, pp. 65–66. London: Hogarth Press.

Strachey, J., et al. (1961b). Editor's note: The ego and the id. In J. Strachey (ed. and trans.), *The Standard Edition of the Complete Psychological Works of Sigmund Freud*, Vol. 19, pp. 3–11. London: Hogarth Press.

Strachey, J., et al., (1961c). Editor's annotation, remarks on the theory and practice of dream interpretation. In J. Strachey (ed. and trans.), *The Standard Edition of the Complete Psychological Works of Sigmund Freud*, Vol. 19, p. 133. London: Hogarth Press.

Sulloway, F. (1979). *Freud, Biologist of the Mind*. New York: Basic Books.

Swanson, D. (1977). On force, energy, entropy, and the assumptions of metapsychology. *Psychoanalysis and Contemporary Science* 5:137–153.

Thistlewaite, D. (1959). College environments and the development of talent. *Science* 130: 71–76.

Thistlewaite, D. (1962). Rival hypotheses for explaining the effects of different learning environments. *Journal of Educational Psychology* 53:310–315.

Thompson, E. P. (1967). Time, work, and industrial capitalism. *Past and Present: Journal of Historical Studies* 38:56–97.

Tolpin, M., and Kohut, H. (1990). The disorders of the self: The psychopathology of the self. In S. Greenspan and G. Pollock (eds.), *The Course of Life. II: Early Childhood*, pp. 229–254. New York: International Universities Press.

Toulmin, S. (1990). *Cosmopolis: The Hidden Agenda of Modernity*. New York: Free Press.

Trevarthan, C. (1980). The foundations of intersubjectivity: Development of interpersonal and cognitive understanding in infants. In D. Olson (ed.), *The Social Foundation of Language and Thought: Essays in Honor of Jerome Bruner*, pp. 316–342. New York: Norton.

Trevarthan, C. (1989). Origins and directions for the concept of infant intersubjectivity. *SRCD Newsletter*, Autumn, 1–4.

Trevarthan, C., and Hubley, P. (1978). Secondary intersubjectivity: Confidence, confiders, and acts of meaning in the first year. In A. Lock (ed.), *Action, Gesture and Symbol*, pp. 183–230. New York: Academic Press.

Vaillant, G. (1977). *Adaptation to Life*. Boston: Little Brown.

Vaillant, G. (1978). Natural history of male psychological health: VI. Correlates of successful marriage and fatherhood. *American Journal of Psychiatry* 135:653–659.

Vaillant, G., and Vaillant, C. (1981). Natural history of male mental health: X. Work as a predictor of positive mental health. *American Journal of Psychiatry* 138:1433–1440.

Vaillant, G., and Milofsky, E. (1980). Natural history of male mental health: IX. Empirical evidence for Erikson's model of the life cycle. *American Journal of Psychiatry* 137:1348–1359.

Vygotsky, L. (1934/1978). *Mind in Society: The Development of Higher Psychological Processes* (M. Cole, V. John-Steiner, S. Scribner, and E. Souberman, trans. and eds.). Cambridge, MA: Harvard University Press.

Wallerstein, R. (1977). Psychic energy reconsidered—Introduction. *Journal of the American Psychoanalytic Association* 25:529–536.

Wallerstein, R. (1986). Psychoanalysis as a science: Response to new challenges. *Psychoanalytic Quarterly* 55:414.

Wallerstein, R. (1987). Psychoanalysis, psychoanalytic science, and psychoanalytic research—1986. *Journal of the American Psychoanalytic Association* 57:3–30.

Weber, M. (1904–1905/1958). *The Protestant Ethic and the Spirit of Capitalism* (T. Parsons, trans.). New York: Scribners.

White, R. W. (1963). *Ego and Reality in Psychoanalytic Theory*. New York: International Universities Press (*Psychological Issues* Monograph 11).

Winnicott, D. W. (1953). Transitional objects and transitional phenomena. In *Collected Papers: Through Pediatrics to Psychoanalysis*, pp. 229–242. New York: Basic Books.

Winnicott, D. W. (1960a). The theory of the parent–infant relationship. *International Journal of Psychoanalysis* 41:585–595.

Winnicott, D. W. (1960b). Ego distortion in terms of the true and the false self. In *The Maturational Process and the Facilitating Environment*, pp. 140–152. New York: International Universities Press.

Wolf, E. (1988). *Treating the Self: Elements of Clinical Self-Psychology*. New York: The Guilford Press.

Wolf, E. (1989). The psychoanalytic self psychologist looks at learning. In K. Field, B. Cohler, and G. Wool (eds.), *Learning and Education: Psychoanalytic Perspectives*, pp. 377–394. Madison, CT: International Universities Press.

Wolff, P. (1960). *The Developmental Psychologies of Jean Piaget and Psychoanalysis*. New York: International Universities Press (*Psychological Issues* Monograph 17).

Wolff, P. (1966). *The Causes, Controls and Organization of Behavior in the Young Infant*. New York: International Universities Press (*Psychological Issues* Monograph 21).

3

History of Milieu in the Residential Treatment of Children and Youth

JOSEPH D. NOSHPITZ

THE FIRST CHAPTER PRESENTED general psychoanalytic perspectives on institutions, and the second focused on schools. This chapter on residential treatment brings us to the heart of Bettelheim's work, in fact, to the very phrase he introduced: *milieu therapy*.

Noshpitz artfully braids several strands in this account: the modern history of institutions for children, starting in 1696; the cultural differences; the sociohistorical forces that determined or impinged on clinical care; the overt or covert religious influences on institutional care (such as the Quaker belief in penitence as curative, from which we have penitentiary); and the conflation of children who are delinquent with those orphaned, those brain-damaged, and those criminal.

The latter admixture of populations reminds us of Erving Goffman's sociological observation that various institutions are more similar than dissimilar—monastery, army barracks, jail, or insane asylum. This may reflect the tendency that bureaucratization of institutions has to homogenize themselves, so that ultimately the institution serves its own need to exist, not its denizens for whom it was created. Here is where a psychoanalytic frame

JOSEPH D. NOSHPITZ • 3141 34th Street N.W., Washington, D.C. 20008.

Educating the Emotions: Bruno Bettelheim and Psychoanalytic Development, edited by Nathan M. Szajnberg. Plenum Press, New York, 1992.

of reference can move the inertia of bureaucratization, by clearly articulating the patients' needs, particularly for a humane environment.

Bettelheim's life was marked by his stay in Dachau. He was deeply impressed with the modern power of managing groups of people. This sociological innovation, like technological innovations, can be used for good or evil. He devoted three decades of his career to showing how an institution can be not only an asylum but also a place to reconstruct an emotionally damaged life.

Noshpitz ends his chapter on a worrisome note. Although Bettelheim and his friends and colleagues, Redl and Ekstein, systematically researched and articulated how to build and run a therapeutic milieu, much of their work is forgotten. Instead, in our American fascination with technological, machinelike language, so-called residential treatment centers use "measurable" behaviors to build automatons with rewards and punishments. What is truly punishing is the damage to the child's soul, the child already emotionally alienated from the world becomes alienated from himself or herself, or simply bides time, waits out the sentence, until released.

We hope that this chapter and this book will rejuvenate greater interest in the person of the child than the mechanistic approach that, as Cohler argued, Freud tried to eschew.

Among the earliest settings created for the care of troubled children and adolescents were two penal environments which appeared at the end of the seventeenth century (Barnes and Teeters, 1951). It would seem that then, as now, the youngster who makes trouble is far more likely to be heard by his society than the child who is troubled. (As Eveoleen Rexford [1969] has noted, society tends first to protect itself from its children.) Nonetheless, it was a great step forward to have these settings arise at all— it meant that somewhere, at last, the fact that youth had special needs and special possibilities was beginning to impress not only the philosophers and the theoreticians, but the implementers, the practical people who created programs and organized institutions.

EIGHTEENTH-CENTURY EUROPE: CORRECTIVE DISCIPLINE, ORPHANAGES, AND PENAL REFORM

In 1695, August Herman Francke opened the first such establishment at Halle, Germany, and in 1704, the then-reigning Pope Clement opened a separate setting in Rome. The central theme in both these institutions was to render the wicked virtuous by corrective discipline. In the Roman setting, the Hospice of San Michele, the means of correction involved silence for the inmates, religious readings by the staff, and ankle chains to maintain a non-acting-out environment. Whipping or isolation were resorted to when these were insufficient. In brief, one gets the impression of an all-powerful, integrated milieu, carefully designed to achieve a specific goal: change in behavior by means of a strong identification model (the Bible reader), ego training through intense discipline, and convincing aversive conditioning through punishment. Evidently there was some measure of regard for the developmental needs of the youngsters; the very fact of an institution designed for youths indicated that from the beginning. On the other hand, it is equally evident that there was little or no conception of individualization. The etiology of the trouble was ascribed to godlessness, and treatment was meted out in keeping with this conception. There was not even a glimmer of seeking for or dealing with the causes of troubled behavior as we would define them today.

Side by side with such correctional settings, orphanages were coming into being; in particular, religious orders were starting to create specialized environments for children without parents. In part, the need for such creations had come about with the breakup of the feudal system in Europe and the rise of cities. The abatement of feudal control released hordes of peasants and serfs from the land who then flocked to the new urban centers. Unfortunately, when they lost their feudal protectors, the former serfs were also left without food and shelter. The Elizabethan Poor Laws created the first almshouses to try to deal with these conditions. All over Europe various religious orders were striving to help the new needy, especially the children.

For the young communities in the New World, a different set of circumstances prevailed. There, no feudal history had established precedents for care, and the several societies that made up pre-Revolutionary America had each to find its own solution. At the start of the eighteenth century, the city of New Orleans, then a French community, was ravaged by a smallpox epidemic. In addition to providing the background for Longfellow's *Evangeline*, this pestilence left a great many orphaned children in its wake. The nuns in the Ursuline convent took pity on these many abandoned waifs, and thereupon established the first orphan's home in America in 1729 (Kirk, 1962).

Nine years later, a second orphanage, the Bethesda Orphan Home, opened in Atlanta, Georgia. Thus was institutional welfare launched into our history.

At that point in its evolution, colonial America was still largely European, but Europe itself was changing and growing. Jean Jacques Rousseau was publishing his philosophical works during these decades;

in particular, *Emile* appeared in 1762 and offered a fictional account of an ideal education (Rousseau, 1762). With its emphasis on individuality and on the natural spontaneity of the impulse to learn, this book turned educational thinking radically from the subject matter to the student and sounded a knell that was to reverberate loudly through the lives of children for many generations thereafter. Among the other elements in *Emile* was a major emphasis on the force of the total environment on the developing mind: milieu had found a champion.

Change was taking place in other spheres as well; in France, Jean Vilain devised a new type of prison (called Maison de la Force) where prisoners were grouped in a planful way and where they had to engage in constructive work in the service of reform. This in turn inspired Mr. John Howard, an English sheriff, to write an exposé of what English prisons were (they were dreadful) and what they might become. His book, *The State of Prisons*, appeared in 1777 and had a profound effect on penal practices both in England and America (Barnes and Teeters, 1951).

Coincidentally, America was going through the rigors of revolution and freeing herself from colonial status. Not until that business was properly accomplished could her energies be freed for social growth and reform. In due time, however, that day did come, and in 1787 Dr. Benjamin Rush set up a new organization, the "Philadelphia Society for Alleviating the Miseries in Public Prisons." This group of dedicated and concerned citizens began actively to study and to make recommendations for change in the theory and practice of imprisoning wrongdoers. In 1790, their work led to a reorganization of the Walnut Street Jail in Philadelphia, along with the provision of a separate bank of cells for isolation of the more hardened offenders. The theoretical position here was that if these harsh men were kept apart from others, in a silent environment, they would be forced to turn inward, to face their consciences, and thus to become penitent. So primary was this conception that this cell block was called the penitentiary. Its lineal descendant continues to be a site where many of our more troubled late adolescents and young adults come to be housed. Alas for the Quaker ideology that conceived of this method; the overall record is that this approach did not work when it was first introduced any better than it works today. But, it continues to be employed (Barnes and Teeters, 1951).

In 1790 another innovation emerged in a different area. By this time a number of orphanages had opened, but always because some religious or charitable group had chosen to marshal its energies and substance in this way. This year saw the first such agency to be run and operated by the state as a public facility in Charleston, South Carolina. The notion that the state should assume responsibility for the care and welfare of its children was a novel idea then; it has moved only gradually since, and not until today is it beginning to approach its fullest expression (Cruickshank and Johnson, 1958).

It was in the ensuing decade that Pinel struck the chains from the mentally ill at the Bicetre in Paris, and Tuke made a similar step forward in England at the York Retreat. Henceforth, moral treatment would be the shining light guiding the idealists and progressives who would better conditions in this area. During the next century the mode of moral treatment for the mentally ill was fated to be found, and lost, and found again many times. It is noteworthy that this modality was essentially milieu therapy; that is, the development of a wholesome, calming, reassuring, and healing environment where the broken spirit might mend and the troubled soul find repair.

A particular impetus to work with children emerged from the celebrated study of the Wild Boy of Aveyron. In 1798 a feral child of perhaps 11 or 12 was found in the woods near this French town. The child had apparently been abandoned as an infant and had grown up in the wild without human contact. Mute, untrained, and animallike, he was given over for study and care to Dr. Jean Marc Gaspard Itard, chief medical officer for the National Institute for the Deaf and Dumb. Itard decided to try to train and indeed to educate this child, took him into his own home, and put him into the hands of his housekeeper, Madame Guerin. This lady thus became the first child care worker; that is, the first paraprofessional to work along with a physician in the planned and systematic milieu treatment for a disturbed child (Danes, 1930).

Itard's efforts over the next five years were only partially successful and, ultimately, he considered his work a failure. Nonetheless, he proved conclusively that such highly deviant children can indeed be helped and treated, even if the final result is less than a total cure. Despite his own discouragement, his work was to be of immense benefit to children thereafter.

Interplay and Impact of Different Populations Upon Juvenile Care

With the advent of the nineteenth century, Free School Societies began to appear all over the eastern United States. Essentially these were made up of groups of philanthropic citizens who attempted to give at least the rudiments of learning to the many illiterates who thronged the cities. Their efforts were presently supported by public grants and in time led to the public school system as we know it today. There was, however, a strong body of opinion that regarded the rearing and education of children as the exclusive province of home and church, and a great controversy arose about state versus church education. It is therefore not by chance that in 1812 Mother Seton established the first school in what was presently to become the Catholic parochial school system (Mulhern, 1946).

Special schools for delinquents, however, were still an institutional form for the future. The hospice of San Michele was now about 100 years old and little further progress had been made on that front. One small light in the darkness was the 1813 opening of a school for delinquents in Weimar, Germany, by Johann Daniel Falk. The real advances in this realm, however, still lay ahead.

The catalyst for such growth in America was again to emerge from that powerful wellspring of good will and philanthropic impulse that had already done so much for the nation's helpless and bereft. This time it took the form of an new group that called itself the Society for the Prevention of Pauperism. Led by Mr. John Griscom, the society took on poverty wholesale. It involved itself in such practices as sending district visitors to the poor, establishing and strengthening the concept of the savings bank, and trying to determine the differences between the worthy poor and the unworthy (a distinction that has haunted our welfare programs until this day). Eventually these charitable and active citizens came to understand that their efforts to deal with the overwhelming issues of poverty in general were doomed to failure. They thereupon decided to focus their energies on a particular sector of the distressed poor, the delinquent youth. In 1819, their second report recommended a separate building within the penitentiary grounds for young offenders. This was the second rung in that long and as yet unfinished ladder—the gradual development of our official residential programs for youngsters in trouble (Barnes and Teeters, 1951).

It is evident in our day that the public gives very little thought to the nature and quality of prison life. In their day, however, this was a matter of great popular interest, an issue that caught the imagination of society. Ingenious theories were elaborated and intricate experiments carried out in an attempt to devise the ideal prison, that is, one that would bring about penitence, correction, reform, and rehabilitation. The Auburn system was created; its model product, Sing Sing, set the style of American prisons for generations. In essence, it defined a highly regimented life in which men kept their eyes downcast, worked in congregate groups, walked in lockstep, and lived in silence.

In keeping with its new focus, in 1824 the Society for the Prevention of Pauperism renamed itself the Society for the Reformation of Juvenile Delinquents. One year later, it opened the New York House of Refuge. This establishment was dedicated to the total reeducation of the delinquent child and was a major breakthrough on this continent in the care for such youngsters. The theory of milieu put forth by this group can be garnered from some of their statement:

These prisons should be rather schools for instruction than places of punishment . . .

The youth . . . should be placed under a course of discipline severe and unchanging but alike calculated to subdue and conciliate. . . .

. . . such an institution would in time exhibit scarcely any other than the character of a decent school and manufactory . . .

But it was not merely the well-disposed private citizen who concerned himself with the unfortunate. State and city governments too were feeling a sense of public responsibility, and a number of experiments were undertaken to do something about the benighted poor. A Mr. Yates of New York walked the streets of the cities of that state and was able to document slum miseries so vividly that the state legislature created a system of almshouses (a new set of milieu arrangements) to take the destitute and the helpless off these streets and care for them at public expense. The psychological skills and the social perspectives of the day, however, were far from able to cope with the multiple problems engendered by such a helter-skelter congregate setting. In short order, the life-style within the almshouses became as chaotic and depraved as the slum conditions they were calculated to correct. A great deal more time, labor, and understanding were going to be necessary before such an operation would be able to work.

A different model of care appeared in Europe in 1834 when Dr. Johanne Wichern opened the Rauhe Haus at Horn, near Hamburg, Germany. This setting was designed to rescue children in difficulties. Chief among its contributions was its organization according to a then rather novel principle, the family plan. In effect, Wichern tried to blend the virtues of family life with the necessity for group care; he accordingly divided the children into "family" groups which were given into the care of "cottage parents." We have little to tell us how well the program worked, but it was a suggestive idea.

The early part of the nineteenth century was a time of great concern for the welfare of the unfortunate, and again and again we can find new developments and new modes of helping in this area. Education was gradually being brought to the public in young America; in France, Seguin was beginning his studies in the training and rehabilitation of the severely retarded; everywhere the concept of moral treatment of the insane was discussed, and in a few settings (a very few), it was coming to be practiced.

In the province of delinquency, a French jurist, Fredric August Demetz, began to struggle with the needs of youngsters brought before him.
In 1840 he established a special school, La Colonie Agricole, at Mettray. He
had traveled about Europe and was inspired by the "family plan" that he
had observed in operation at the Rauhe Haus. At the same time, as a matter
of personal conviction, he was a profound believer in the virtues of
working the land as a means of building character. He thereupon put these
two concepts together and developed a program that provided a cottage
parent, group life, and a farm setting for youngsters that would collec-
tively emulate an agricultural family living close to the soil. The youngsters were required to work hard at farming during their stay, and the
motto of this novel establishment was "Moralization of Youth by the
Cultivation of the Soil" (Barnes and Teeters, 1951).

Since the groups were small and supervision intensive, this was a
relatively expensive proposition and aroused a storm of criticism: after all,
these were malefactors who were thus being allowed to consume so much
of society's substance. To this Demetz replied that it was vital to reform, as
cheaply as possible, but in any case, to reform.

Thus was the reform school born, with its cottages and its special kind
of group life and work patterns. The intention was noble and the practice
imaginative and creative. Alas for innovations. This great breakthrough
effort, which was destined to be copied and refined until no state in our
country lacked its version of this original, is in our day the expression of all
that is most evil, backward, and reactionary in care patterns for the young.

NINETEENTH-CENTURY AMERICA

Dorothea Dix

At almost the same time, moral treatment for the insane, long available but still not widely practiced, was given a new surge of life when
Dorothea Dix took up the cudgels for these helpless and unrepresented
inmates. It seemed miraculous in her own day, and truth to tell appears no
less so today, that this little sickly woman, through the vibrant strength of
her own extraordinary spirit, castigated, cajoled, dominated, and ultimately coerced an unwilling world into reforming its old asylums and
building a host of new ones. Miss Dix began her work in 1841. Within the
next decade she had literally rammed through changes in most of the state
legislatures and had a considerable impact in Europe as well. It is not mere
coincidence that in 1844, 13 American hospital superintendents got to-

gether to found the first version of the American Psychiatric Association (long before the founding of the American Medical Association).

The decade of the 1840s was a great one: it was the time when state care for the insane, for the delinquent, and for the severely retarded first began to take hold. Prophetically, it was during this same period that in France, Itard's work with the wild boy of Aveyron bore rich fruit. One of Itard's students, Seguin, published a powerful and optimistic work in which he contended that all the feebleminded could be reeducated. He detailed a series of careful and reasonable measures involving education of the senses to accomplish this goal, and a wave of hope swept over educators and physicians everywhere. A number of state schools were opened in America to try to apply the new methods, and the movement itself gained enormous impetus when, in 1850, Seguin emigrated to America to take up residence here. The Perkins School for the Blind near Boston, in which Dr. Samuel Howe was deeply interested, was able to induce Seguin to become its director (Kirk, 1962).

Meanwhile, however, the sheer weight of care for the hungry and the deprived was mounting enormously. In 1852, for example, the New York chief of police estimated that there were 10,000 vagrant children haunting the streets of the city. Even for those with enough to eat there were problems aplenty. Thus, in 1853, in New York's 11th ward there were 12,000 children aged 5 to 16; of these, only 700 attended public school. Large institutions came into being to care for the many waifs and strays (e.g., the Children's Village at Dobb's Ferry, New York opened in 1855), and authoritative voices led by Horace Mann and Henry Barnard called for free, universal, publicly supported education for all children (Mulhern, 1946).

The Children's Aid Society

At almost the same time, Charles Loring Brace, a New York minister, organized the Children's Aid Society, and in 1853 began a program of child rescue and foster home placement that presently affected the lives of nearly 50,000 children. Like Demetz, Brace too believed in the powerful impact of family life and farm culture. Since Brace concerned himself with waifs and orphans rather than delinquents, however, his ideas developed in the direction of home placement rather than institutionalization. In time he developed a program through which a tremendous number of youngsters were literally loaded onto trains, shipped out West en masse, and given over to the care of foster parents to grow and work on farms. There was some follow-up in subsequent years, and it would appear that the great bulk of these placements were successful! Brace also devoted his energy to many community projects such as providing a home for city newsboys, conducting prayer meetings for disadvantaged youth, and the like. He even originated a form of "advocacy," in which a man was stationed in a given part of the city whose task it was to get to know all the deprived children in his territory and to bring them help as they needed it (Cruickshank and Johnson, 1958).

The decade of the 1860s dawned and the guns of the Civil War were heard throughout the land. When the smoke of battle finally dispersed, a great army of orphans remained in its wake, and a large number of settings were established to deal with them. Among these was the Cleveland Jewish Orphan Home which was opened in 1868. This has since become Bellfaire, the highly regarded residential treatment center that was for many years directed by Morris ("Fritz") Mayer (Reid and Hagan, 1952).

At the same time that such new establishments were opening, old ones were being reviewed. In 1868, a Mr. Letchworth reported that living conditions within the New York almshouses were dreadful, and presently a great debate was under way between the proponents of residential settings and those who espoused foster care. Currently, this issue is by no means settled.

Elmira Reform School

Meanwhile, penology was making great strides. A national prison congress met in Cincinnati in 1870 and, in a curious, prayer-meeting atmosphere, set forth a body of principles for the care and rehabilitation of prison inmates that could still stand today as model goals for most of our penal institutions. A direct consequence of this current in our national thought was the creation in 1876 of the prototypic American type of reform school at Elmira, New York. Among its features were a system of grading prisoners, indeterminate sentences, parole, and physical training, plus vocational or academic education for each inmate. Alas, it also included such elements as a maximum security structure, too many prisoners, onerous discipline, and a program that took on the character of dehumanizing treadmill. Now, over a century later, in many a setting we still march to that same drum (Barnes and Teeters, 1951).

In vivid contrast is the story of a radically new social creation that suddenly came into being, the settlement house. First invented in London in 1884, it leapt the ocean to come to America in 1886. Much that we call community service, community organization, and even community psychiatry today is no whit different from what was there developed and practiced. The great exemplar of this movement is, of course, Hull House in Chicago. There, Jane Addams inspired a whole generation of budding social scientists with the values of tendering service to people by meeting and helping them in their own settings (Cruickshank and Johnson, 1958).

Medicine too was making advances in its understanding of children. In 1887 Eminghaus wrote the first text devoted entirely to children's mental and nervous diseases, and one year later Thomas M. Rotch became the first full-time professor of pediatrics in America when he was appointed to the first Department of Pediatrics at Harvard Medical School.

But the direction was not only forward and upward. Seguin's optimistic promises about the trainability and educability of the severely retarded had not borne fruit, and serious attempts to work with many such children had produced an ever-increasing sense of despair among numerous devoted professionals. In 1894, this disillusionment was reflected in public action when the first State Custodial Asylum was opened in Rome, New York. Hopelessness was now settled firmly on the shoulders of the retarded, the bright yearnings of only a decade before had dimmed almost to nothingness, and the new commitment was not to training or educating, but only to keeping and protecting (Danes, 1930).

Meanwhile society's hair shirt, the endless discomfort of trying to cope with the delinquent, led to more and more social experiments. A new note was struck in 1896 when William Reuben George founded the George Junior Republic in upper New York State. The emphasis in this setting was on a tactic that had received relatively little expression in the past, namely providing delinquents with genuine possibilities for self-government. It is true that in Mettray there had been some choice for the youngsters in electing their own monitors, but George went much farther and attempted to give his charges real responsibility.

This idea led to a transient "movement," and in short order a series of Junior Republics were established. The nature of the outcome was so problematical, however, that few such institutions survive today. Nonetheless, the basic theoretical stance of using responsibility and a measure of self-governance in the service of rehabilitation is a powerful idea, the fullness of whose dimensions remains to be explored (Barnes and Teeters, 1951).

This time of waning interest in "curing" retardation was also the epoch of one of the most progressive, practical, and forward-thinking physicians ever to work in this realm. Walter Fernald, a man of most unusual stature, developed a series of innovative approaches during these years. These included outpatient services, the first "special ed" classes, a host of contributions to legislation, a technique for systematic and definitive evaluative studies, and many other conceptual and empirical advances. He was the greatest exponent of his day for the careful, detailed diagnosis of all institutionalized children and for the provision of specific programs in line with identified individual needs. This conception remains basic to all scientific residential treatment and, indeed, to all child psychiatric treatment of any kind (Kirk, 1962).

The closing years of the nineteenth century were exciting and rich with promise. In 1899 the first Juvenile Court in the United States was established in Chicago. John Dewey was setting forth his ideas on education and Sigmund Freud wrote the *Interpretation of Dreams* in that same year. The stage was set for great things to come.

THE TWENTIETH CENTURY

As the twentieth century dawned, the accumulated skills and experiences of the late nineteenth century began to bear fruit. By 1905, Binet and Simon had developed the first modern standardized psychological test and thus opened a whole new universe of technique for the evaluation of children. At almost the same time, Freud published his *Three Contributions to a Theory of Sex*, and at a stroke the world of childhood took on richer and deeper meanings. The year 1906 saw the breaking of ground at Hawthorne, New York, for a model reformatory based on the cottage plan. In time, after several metamorphoses, this institution was to become the Hawthorne Cedar Knolls School (Reid and Hagan, 1952).

On the theoretical front, this first decade of the twentieth century was an incredible time. The works of Sigmund Freud, John Dewey, and Adolph Meyer were all coming into their fullest flower. Parallel with this, Durkheim (1938) was expanding the frontiers of sociology. This ferment coincided with political change as well: the first White House Conference on Children was convened by Theodore Roosevelt in 1909. And in that same year, William R. Healy established a study section at the Cook County Court, and the child guidance clinic was born. Healy and Augusta Bronner opened the Judge Baker Guidance Center in Boston in 1912 to work with Judge Cabot of the Boston Juvenile Court, and in 1915 Healy published the fruits of his studies, *The Individual Delinquent*.

This was also the time of the appearance of psychiatric social work and of rich and active developments in psychology. Earnest Southard and Mary Jarrett developed a multidisciplinary team at the Boston Psychopathic Hospital and began to work with children in the outpatient department. In Paris, we had noted that in 1905 the psychologist-alienist team of Binet and Simon had published the first standardized measuring instrument for the intelligence of children. Goddard, an American psychologist who had recently been appointed director of research for the Vineland, New Jersey school for the retarded, visited Europe and brought this test back with him. He had many doubts about it and was astonished to discover how accurate and precise it was when compared to clinical estimates of children's intelligence. Through his energetic support, this test and a later, more sophisticated version that Binet and Simon published in 1908, became familiar to American psychologists and were the basic structures upon which all later psychometric techniques were built (Cruickshank and Johnson, 1958).

With new knowledge came new conflicts. The organic neuropsychiatrists and the dynamic psychoanalysts were at odds, each wielding new insights and new discoveries. The organicist had unraveled the secrets of paresis; Moore and Naguchi traced the spirochete to the brain in 1913. Freud, on the other hand, had produced the first approach to a scientifically based comprehensive human psychology and opened new vistas for understanding and research.

At about the same time, the psychologists too were developing new methods and new theories. Psychological testing gave its practitioners a sense of diagnostic strength, an ability to evaluate and to predict. But it did not make for treatment. Then Watson published his work on behaviorism in 1914; it seemed that all questions were answered, or on the verge of an answer.

In responses to these developments, Fernald, at that time director of an institution for the retarded, published his definitive statement about the nature of evaluation: to study a child, one had to observe and measure its function in ten fields. These included: physical examination, family history, personal and developmental history, school progress, examinations in school work, practical knowledge and general information, social history and reactions, economic efficiency, moral reactions, and mental examination. Thus, to study a person, a wide range of skills was required; ultimately, it would take a mental health team to live up to the standards that Fernald set forth. More to the point, to plan for a child rationally (whether in or out of an institution), one had to have all this information immediately at hand. With this type of approach a staff was now able to create a program to fit the child rather than to make the child adapt to the existing program (Danes, 1930).

A curious by-product of World War I was the fact that mental health work gained national prominence. When the draft boards began to process large numbers of young men for the army, the nation was shocked to discover how many and how widespread were the intellectual and emotional defects throughout the population. Clifford Beers had founded the mental hygiene movement in 1909. The experiences of World War I gave added impetus to its growth and additional vigor was injected when, in 1922, the Commonwealth Fund supplied leadership and funds for a series of demonstration child guidance clinics. Based on Healy's professional team approach, these clinics proposed to prevent delinquency by treating children early. The hope was that early diagnosis and intervention would head off later serious problems. Once established, the new clinics were funded for five years. When this initial demonstration period had run its course, support would be taken over by the local communities. The first clinic opened in 1922. Two years later, the American Orthopsychiatric Association was founded to provide a forum for scientific exchange about the new methods and ideas for treating emotionally disturbed children (Stevenson, 1934). Despite these efforts, however, delinquency continued to flourish. The clinics were a success and provided much needed help to many children, but not to their original target population.

Adding Psychiatric Care to Institutions

To benefit from the new knowledge, the Hawthorn Reform School added a part-time psychologist to its staff in 1915. This was an important shift and quite a step forward for a penal institution. Within a few years, Hawthorne had a full multidsiciplinary group at work within its structure and collaborative inpatient work among psychiatrist, psychologist, social worker, and paraprofessional was a reality. At nearly the same time, throughout the country a similar change was overtaking the many orphans' homes. Thus, in 1924, the Cleveland Jewish Orphans' Home introduced psychiatric services for its children. In the ensuing decades, the metamorphosis undergone by these agencies in the 1920s was due to be repeated in many places; today there is scarcely an "orphanage" in the old sense to be found anywhere in the United States.

August Aichorn: Psychoanalytic Work with Delinquents

A strong theoretical support for a new kind of institution came from the work of August Aichorn in Vienna. An educator who directed an institution for delinquents, Aichorn became a psychoanalyst and turned the full force of his remarkable gifts to the treatment and rehabilitation of his young charges. He developed a philosophy of management that involved a great deal of permissiveness and a primary emphasis on understanding. In a sense he attempted to wed psychoanalytic theory to institutional practice. Although his methods were not much emulated, his basic conception of trying to fit milieu work into a context of general personality theory was to have a powerful effect on the thinking and methods of many later practitioners. His book, *Verwahrloster Jugend (Way-*

ward Youth), appeared in 1925 (the English translation did not become available until 1935).

In the nature of things, psychoanalysis does not lend itself in any obvious way to the establishment of milieu practices or to the organization of institutional care. Instead, this approach stipulates that all behavior has meaning, that the meaning is usually not understood (or not completely understood) by the individual who acts, and that with help, many people can achieve insight into the motives underlying their behavior and thus be empowered to come to grips with what they are doing. Hence, the essential message of the psychoanalytic approach has been to seek to create an environment that will foster self-understanding. How to do that is the challenge posed to the ingenuity and imagination of the individual practitioner or team. Aichorn, for example, sought to accomplish this by allowing a group of youngsters unrestricted freedom. This soon proved so disastrous that the children became aware of their own self-destructiveness and turned to the adults for protection from and help with their impulses. Bettelheim focused on the need for more than mere affectionate care. Love was not enough; there had to be a response to the meaning of the child's behavior. Only this would open the path to the critical ego growth and dynamic self-understanding (which would ultimately be arrived at by means of support and interpretation). Redl emphasized the need for carefully designed controls as essential ingredients to allow containment of the defensive acting out. This in turn would make it possible for the necessary understanding to be achieved (Bettelheim, 1950; Redl and Wineman, 1951).

During this epoch, many Americans were finding their way to Vienna to study the new theories and methods developing there. They met Freud, they met the circle of colleagues that had grown up about him, and presently the influence of Aichorn and Anna Freud and other pathfinders in child treatment began to filter back into America.

In contrast to this influx of dynamic thinking, the early 1920s brought with them some signal lessons in organicity. During those years a severe epidemic of von Economo's encephalitis attacked many children all over the United States. The result was a dramatic display of the effects of brain injury on behavior. The radical changes in deportment and personality that followed the subsidence of the acute phases of the disorder gave a striking demonstration of the role of physiology and anatomy in such areas as activity level, impulse control, attention span, distractibility, learning, cognition, and so forth. Of special interest to us, it led directly to the opening of a number of settings for brain-injured children. Karl Menninger opened one such center at the Menninger Foundation, naming it the Southard School in memory of his revered teacher, Ernest Southard.

The school was designed both for brain-injured and retarded children; in essence it was a custodial institution. In Philadelphia, the Franklin School of the Pennsylvania Hospital was created in 1926 under the direction of Earl Bond specifically for the postencephalitic child (Reid and Hagan, 1952).

The mental hygiene clinic approach was also spreading far and wide throughout the land; it penetrated some of the large welfare settings and helped catalyze their conversion to a residential treatment milieu. Thus, in 1926, the Pleasantville Cottage School for orphans at Pleasantville, New York introduced a child guidance clinic into its structure. The cottage parent concerned about a behavioral problem could now refer the child to a clinic right on the grounds. It was only a matter of time before the clinical tail began to wag the welfare dog; from the 1950s onward, Pleasantville has regarded itself as and has, in fact, become a treatment center (Child Welfare League of America, 1963).

Other such institutions took a similar tack in ways that were analogous if not identical. Thus the Cleveland Jewish Children's Home grew by changes in internal structure rather than by tacking on such clinical additions. As noted, in 1926 casework had become part of the basic cadre of this institution, and child guidance principles now began to set the tone for children and staff alike. It is not surprising, then, that in New York City the Institute for Child Guidance came into being that same year as a center for research and as the principal site for training personnel for child guidance work. Marion Kenworthy was the first director and David Levy was director of research.

In New England, a bequest established the Emma Pendelton Bradley Home in Providence, Rhode Island in 1931. Originally the mission of this organization was to care for the brain-injured child, the postencephalitic, the convulsive, and the spastic. Shortly, the Bradley Home too was to remake itself into a residential treatment center within a basic hospital structure (Reid and Hagan, 1952).

The early 1930s saw Hitler's rise to power in Germany. The tide of refugees that thereupon poured out of Europe had an enormous impact on mental health practices in many places. In America, a great many psychoanalysts and child analysts found haven, began to work, and were presently playing a major role in teaching, training, and the refinement of mental health practices on every level.

The theoretical literature about treatment of children was increasing even more rapidly. In 1933 Melanie Klein's book, *The Psychoanalysis of Children* (1932), appeared in England, and Jessie Taft's *Dynamics of Therapy in a Controlled Relationship* was published in the United States. Taft, a psychologist, was actively introducing the principles of Otto Rank into the clinic treatment of children, while Klein, a psychoanalyst, was defining new theory and a novel method of child analysis that were to play a major role in sharpening the issues in that field. Today, Taft is less well known than her student, Fred Allen, whose book, *Psychotherapy with Children*, was the basic text in this area for many years and who was the chief exponent of Taft's ideas (Allen, 1942).

Empirical strides were being made as well. Howard Potter in 1933 published a description of a group of aberrant children he found in institutions for the mentally retarded. He was able to demonstrate symptoms closely akin to those of adult schizophrenia, and thus gave us the first picture of childhood schizophrenia. In 1934, Lauretta Bender took over the children's ward at Bellevue Hospital in New York City; her studies in childhood schizophrenia were to be among the classics in the field.

The year 1934 was notable in yet another way. The American Board of Psychiatry and Neurology was created and psychiatry was given recognition as a new specialty. It would take almost 25 years, however, before the subspecialty Committee on Certification in Child Psychiatry would come into being.

Meanwhile the depression was ravaging the country, and in response to this, at a government level, vast changes were occurring. In 1935, the Social Security Act was passed with a provision for Aid to Dependent Children. This program would lead to a pattern of more children remaining in the home or going into foster placement, and only the most disturbed finding their way into institutions.

More clinics and constantly improving theoretical and diagnostic tools led to the detection of ever more disturbance in children in schools, in courts, and in the community at large. Since facilities simply did not exist for the very sick ones, soon an unprepared state hospital system the country over began to encounter a steady and steadily growing stream of child admissions. A number of articles appeared (stemming chiefly from New York State institutions) describing some of these events. The authors could, alas, only document the problem; at the time there were no "solutions."

Changes continued as well in the existing settings, and on both coasts the transformation of agencies went on apace. In 1935, in Seattle, the Ryther Child Home with a 50-year history of care and shelter for needy children and mothers now became the Ryther Child Center and began to offer expert intake, treatment, and placement services. In New York, Hawthorne Cedar Knolls took yet another step away from its penal character by adding a guidance clinic to its structure. Two years later, Hawthorne completed its conversion and dedicated itself to the achievement of inner change in children through treatment (Reid and Hagan,

1952). This was at the very time that Aichorn's *Wayward Youth* was translated into English.

An important event in the development of child psychiatry came from the work of Leo Kanner. A pediatrician who had gone into psychiatry, Kanner was trained by Adolf Meyer and carried his psychobiological orientation along with a healthy eclecticism into his work with children. In 1935 he published a remarkable text, *Child Psychiatry*, which was destined to dominate the field for decades. The following year, Otto Rank's *Will Therapy & Truth & Reality* was published; it offered a straightforward way to conceptualize psychotherapy and had a considerable influence on child guidance practice. Institutional work was also being addressed.

Almost every year brought new and important developments. In 1937 Bradley discovered that Benzedrine could quiet hyperactive children. Soon after, Lauretta Bender published the Bender–Gestalt Test.

The Shift from Treating Brain-Damaged to Emotionally Disturbed

By 1938 the Ryther Child Center had firmed up its identity; henceforth, it divested itself of intake and placement and devoted itself primarily to residential treatment. A similar series of changes overtook the Home for Friendless Children at Wilkes-Barre, Pennsylvania. Under the leadership of J. Franklin Robinson it became the Children's Service of Wyoming Valley and joined the ranks of the earliest residential Treatment Centers in the country (Reid and Hagan, 1952).

During the decade of the 1930s, pediatricians and child psychiatrists were eying one another with mixed feelings. On the one hand, William Langford, a child psychiatrist, had opened a pediatric psychiatric clinic at Columbia Medical Center. On the other hand, an influential pediatrician, Dr. J. Brennemann (1931), wrote an article entitled "The Menace of Psychiatry," in which he took arms against both behaviorism and the Oedipus complex. Perhaps the state of affairs is best described by the title another pediatrician, Dr. Crothers, gave to his 1937 paper: *The Pediatrician in Search of Mental Hygiene*. Between the two disciplines a state of expectant engagement and chronic unease continued to prevail.

The work of the children's ward at Bellevue was now beginning to be reported. For the first time, the richness of the possibilities of a therapeutic milieu within a hospital were described when Curran and Schilder (1940) published *A Constructive Approach to Problems of Childhood and Adolescence*.

One year later the Southard School at the Menninger Clinic joined the new surge and formally converted from a custodial center for retarded and brain-injured children to a residential treatment unit for the emotionally disturbed. Within two years, Bellfaire, in Cleveland, which had long been moving in that direction, made the same definitive commitment. Then the Bradley Home in Rhode Island followed suit. At this point, these were among the pioneer agencies to take this step. In time, such a style of conversion became the national practice.

In part, these events marked a critical change in the role and expectations of the guidance clinics. Over the previous two decades, it had become very clear that there were many children who were too disturbed or too disturbing to be treated on an outpatient basis. But they were not too disturbed to be diagnosed, and, with the spread of clinics and skills, more and more such children were in fact being identified. Thus the pressure for placement grew steadily. Parallel with the increase in diagnostic sophistication, another change of social character was taking place. At this point, as we noted, orphans were by and large no longer going into institutions; they were being placed in foster homes. But the foster homes functioned as a sort of social sieve; they screened out the manageable ones and kept them, whereas their failures, the impossible ones, began to concentrate in the institutional welfare settings. Over and beyond this, still another element was at work: there was a fresh body of theory emerging. Aichorn had set the pace; the child guidance concepts had added a rich mix of possible practices, and the stage was set for a new crystallization. Then, in the early 1940s, World War II intervened and soaked up the nation's energies. Once the war was over, however, a tremendous spirit of revitalization was felt everywhere. All the potentials formerly devoted to the conflict were now freed for growth. And growth ensued.

In 1946, 54 clinics banded together in order to form a new standard-setting agency, the American Association of Psychiatric Clinics for Children (AAPCC). For many years this was the only agency to certify clinics, child psychiatry training programs, and child psychiatrists. At the same time the Group for the Advancement of Psychiatry was established, the Society for Biological Psychiatry came into being, and the first T groups were organized by Kurt Lewin at MIT.

A Therapeutic Milieu: Bettelheim, Ekstein, and Redl

In the arena of residential treatment, Bruno Bettelheim at the University of Chicago set an established agency, the Sonia Shankman Orthogenic School, on a new course. Henceforth it would treat only the very sickest mentally ill children. In nearby Detroit, Fritz Redl opened Pioneer House for the study and residential treatment of hyperaggressive children and for research into the process of residential treatment itself. Working in their respective settings, these two men were to give rise to a wavefront of theoretical and creative conceptualization in the field of milieu care that was extraordinary in its impact. Not far behind was the work of Stanislaus Szurek, begun that same year, 1946, at the Children's Inpatient Service of Langley Porter Hospital with very regressed schizophrenic children.

The Therapeutic Community

In a very short time a group of books and papers began to appear that gave residential treatment definitive form. Bettelheim and Sylvester were the first authors in the American literature to use the term "therapeutic milieu." Their 1948 article (to which they gave this title) was epoch making. It set down firmly many of the basic principles that were to characterize residential treatment thereafter. It spoke of an environment with an ". . . inner cohesiveness which alone permits a child to develop a consistent frame of reference" (Bettelheim and Sylvester, 1948). The authors mentioned the structured use of regression in the service of mastery, the unconditional gratification of primitive needs, the use of holidays and ceremonies to structure time, the importance of fun in a child's life, the identification of what gives a child a feeling of worth and providing it, the need to avoid posing tasks beyond the child's capacity to master, the limiting of relationship demand to the immediate caretakers, and the primacy of this caretaker in the child's life. One of their central concepts was the need for a single governing framework for all the staff to share about the nature of the child's pathology; this must be worked out with great care and the therapeutic program must be a direct reflection of and response to this model.

In particular, they emphasized the need to understand the child, dynamically and in depth, in order to help him. These principles, along with constructs of similar character, have continued to be central in formulating programs and practices in this work. And the concept of milieu therapy was given at once both name and form.

One can list many units that opened up during the next few years, in Chicago, in Ann Arbor, in Cincinnati, and so on. A setting of special interest was Fritz Redl's Pioneer House in Detroit; it existed for only two years and closed in 1949. It was unique in that its main purpose was research. It was one of the few situations at the time (perhaps the only one) that formally dedicated itself to study the process of residential treatment and the elements of therapeutic milieu. From this, and from many other sources, important books began to appear. Bettelheim published *Love is not Enough* in 1950 and Redl and Wineman's *Children Who Hate* appeared in 1951. Thus were two of the most penetrating studies of the meaning and methods of residential treatment made available almost at once; a new level of theory and practice had emerged.

What these authors spoke for was the primary power of the immediate environment to shape and mold human behavior. Children are profoundly dependent on and deeply involved with their caretakers; much of the primary pathology that disturbed youngsters bring to therapy is a mirror of the original caretaking behavior to which they had been exposed. A distorted mirror, to be sure, but nonetheless an expression of the quality and even of the events that took place in interaction with these primordial figures. The remedy must follow suit; the interaction of the child with its milieu, especially with those persons in the milieu who feed and clean and watch over health and play with and protect—in short, the child care staff—this interplay is critical. It can serve to foster pathology and drive the child ever more irreversibly into maladaptive forms of adjustment or it can become the primary means for healing and repair. The essential substance of the message these authors presented was the skillful use of the details of everyday living in the service of achieving therapeutic change. Redl had at once to distinguish the work of the child care staff from that of the psychotherapist, and at the same time recognize the child care work as profoundly therapeutic. He did this by designating the interactions of the child care staff with the youngsters as "life space interviews." Thus, at a stroke, these interactions became official therapy, they were interviews, and at the same time they occurred ad hoc, without appointment, without set time frames, and without set sites of encounter. They happened anywhere, in the corridor, in the day hall, in the child's own room. They were initiated by either staff or child, perhaps because something had happened and the staff wanted to confront the child, or because the child became upset in response to a disturbing phone call or letter and needed to talk it over. In any case, these interviews were vital components of the therapeutic mix.

It does not do justice to Redl's conceptual power to focus on this one contribution, however. His notion was to englobe the child in a mantle of therapeutic activities so that every moment of the child's experience allowed for something to happen that was constructive. Redl brought enormous creativity and imagination to bear on designing such a life, and he subjected his ideas to critical study.

Bettelheim, on the other hand, regarded his counselors (child care workers) as the child's primary therapists. There was no distinction between life space and therapy sessions; all were therapy sessions. The counselors were supervised intensively and taught to interpret to the child in depth psychological terms. Bettelheim too designed a magnificently wrought therapeutic tapestry in which to wrap the child. The result was an environment within which even the most deviant child was fostered and could grow. Bettelheim's work is characterized by meticulous attention to the details of everyday living as critical bits of the mosaic of therapeutic engagement. Thus the way a child was awakened in the morning was worth an extended passage in his book.

It is probably no exaggeration to say that the depth, beauty, and power of the work of these two authors literally revolutionized the field. Up to that time, most practitioners had simply failed to give anything like the concentrated attention to the ingredients of therapeutic milieu that these works now spread before them. It is unlikely that many environments as carefully achieved as the settings they described are to be found today; it is, however, certain that the more informed settings strive to cast themselves in that mold.

In any case, the growth of the field had now come to a point where the Child Welfare League of America undertook a major examination of existing residential methods and practices. Joseph Reid and Helen Hagan (1952) traveled to 12 different centers all over the United States and published a detailed study of each in a comprehensive volume, *Residential Treatment of Emotionally Disturbed Children*. The authors wrote of these agencies: ". . . they have one thing in common—the development of a total approach to therapy" (Reid and Hagan, 1952). This total approach has continued to be the hallmark of such work.

There were many changes taking place in the professional and governmental world that were to have considerable bearing on residential care. In 1952, the Social Security Agency became the Department of Health, Education and Welfare. In the same year, the American Academy of Child Psychiatry was formally organized. Two years later, the Supreme Court decided that public schools could no longer be segregated.

Among the first acts of the new American Academy of Child Psychiatry was to join with the American Psychiatric Association to co-sponsor a National Conference on Inpatient Psychiatric Treatment of Children. After many months of patient preliminary work, a plenary session was held in Washington in 1956. Residential treatment had now attained the level of a consolidated technique, and, of major importance, the role of the child care worker received a new and vivid valuation (Robinson, 1957).

The end of the World War II brought with it many other changes and developments that had profound implications for the way children were managed in congregate settings. Some of the concepts derived directly from the war experience itself. Thus, in England, Maxwell Jones found himself dealing with a hospitalized population of character-disordered soldiers for whom no adequate treatment had yet been devised. To cope with these difficult patients, Jones (1953) developed a novel technique, a milieu method he called the "therapeutic community." The underlying concept was that people behaved badly because they felt helpless. If this feeling could be overcome, they would feel more effective and would no longer need to resort to the manipulative and dishonest techniques with which they had run their lives. Some of the core concepts, then, focussed on empowerment. There was empowerment of the individual, of the patient group, and of the staff. Jones postulated that the emergence of a common value system would then unify the group in reclaiming its right to responsibility.

The innovations this implied were rather extreme. For example, all decision making must be carried out at community meetings where all staff and patients came together. Within that context, there was to be no hierarchical difference between staff members or between staff members and patients; everyone had a right to speak and be heard; everyone's voice was of equal weight. Given the traditionally highly stratified hierarchy of senior doctor, junior doctor, nurse, and aide, this made quite an extraordinary demand on staff. Ultimately, very few programs in America were able to convert to the ideal which Jones's idea demanded; on the other hand, the use of community meetings as a central facet of milieu therapy caught on and is quite universally practiced. In many settings, anybody, staff or patient, has the right to call a community meeting whenever they feel they have a grievance or a problem that involves community decision.

Behavioral Approaches

Indeed, within the world of residential care, the community approach has given rise to several different styles of milieu organization. Thus a method called "positive peer culture" (Vorrath and Bendtro, 1985; Bendtro and Wasmund, 1989) requires the staff to seek to effect change through frequent small-group discussions. The emphasis falls on the assets that youngsters bring to the setting; the assumption is that every youth has the potential for strength and greatness, and that these can be achieved through learning to love and to care for others. The adults make a point of concentrating on values; positive helpful behavior is relabeled as strong, cool, and sophisticated; hurtful behavior as weak, immature, and inadequate. Another tactic that characterizes the method is the assigning of responsibility to the youngster instead of allowing him or her to perceive it as coming from the outside. The effort throughout is to build social competencies within a group context. The adults do not lead the groups so much as they raise questions for the group to consider. The spirit of the meeting is that of support rather than confrontation.

Another approach was developed by Kurt Hahn, a German educator (Bacon and Kimball, 1989). He had been at Salem School in Germany during the 1920s. With Hitler's rise to power, Hahn went to England in 1933 and began to develop a new approach. He regarded the goal of education as toughening the human spirit; accordingly, he developed a mode of character training that thrust the student into situations where one would have to act in order to survive. Given the nature of the stresses imposed on the student, one had to learn self-denial, tenacity, cooperation, and compassion for others. To bring this about, each youngster had to be pressed to engage in health-giving but stressful experiences to which each would have to find his or her own solutions, with guidance to be sure, but without opinions being forced on them.

If properly organized, the program would drive students to discover a code of ethics as a practical and utilitarian element in their lives. Hahn found that if youngsters were required to adapt to wilderness living and to engage in rescue work, this was particularly conducive to the formation of such values. Hahn's fundamental conception was that properly designed experiences would naturally and inevitably give rise to constructive values.

Brought to the United States in 1962, the idea caught on immediately. The program was called Outward Bound, and five such schools were established. More than that, many other programs began to incorporate elements of this method into their address to their clients. More generally, all sorts of wilderness-challenge programs are coming to be included in remedial approaches and even into more straightforward educational settings.

The Outward Bound strategy involves several typical characteristics. Since it is seeking to create a group ethic, of necessity it is always a group program, normally with about ten members or less. The group is led to face a series of challenges that become increasingly difficult and demanding as the group gains experience. Coping with these challenges requires mutual reliance and cooperation among the group members, a great deal of problem-solving activity, a need to stick to a difficult course in the face of meaningful obstacles, the use of training and acquired skills, and often some element of imaginative or creative address to difficulties.

There is generally a degree of physical danger involved, more perceived than real for the most part, but real nonetheless. This might be associated with climbing a dangerous rock face while securely attached by a rope, exploring an underground cave where one could realistically get lost or stuck, white water rafting or canoeing where a craft could overturn or one could be swept away, and the like. Sometimes such a program is carried out aboard sailing vessels, sometimes by being thrust into an unfamiliar urban environment. The leaders seek to manage the group process in such a way as to encourage group members to distill appropriate social values from the experience. Students are asked to keep journals;

they may have individual counseling sessions, and other forms of support are available as needed. Such programs can last from a day (as an adjunct activity of some other therapeutic modality) to a year. By and large these are colorful and dramatic undertakings; in fact, they tend to build trust and affiliation.

To shift now to quite a different milieu conceptualization, in the early 1960s, Nicholas Hobbs developed what he called Project Re-Ed (Hobbs, 1982). This has been elaborated into what is called the psychoeducational approach, and a number of treatment centers employ this strategy. Hobbs was impressed by the work done in France as part of the postwar reconstruction effort. The French had to find a way to deal with the large number of waifs and strays who roamed the cities and the countryside in the wake of the battles and bombings. The French approach had been to marshal the efforts of young educators who took on the burden of treatment and guidance for the many youngsters in need at the various centers that accommodated them. These "educateurs" modeled behavior, encouraged prosocial activity, gave counseling and support as needed, taught the children, and were the realistic caretaking presences in their lives.

Hobbs saw this as the nucleus for a short-term type of intervention with emotionally disturbed children where they could be reeducated into more prosocial patterns. As it came to be organized in America, the "re-ed" programs usually held a child in five-day a week residence for some six to eight months; the child spent weekends at home with his or her parents. Within the setting, the youngsters were seen as members of an ecological unit. For each group of eight children, one teacher-member of the team worked with the youngsters in their setting, one worked in their educational program, and one with their group living.

The program is designedly educational in orientation and notably free of mental health personnel. The school is central to the program. There is much emphasis on keeping kids in class. Most of the instruction is individualized, and much of the teaching is by doing; the teachers are also likely to drop a prepared program in order to follow the child's indication of interest and to build on that. Behavioral methods are prominently in evidence: the program employs levels to be attained, written goals to be measured against, and contracts to define expected performance. A group-process structure is also part of the approach, for example, each child sets a goal at the start of the week and behavioral group meetings are then called in order to have the other youngsters evaluate how that youngster is doing. Those who meet their goals get something special, like a valued trip. Problem-solving meetings and planning meetings are also part of the structure.

The nature of the program does not involve seeking the causes of the disturbed behavior. Instead, emphasis falls on increasing the ability of the entire ecological unit to function well. This might involve changing unrealistic parental expectations and working to increase a given child's social skills. Hobbs proposed 12 principles of reeducation. These include such assertions as: (1) life is to be lived now; (2) trust is essential; (3) competence is crucial; (4) time is an ally; and so forth.

I have referred to the use of behavioral principles in residential treatment. Behavioral therapy applied to humans has been on the scene only since the late 1950s and early 1960s. However, because it is allegedly effective and easily taught, its techniques have become so widespread and so well established that their use is taken for granted as the "normal" way to do things. Actually the principles of social learning theory are still not completely realized as methodology and important new advances are likely to appear in that realm. To date, however, certain practices such as token economy, the use of "time-out," behavioral contracts, star charts, and level systems have permeated the field; they are accepted management routines rather than a conscious application of behavioral principles. Indeed, other kinds of therapeutic models (medical inpatient or psychoanalytic) employ these practices to serve the ends of very different conceptual arrangements.

In certain contexts, however, behavioral thinking has grown along its own unique lines. A number of settings sought to build programs around behavioral principles from the ground up. Ever since 1967, there has been an organized attempt to apply behavioral theory to the management of delinquents housed in residential settings. The arrangement that has emerged is called the teaching-family model (Blase *et al.*, 1989). There are now said to be between 200 and 300 such settings in North America.

This theoretical position holds that the child does not need treatment for his- or herself; it is rather the ecological niche within which the child resides and the youngster's interactions with other occupants of that ecological setting that require therapeutic address. Hence one studies behavior in context and seeks to bring about change in that way. This approach serves for outpatient care as well as for work within a setting. Moreover, since behavioral work is research based, ongoing research is continually defining improvements in technique and in the means of evaluating what one does.

Since this method grows out of behavioral research, it implies that it is built around measurable parameters. This in turn affords ready access to community agencies and third-party payers who seek clear measures of progress and means for evaluation of what is done. An additional advantage of the approach is that it lends itself to relatively inexpensive community-based group home management. Over time, it has proven itself to be a relatively flexible strategy and has come to adapt to the complexities of administration, personnel and staffing issues, and community requirements. It has developed training strategies for staff, it has learned to meet standards, and it has begun to cope with issues of accreditation, licensure, peer review, and the like.

An emphasis has been placed on making it a replicable program, that is, developing principles and techniques that can be communicated and applied with predictable outcome. This has been a direct outgrowth of the research strategy on which the program is based.

The primary tactic employed by these programs is teaching. In a sense, all of living is conceptualized as a complex set of learned skills; the technique of treatment is to impart these skills by breaking them down into simple, manageable components. Taken individually, these fragments should be relatively easy to impart and relatively easy to learn. For example, the child is taught that when addressed by a teacher, the first skill to be mastered is to look at the person addressing you. The second skill is then to listen to what is said, a task that is not necessarily easy. The third, harder still, is to listen without arguing or fussing. Once some success is registered on that score, the child can be taught to try to do the task and then to carry through the task to the end. The next skill is to report back that the task is done. And so on step by step. A separate line of training is to learn the skill of accepting criticism, again a stepwise set of accomplishments. In this way, the groundwork is laid on which further elaborations of training and education can be built.

The basic organization of the program is to offer a community group home setting where a pair of teaching parents care for a small number (approximately six) of troubled (usually borderline retarded and emotionally disturbed) teenagers. These teaching parents are a married couple, often with their own children, who seek to be both teachers and parents to their charges. The couple works with the school, with community services, and with the family of each youngster in an effort to integrate the services each child receives. The teaching parents seek to establish a close personal relationship with each youth and to use that as the context within which to impart the necessary skills. Careful attention is given to the need to foster autonomy in order to avoid the inevitable tendency for an ever-increasing state of dependency to develop. The teaching parents in turn are taught to use what is designated as "teaching interaction" as their principal modality for serving their charges. Early on, this involves a skillful reward design in order to motivate the youngsters to learn. Later, it requires the use of praise, redirection toward alternative behaviors, practice of appropriate behaviors, the use of positive and negative consequences, and so forth. A roster of skills is thus inculcated in each child. Where the teaching parent is a good observer and can grasp the circumstances that evoke negative reactions within each child, much useful behavioral change can follow.

A daily "family conference" is held. Attended by the whole group of youngsters along with their caretakers, it is a site where a measure of self-government is encouraged. The youngsters can create or change existing rules and engage in a variety of self-regulatory activities. They are encouraged to gain a sense of realistically affecting their world by the decisions they make, and they learn as well a variety of essential social competencies. In addition to the group context, the teaching parents offer individual counseling as well in order to shore up and reassure the youngsters in sensitive areas. But these are not scheduled meetings; they form part of the fabric of daily life and emerge from the natural interplay of encounter. In effect, each interaction is a site for teaching.

CONCLUSION: THE LOSS OF THE THERAPEUTIC MILIEU

In sum, then, residential treatment and the formulation of the concept of a therapeutic milieu confronts many of the same problems that engage psychotherapy in general. Should one deal with the dynamic roots of behavior, its causes, its beginnings, and its origins, or should one confine oneself to the immediacies of how the child acts and seek only to change the external forms of behavior in order to improve social adjustment? In a time when medicine in general is under considerable critical social scrutiny and when the financial structures on the delivery of care are a matter of profound public concern, short-term surface solutions are inevitably the runaway favorite as the likeliest course to follow. In the nature of things, in-depth understanding is not to be arrived at quickly, and long-term residential care is expensive. Nor do empiric observations support the concept that the attainment of insight leads to any better outcome than changes arrived at without any great degree of self-understanding. Withal, however, those who work in the trenches have a sense of a sizable coterie of youngsters, in particular those with nascent or fully realized characterological disorders, who cannot be helped readily on the fly. It is altogether too easy for such youngsters to adopt a patina of correct behavior only to regress immediately to type once they are outside the walls of the setting. The "mask of sanity" is still with us as an ongoing problem, and the role of long-term skilled milieu therapy remains the only available modality to address such issues meaningfully.

References

Aichorn, A. (1935). *Wayward Youth*. New York: Viking Press.
Allen, F. (1942). *Psychotherapy with Children*. New York: Norton.
Bason, S. B., and Kimball, R. (1989). The Wilderness Challenge Model. In R. D. Lyman, S. Prentice-Dunn, and S. Gabel (eds.), *Residential Inpatient Treatment of Children and Adolescents*, pp. 115–144. New York: Plenum Press.
Barnes, H. E., and Teeters, N. K. (1951). *New Horizons in Criminology* (2nd ed.). New York: Prentice-Hall.
Bendtro, L. K., and Wasmund, W. (1989). The peer culture model. In R. D. Lyman, S. Prentice-Dunn, and S. Gabel (eds.), *Residential Inpatient Treatment of Children and Adolescents*, pp. 81–95. New York: Plenum Press.
Bettelheim, B. (1950). *Love Is Not Enough*. Glencoe, IL: Free Press.
Bettelheim, B., and Sylvester, E. (1948). Milieu therapy: Indications and illustrations. *Psychoanalytic Review* 36(1):54–68.
Blase, K. A., Fixsen, D. L., Freeborn, K., and Jaeger, D. (1989). The behavioral model. In R. D. Lyman, S. Prentice-Dunn, and S. Gabel (eds.), *Residential Inpatient Treatment of Children and Adolescents*, pp. 43–59. New York: Plenum Press.
Brennemann, J. (1931). The menace of psychiatry. *American Journal of Diseases of Children* 42:376–402.
Child Welfare League of America. (1963). *What We Have Learned*. New York: Child Welfare League of America.
Crothers, B. (1937). *The Pediatrician in Search of Mental Hygiene*. New York: Commonwealth Fund.
Cruickshank, W. H., and Johnson, G. O. (1958). *Education of Exceptional Children and Youth*. Englewood Cliffs, NJ: Prentice-Hall.
Curran, F. J., and Schilder, P. (1940, 1941) A Construcitve Approach to the Problems of Childhood & Adolescence. *Journal of Criminal Psychopathology*, 2:125–142; 3:305–321
Danes, S. T. (1930). *Social Control of the Mentally Deficient*. New York: Thomas Y. Crowell.
Dewey, J. (1899). *The School and Society*. Chicago: University of Chicago Press.
Dewey, J. (1938). *Experience and Education*. New York: Macmillan.
Durkheim, E. (1938). *The Rules of Sociologic Method* (S.A. Solovay and J. Mueller, trans.; G. E. Catlin, ed.). Chicago: University of Chicago Press.
Emminghaus, H. (1887). *Die Psychischen Storungen des Kindesalters*. Tubingen: Laupp.
Healy, W. R. (1915). *The Individual Delinquent*. Boston: Little Brown.
Hobbs, N. (1982). *Troubled and Troubling Children*. San Francisco: Jossey-Bass.
Jones, M. (1953). *The Therapeutic Community*. New York: Basic Books.
Kanner, L. (1935). Child Psychiatry. Springfield, IL: Charles C. Thomas.
Kirk, S. A. (1962). *Educating Exceptional Children*. Boston: Houghton Mifflin.
Klein, M. (1932). *The Psychoanalysis of Children*. London: Hogarth.
Mulhern, J. (1946). *A History of Education*. New York: Ronald Press.
Rank, D. (1945). *Will Therapy and Truth & Reality*. New York, Knopf.
Redl, F., and Wineman, D. (1951). *Children Who Hate*. Glencoe: Free Press.
Reid, J. H., and Hagan, H. R. (1952). *Residential Treatment for Emotionally Disturbed Children: A Descriptive Study*. New York: Child Welfare League of America.
Rexford, E. (1969). Children, Child Psychiatry, and Our Brave New World. *Archives of General Psychiatry*, 20:25–37.
Robinson, J. F. (1957). *Psychiatric Inpatient Treatment of Children*. Washington, DC: American Psychiatric Association.

Rousseau, J. J. (1762). *Emile; ou de l'Education*. Amsterdam, Neaulme. [In English: Rousseau, J. J. (1911). *Emile*. (B. Foxley, trans.). London: Dent.]

Stevenson, G. S. (1934). *Child Guidance Clinics, A Quarter Century of Development*. New York: Commonwealth Fund.

Taft, J. J. (1933). *The Dynamics of Therapy in a Controlled Relationship*. New York, Macmillan.

Vorrath, H. H., and Bendtro, L. K. (1985). *Positive Peer Culture* (2nd ed.). Hawthorne, NY: Aldine Publishing.

4

Orthodoxy and Heresy in the History of Psychoanalysis

ELIO FRATTAROLI

FRATTAROLI, LIKE COHLER AND GALATZER-LEVY, explores a divisive, malignant conflict within the psychoanalytic community, tracing it back to an intrapsychic conflict of Freud. In this case, Frattaroli identifies it as the disagreement over whether our personal miseries are due to intrapsychic origins (the orthodox psychoanalytic position) or interpersonal origins (the heretical psychoanalytic position).

Most intriguing, Frattaroli suggests that this psychoanalytic controversy is an issue of Western culture, translated into psychoanalytic terminology. That is, he puts psychoanalysis in the tradition of Western philosophy, trying to resolve "Where does evil arise?" Is man tragic or guilty? In that sense, psychoanalysis can be seen to arise in Western intellectual thought at a time when previous *Weltanschauungen*, religion, and later the Enlightenment's faith in reason were no longer universally held to answer our fundamental questions. Psychoanalysis arose to explore this issue of humankind's nature by bringing unreason into the realm of reason.

Frattaroli elegantly develops the two conflicting lines of thought, beginning with philosophy, through psychoanalytic theories of etiology, to implications for technique. The "orthodox" psychoanalytic position is this: If man is inherently guilty, childhood sexuality is the etiological agent, neurosis is primarily intrapsychic, and the cure is recovery of the repressed fantasy. The

ELIO FRATTAROLI • 168 Gramercy Road, Bala Cynwyd, Pennsylvania 19004.

Educating the Emotions: Bruno Bettelheim and Psychoanalytic Development, edited by Nathan M. Szajnberg. Plenum Press, New York, 1992.

"heretical" psychoanalytic position is this: If man is inherently tragic, his vicissitudes are due to poor nurturing, the seduction theory accounts for etiology, neurosis is primarily an interpersonal issue, and the cure is recovery of the repressed memory of a true event. Interestingly, the "orthodox" theory is not so purely intrapsychic. For Freud recognized in his working papers that this "intrapsychic" neurosis needs to be recreated interpersonally in the transference (and we would now add countertransference) interaction.

Freud approached a resolution of this interpersonal–intrapsychic conflict in his paper *Inhibitions, Symptoms and Anxiety*. As Frattaroli carefully argues, however, this was a compromise formation, not a comfortable concordance of opposites or recognition of multiple functions. For Freud, under sway of nineteenth-century physicalism, or "scientistic" influence, as Cohler and Galatzer-Levy call it, still placed the ego as subordinate to the more physiological id.

Frattaroli concludes with how this controversy persists with destructive results for the psychoanalytic community, yet on a more hopeful note, how there is some working through and resolution. After demonstrating that Freud's intrapsychic conflict became interpersonal in the psychoanalytic community, Frattaroli implicitly describes how this community functions like the human mind. When a part of our self or community is felt threatened by another part, one defensive maneuver is to attack the interloper and expel him, as Freud did to Adler and Jung. Ironically, after exiling that part of ourself or our community, we may take in that formerly heretical belief, as Freud could later develop a theory of aggression, years after attacking Adler for his emphasis on aggression. On the other hand, when we are honest with ourselves, we may recognize when such a felt threat is in fact a part of ourselves, and by working this through, we function more complexly and richly as a person or as a psychoanalytic community.

CONFLICTING PHILOSOPHIES IN PSYCHOANALYSIS: ORTHODOXY AND HERESY IN THE TEACHING OF BRUNO BETTELHEIM

The Orthodox Position

My first experience of what I later came to think of as psychoanalytic orthodoxy was the teaching of Bruno Bettelheim in staff meetings at the Sonia Shankman Orthogenic School. A staff member would present him with a problem in an interaction with a particular child. Bettelheim would then, with a few well-chosen questions, demonstrate how a conflict or inhibition in the staff member had interfered with his or her ability to understand the child's communication. We learned that even the stormiest encounters became problems only when our own anxiety prevented us from thinking clearly about what need the child was expressing, however distortedly, or from feeling free to respond in a way appropriate to the child and the current state of the therapeutic relationship. The message was clear: if a problem arose between therapist and patient, it was caused by the intrusion of the therapist's intrapsychic conflicts. If we mastered our own inner psychic reality, we would have relatively little difficulty dealing with external patient realities. Although this is the completely traditional analytic approach to countertransference, it also felt like a profoundly moral teaching. Problems were our responsibility and also our fault. If we wanted to love the children and not mistreat them, we must struggle with our own sinfulness and work for salvation through psychoanalysis. Although Bettelheim did not use such religious concepts in his teaching, they capture an important aspect of what his teaching meant to us. On the one hand, it was inspiring. On the other, it could all too easily be incorporated into the predominantly Catholic and Jewish guilt complexes we had brought with us to the Orthogenic School.

The Heretical Position

Then Bettelheim retired and some of the teaching responsibilities devolved upon Alfred Flarsheim, who, since he had been a long-time student of Bettelheim, we expected to follow the same approach to teaching. Instead, we got our first taste of what I now respectfully call psychoanalytic heresy. Presented with a problem between patient and staff, and with a staff member prepared to search his own soul for his countertransference sin, Flarsheim invariably posed the following questions: "I wonder why the child needed to evoke such feelings in you. Why did he need to create precisely this kind of problem between you? How might creating such a crisis be seen as his attempt to make his life more bearable?" Again, the message was clear, but it was a very different message: it was not our fault. It was the average expectable impingement of the child's illness on someone trying to help him. Whatever conflicts were stirred up in the therapist were best understood in reference to the inner reality of the patient. Our conflicts were in fact caused by the children. Years later I recognized this as an inversion of Freud's seduction theory, which has in common with it the emphasis on interactional trauma rather than intrapsychic conflict. At the time what felt important was that we had not sinned; we were doing our best, but were overwhelmed by our patients. Justification by works was not necessary. Of course we loved the children and wanted what was best for them. This was our justification by faith alone. Our relief and even joy at this liberating outlook was mitigated only by Flarsheim's astonishment at our reaction. He could not believe that his approach was new to us—he had learned it from Bettelheim.

Two Hypotheses

For me this unexpected news brought with it a profound but ill-defined shock of recognition, the implications of which I did not begin to understand until years later. I would now say that I learned two invaluable lessons from this experience, involving essential but controversial elements in psychoanalysis. The first is that psychoanalysis is not simply a science of man's sexual and aggressive drives, but is more broadly a philosophy of human nature, including the moral dimension and the problems usually associated with it—love and hate, good and evil, responsibility and blame. The second lesson was that more than one frame of reference is necessary to understand and describe human experience. Man must always contend simultaneously with both internal needs and external influences, integrating them in what we call motivation. Theoretically we require two distinct frames of reference to describe these two motivational axes, one intrapsychic and the other interpersonal.

The shocking thing was that these two ways of understanding a problem felt so dramatically antithetical, and yet they came from the same man. Bettelheim's ability to integrate the intrapsychic and the interpersonal in his approach to clinical problems is surprisingly rare in the history of psychoanalytic thought, which has been marked by controversy precisely because of a failure to recognize that both points of view are applicable to any human experience, although only one at a time can be applied. Instead, psychoanalysis has struggled with an either–or dichotomizing that has led to polarization and repetitive splits between those working exclusively from one frame of reference and those working exclusively from the other. Analysts emphasizing the interpersonal perspective have repeatedly attacked what they perceived as the reductionism of classical analysis, while the "Freudian" analysts, feeling threatened with the erosion of their hand-won insights, have counterattacked by dismissing interpersonal theories as superficial and naive.

Although it might be questioned whether the words "heresy" and "orthodoxy" are applicable to these conflicting points of view as they have become institutionalized into mainstream and dissident schools of thought, I would contend that they are particularly appropriate in conveying the sometimes-incendiary intensity of psychoanalytic controversy. The religious origin and overtones of the terms are not misplaced. The issues at stake in psychoanalytic controversies are ultimately the same as those which inform religious controversy; namely, conflicting philosophies of human nature and of man's relationship to the Good. Although many analysts on both sides would object to the implication that their disputes are doctrinal rather than scientific, the plain fact is that psychoanalytic controversies are based not on discoverable facts but on conflicting philosophical premises.[1]

Take the well-known story of Joseph Breuer and Anna O. Breuer abandoned the treatment of his patient precipitously at the point when she fell in love with him. What was his motivation? Was it the external danger of her erotically aggressive assault on him and his marriage, or was it the internal danger posed by the coming true of his unconscious wish to seduce her? Analysts have traditionally answered such questions in an either–or way. Those of the dissident schools would stress that Breuer was fleeing the interpersonal danger, while mainstream analysts would say he was fleeing the intrapsychic one. This is not a difference that could ever be settled by appealing to evidence. Evidence can be found for either position, depending on whether one chooses to look for it in Breuer's feelings about Anna O. or in his feelings about himself. This choice in turn would depend on the philosophical premises that I am calling heretical and orthodox. The orthodox position is that man is fundamentally at war with himself and must strive to achieve inner peace through accepting responsibility for his own contradictions. The heretical position is that man is fundamentally loving and at peace with himself but develops problems as a result of the traumatic influence of a hostile environment; that he can achieve inner peace by changing that environment.

Bettelheim was able to integrate these two points of view and apply both to the same situation. In teaching, he emphasized one side or the other depending on the needs of his students. Psychologically naive and emotionally unsettled children of the 1960s, like the staff of which I was a member, needed to develop their sense of responsibility. Experienced, well-analyzed psychiatrists like Flarsheim needed new, even unorthodox perspectives on treating their "untreatable" patients. But Bettleheim was always aware of both perspectives. If Breuer had presented his problem to the staff's Bettelheim, he would have been told that he was having difficulty with his own sexual feelings for his patient, and that this prevented him from responding comfortably to her wish for love even though she was expressing it in an uncomfortable, sexualized way. If he had presented to Flarsheim's Bettelheim he might have been told that his patient was trying to force him to reject her, that she felt she deserved a terrible punishment for her sexual feelings toward him, so that getting him to reject her would both provide the needed punishment for her forbidden wish and protect her against the danger of actually achieving that wish. Interestingly, each explanation actually involves both orthodox and heretical propositions.

According to the staff's Bettelheim, Breuer is fundamentally conflicted while Anna O. is traumatized in her naturally loving disposition. According to Flarsheim's Bettelheim, Anna O. is fundamentally conflicted while Breuer is forcefully turned away from his naturally loving course. According to Bettelheim himself, both explanations are correct.

It is certainly no accident that Bettelheim has always been an outsider in relation to organized psychoanalysis, which is still struggling to achieve such a "both–and" integration out of the either–or struggle between orthodox and heretical schools. The most recent example is the debate between self psychology and classical analysis. Kohut (1977) accurately suggests that the point of contention involves differing models of human nature, self psychology's "tragic man" and classical analysis's "guilty man." Guilty man is man by nature in conflict over his innate drives, as epitomized in the Oedipus complex. Tragic man is innocent man forced into a state of inner fragmentation by traumatic parenting, as epitomized in pathology of the self. Guilty man has original sin, in the form of the drives, whereas tragic man is born guiltless. These are precisely the categories, implicit in Bettelheim's two teaching approaches, which I have described as orthodox and heretical points of view. By articulating these categories so clearly, Kohut has facilitated the recognition that the controversy is a philosophic rather than scientific one, but he has also contributed to the continued polarization of the two points of view. Both sides want to resolve the debate by showing their point of view to be right and the other wrong. Self psychologists argue that tragic man is at the core of all psychopathology, reducing guilty man to the status of "disintegration products." Classical analysts dismiss tragic man as merely manifest content that disguises the real basis for psychopathology, guilty man's Oedipus complex. But the fact is, while one perspective may be more useful than the other in a particular situation with a particular person, no situation or person can be fully understood without taking both perspectives into account. There is no oedipal pathology without trauma and no self-pathology without guilt.

According to Niels Bohr's principle of complementarity (Bohr, 1958; Holton, 1970; Folse, 1985), a complete psychological description requires the use of mutually exclusive but equally valid frames of reference. In the same way that the physicist must use mutually exclusive experimental arrangements to observe the wave or the particle nature of light, so the psychoanalyst must use mutually exclusive mind sets (conceptual frameworks of philosophical assumptions) to observe the tragic or the guilty nature of man.[2] The choice to focus on one precludes our being able (for the moment at least) to observe the other. Bohr stressed the fundamental paradox that apparently contradictory phenomena can be equally and simultaneously real. He is reported to have said, "There are the trivial truths and the great truths. The opposite of a trivial truth is plainly false. The opposite of a great truth is also true" (see Waelder, 1963; H. Bohr, 1967). The lesson for psychoanalysis is that tragic man and Guilty Man have equal claim to being the "real" human nature. A good psychoanalyst must therefore be able to shift easily from one point of view to the other, appreciating both realities and resisting the reductionistic temptation to dismiss one as an epiphenomenon.

For example, in *The Uses of Enchantment*, Bettelheim (1976) presents the orthodox position on the Oedipus complex:

> There is a widespread refusal to let children know that the source of much that goes wrong in life is due to our very own natures—the propensity of all men for acting aggressively, asocially, selfishly, out of anger and anxiety. Instead, we want our children to believe that inherently, all men are good. (p. 7)

> It is not just since Freud that the myth of Oedipus has become the image by which we understand the ever new but age-old problems posed to us by our comlex and ambivalent feelings about our parents. Freud referred to this ancient story to make us aware of the inescapable cauldron of emotions which every child, in his own way, has to manage at a certain age. (p. 24)

In *Children of the Dream*, Bettelheim (1969) presents the other side:

> It is . . . the parent's power over the very life of his infant that sets the tragedy of Oedipus in motion. Had the father of Oedipus not had (and used) the power he held over his son's existence, his son would never have slain him. We cannot separate the receiving of dependent care from the power relations within which they are given and received. (p. 69)

Likewise, in *The Empty Fortress*, Bettelheim (1967) writes:

> All psychotic children suffer from the experience of having been subject to extreme conditions of living, and . . . the severity of their disturbances is directly related to how early in life these conditions arose, for how long they obtained, and how severe was their impact on the child. (p. 63)

Bettelheim does not refer to Bohr in his writings, but does refer to the fundamental insight of complementarity in terms of a much older philosophic tradition. In *The Informed Heart*, Bettelheim (1960) describes his own ambivalent struggle as a young man trying to come to terms with the nature–nurture controversy in his "quest for a better man in a better society":

> I thought if I could only plumb deep enough, I might find the one right answer. Philosophy seemed to plumb deepest, so it was that discipline I turned to at one period. There I encountered the theory of the concordance of contraries, but since I was still looking for unilateral solutions, it helped me

little in my search. I did not then realize how it could be applied to understanding the dynamic interdependence of the organism and its environment, and how life consists of struggles to reach higher stages of integration within a basically irreconcilable conflict. To accept this last as fact was not possible for me at the time. . . . Self-realization I could not yet see as existing within a *conjunctio oppositorum*. (p. 8)

Psychoanalysis as a whole has had the same difficulty and has not yet achieved this integration. It remains split today, as it has been split throughout its history, into warring factions, whose theoretical disputes take on the flavor and intensity of religious ones, with excommunication the punishment for heresy. There has been a kind of group repetition compulsion in which, time and again, original psychoanalytic thinkers have been treated as heretics and ostracized by the psychoanalytic establishment. No sooner has one heretic been ostracized than another has arisen. Among the most prominent are Carl Jung, Alfred Adler, Melanie Klein, Karen Horney, Erich Fromm, Franz Alexander, John Bowlby, W. R. D. Fairbairn, and Heinz Kohut.

Origins of the Controversy in Freud's Unconscious Conflict

The Conflict: Freud as Heretic

Two factors account for the persistence and acrimony of this psychoanalytic controversy. The first is that it is a repetitive reenactment of a conflictual unconscious fantasy that was originally Freud's. Evidence for this is abundant in Freud's autobiographical writings, *On the History of the Psycho-Analytic Movement* (1914) and *An Autobiographical Study* (1925), which document that psychoanalysis had its origin in heresy, with Freud himself being the first heretic:

When, in 1873, I first joined the University . . . I found that I was expected to feel myself inferior and an alien because I was a Jew. I refused absolutely to do the first of these things. . . . At an early age I was made familiar with the fate of being in the Opposition and of being put under the ban of the "compact majority." (1925, p. 9)

In classical antiquity great importance was attached to dreams as foretelling the future; but modern science would have nothing to do with them, it handed them over to superstition, declaring them to be purely "somatic" processes—a kind of twitching of a mind that is otherwise asleep. . . . *But by disregarding the excommunication that had been pronounced upon dreams.* . . . psychoanalysis arrived at a different conclusion. (1925, p. 43; emphasis added)

This time I was applauded, but no further interest was taken in me. The impression that the high authorities had rejected my innovations remained unshaken . . . I found myself forced into the Opposition. . . . I was soon afterwards [1886] excluded from the laboratory of cerebral anatomy. (1925, pp. 15–16)

I unhesitatingly sacrificed my growing popularity as a doctor . . . by making a systematic enquiry into the sexual factors involved in the causation of my patients' neuroses. . . . I innocently addressed a meeting of the Vienna Society for Psychiatry and Neurology. . . . But the silence which my communications met with, the void which formed itself about me, the hints that were conveyed to me, gradually made me realize that from now onwards I was one of these who have "disturbed the sleep of the world" . . . and that I could not reckon upon objectivity and tolerance. (1914, pp. 21–22)

Meanwhile my writings were not reviewed in the medical journals, or, if as an exception they were reviewed, they were dismissed with expressions of scornful or pitying superiority. (1914, pp. 22–23)

For more than ten years after my separation from Breuer I had no followers. I was completely isolated. In Vienna I was shunned; abroad no notice was taken of me. (1925, p. 48)

I have long recognized that to stir up contradiction and arouse bitterness is the inevitable fate of psycho-analysis. (1914, p. 8)

[Breuer] was the first to show the reaction of distaste and repudiation which was later to become so familiar to me, but which at that time I had not yet learnt to recognize as my inevitable fate. (1914, p. 12)

The Conflict: Freud as Orthodox

Distaste and repudiation is the mark of either–or thinking and also of unconscious conflict. Breuer had been the first psychoanalyst to show this orthodox response to heresy. Freud himself was the second, when he repudiated the theories of his former disciples, Jung and Adler, describing them explicitly as heretics:

The criticism with which the two heretics were met was a mild one; I only insisted that both Adler and Jung should cease to describe their theories a "psycho-analysis". . . . If a community is based on agreement upon a few cardinal points, it is obvious that people who have abandoned that common ground will cease to belong to it. Yet the secession of former pupils has often been brought up against me as a sign of my intolerance or has been regarded as evidence of some special fatality that hangs over me. (1925, p. 53)

[P]sychoanalysis is my creation; for ten years I was the only person who concerned himself with it, and all the dissatisfaction which the new phenomenon aroused in my contemporaries has been poured out in the form of criticisms on my head. . . . no one can know better than I do what psycho-analysis is, how it differs from other ways of investigating the life of the mind, and precisely what should be called psychoanalysis and what would better be described by some other name. In thus repudiating what seems to me a cool act of usurpation. . . . (1914, p. 7)

[I]t has never occurred to me to pour contempt upon the opponents of psycho-analysis merely because they were opponents. . . . I knew very well how to account for the behaviour of these opponents and, moreover, I had learnt that psycho-analysis brings out the worst in everyone. . . . Experience shows that only very few people are capable of remaining polite, to say nothing of objective, in a scientific dispute, and the impression made on me by scientific squabbles has always been odious. Perhaps this attitude on my part has been misunderstood; perhaps I have been thought so good-natured or so easily intimidated that no further notice need be taken of me. This was a mistake; I can be as abusive and enraged as anyone. (1914, p. 39)

It is no easy or enviable task to write the history of these two secessions, partly because I am without any strong personal motive for doing so—I had not expected gratitude nor am I revengeful to any effective degree—and partly because I know that by doing so I shall lay myself open to the invectives of my not too scrupulous opponents and offer the enemies of analysis the spectacle they so heartily desire—of "the psycho-analysts tearing one another limb from limb." After exercising so much self-restraint in not coming to blows with opponents outside analysis, I now see myself compelled to take up arms against its former followers or people who still like to call themselves its followers. I have no choice in the matter, however; only indolence or cowardice could lead one to keep silence . . . I shall . . . restrict to a minimum my use of analytic knowledge, and, with it, of indiscretion and aggressiveness towards my opponents; and I may also point out that I am not basing any scientific criticism on these grounds. *I am not concerned with the truth that may be contained in the theories which I am rejecting,* nor shall I attempt to refute them. . . . I wish merely to show that these theories controvert the fundamental principles of analysis. (1914, pp. 49–50; emphasis added)

I was either compared to Columbus, Darwin and Kepler, or abused as a general paralytic. I wished, therefore, to withdraw into the background . . . transferring (my) authority to a younger man, who would then as a matter of course take my place after my death. This man could only be C. G. Jung, [because of] his exceptional talents, the contributions he had already made to psycho-analysis, his independent position and the impression of assured energy which his personality conveyed. In addition to this, he seemed ready to enter into a friendly relationship with me and for my sake to give up certain racial prejudices which he had previously permitted himself. I had no inkling at that time that . . . I had lighted upon a person who was incapable of tolerating the authority of another, but who was still less capable of wielding it himself, and whose energies were relentlessly devoted to the furtherance of his own interests. (1914, p. 43)

To be sure, I see nothing reprehensible in a younger man freely admitting his ambition, which one would in any case guess was among the incentives for his work. But even though a man is dominated by a motive of this kind he should know how to avoid being what the English, with their fine social tact, call "unfair"—which in German can only be expressed by a much cruder word. How little Adler has succeeded in this is shown by the profusion of petty outburst of malice which disfigure his writings and by the indications they contain of an uncontrolled craving for priority. (1914, p. 51)

The view of life which is reflected in the Adlerian system is founded exclusively on the aggressive instinct; there is no room in it for love. . . . with Jung, the appeal is made to the historic right of youth to throw off the fetters in which tyrannical age with its hidebound views seek to bind it. (1914, p. 58)

Adler [finally] took a step for which we are thankful; he severed all connection with psycho-analysis. . . . Adler's "Individual Psychology" is now one of the many schools of psychology which are adverse to psycho-analysis and its further development is no concern of ours. (1914, p. 52)

Interpretation

Freud's disparaging *ad hominem* remarks about Jung's incapacity to tolerate authority and relentless devotion to his own interests and about Adler's uncontrolled craving for priority, together with the obvious bitterness and self-righteousness with which he describes his own relentless pursuit and defense of *his* psychoanalysis, strongly suggest that he was indeed intolerant of qualities in Jung and Adler that were all too similar to qualities in himself. These autobiographical passages show Freud's pervasive disavowal and projection of his hostile aggression. Specifically, he seems to be conflicted about his revolutionary, iconoclastic motive, his need to challenge received wisdom and attack its orthodox purveyors. For Adler such a motive was explicit in the "masculine protest," for Jung in the assertion of "the historic right of youth to throw off the fetters (of) tyrannical age." Freud needed to deny this motive in himself and in his theory (which at the time of the break with Adler and Jung contained a sexual, but not an aggressive drive), while repudiating it in Jung and Adler and in their theories.[3]

Freud is unable to empathize with the iconoclasm of Adler and Jung because it is too openly attacking and threatens his need to disown hostility. His uneasiness about this motive leads him to describe his own iconoclasm as essentially involuntary, in pointed contrast to the willfulness he ascribes to Jung and Adler. He describes himself not as an aggressor, but as an unsuspecting victim of the "compact majority," unfairly shunned and attacked for his blamelessly disinterested pursuit of scientific truth. He thinks of himself as *"innocently"* seeking the approval of the scientific establishment and as *"forced"* into the Opposition" as if against his will. He views the tendency to provoke bitter controversy as "the inevitable fate of psychoanalysis" rather than the result of his own aggressive provocativeness.

Another example of this disavowal of iconoclastic intent is Freud's *apologia* for his radical emphasis on sexuality. He disclaims responsibility for any active wish on his part to shock, scandalize, incite, or otherwise "disturb the sleep of the world" by announcing that this emphasis on sexuality was not really his idea in the first place:

> There was some consolation for the bad reception accorded to my contention of a sexual aetiology in the neuroses even by my more intimate circle of friends—for a vacuum rapidly formed itself about my person—in the thought that I was taking up the fight for a new and original idea. But, one day, certain memories gathered in my mind which disturbed this pleasing notion, but which gave me in exchange a valuable insight into the processes of human creative activity and the nature of human knowledge. The idea for which I was being made responsible had by no means originated with me. (1914, pp. 12–13)

He goes on to explain that Breuer, Charcot, and the eminent gynecologist Chrobak had all unwittingly suggested the idea to him. The story about Charcot is most striking. Freud recalls the time he heard him animatedly telling a colleague that "in this sort of case it's always a question of the genitals—always, always, always":

> I know that *for a moment I was almost paralysed with amazement* and said to myself: "Well, but if he knows that, why does he never say so?" [emphasis added] But the impression was soon forgotten. . . . I have not of course disclosed the illustrious parentage of this scandalous idea in order to saddle other people with the responsibility for it. I am well aware that it is one thing to give utterance to an idea once or twice in the form of a passing *apercu*, and quite another to mean it seriously—to take it literally and pursue it in the face of every contradictory detail, and to win it a place among accepted truths. It is the difference between a casual flirtation and a legal marriage with all its duties and difficulties. *"Espouser les idees de . . ."* is no uncommon figure of speech, at any rate in French. (1914, pp. 14–15)

Freud was willing to take responsibility for his very legal impulse to "espouse an idea," but we can guess that in his moment of paralyzed amazement with Charcot he was on the verge of feelings and impulses he was not so ready to take responsibility for, both the excitement of shocking and scandalizing the civilized world and the impulse to steal Charcot's idea and his thunder precisely in order to do so.[4] Freud's focus on banishment, ostracism, excommunication, isolation, being in a vacuum like a pariah, all suggest a need to see himself as punished (though, in keeping with the principle of multiple function, he also seemed to relish the sense of distinction his isolation and ostracism gave him) for the iconoclastic crime he was reluctant to take credit for.[5]

My claim then is that the struggle between orthodoxy and heresy, which stirred such strong feelings in Freud and in which he took now one side, now the other represented for him an important unresolved intrapsychic conflict. *Ostracism of the iconoclast–scapegoat* is the enactment of a conflictual unconscious fantasy. The iconoclastic–scapegoat is Oedipus. His heresy combines the unconscious oedipal elements of patricide (overthrowing the establishment) and incest (waking the sleep of the world), and his punishment is also oedipal, banishment from the kingdom (the mainstream of orthodoxy). But the iconoclast–scapegoat is also a hero. In fact, he is Joseph Campbell's (1949) "hero with a thousand faces." He is Prometheus and he is Christ, scapegoated and crucified for trying to bring enlightenment to the world.

I submit that this fantasy is intimately bound up with the motive force in Freud's lifework, and I would argue that it continues to exert a strong influence on the development of psychoanalysis today. We can still feel the bitterness of the 25-year-long dispute between Melanie Klein and Anna Freud (see Segal, 1979). Many analysts still bristle at the mention of Franz Alexander's (1946, 1950) "corrective emotional experience." The provocative, rebellious need that Freud disavowed but enacted has lived on in psychoanalysis. So has his intolerant repudiation of that need. The combination of the iconoclastic "drive" of the analytic dissidents (the intrapsychic component) with the oppressive intolerance for new ideas of the analytic "compact majority" (the interpersonal component) has repeatedly driven heretical analysts like Klein and Alexander to a kind of stridency that became self-defeating. They seemed to court their own excommunication by their polemical radicalism, while at the same time they were driven to it by the equally polemical conservatism of the "Freudian" establishment, with the result that they have indeed been shunned and their theories dismissed out of hand, often without being understood.

Alexander's case is particularly interesting because he had published a thoughtful critique of the radical polarizing tendencies of Karen Horney only a few years before he would succumb to the same tendencies himself (and in the process become associated with Horney in the minds of the orthodox as a heretical "interpersonal-culturalist"):

Her polemic ardor involves [Horney] in greater difficulties and more serious issues than those of questionable taste and lack of perspective. As is often the case when one attacks an enemy, one is likely to adopt the enemy's worst weaknesses. Horney attacks the libido theory and replaces the idea of a vague and mystical biological substance—the libido—with an equally empty sociological slogan—culture. She tries to expel Satan with Beelzebub. Just as human behavior cannot be explained satisfactorily by a solely biological principle which is immanent in the organism (libido), neither can it be explained by a sociological principle alone (culture). Cultural influences obviously act upon a highly complex biological system which has to an amazing degree a preformed individual structure. Furthermore, culture itself is originated from the dynamic qualities of biological systems. Obviously we deal here with a complex interplay between biological systems (men) which create a society and become modified by their own creation. (1940, pp. 140–141)

Clearly, Alexander had more of a sense of the integration of orthodox and heretical perspectives than he is usually given credit for nowadays.[6] Ironically, the concept of corrective emotional experience over which he was ostracized has become intregated into orthodox theory without acknowledgment and (importantly) without polemic in the writings of Loewald (1960), Dewald (1976), and others. Similarly, many of the ideas of Melanie Klein have become part of orthodox thinking through the non-polemical writings of Winnicott (1958, 1965), Kernberg (1976, 1980), Modell (1968, 1984), and others.

Is Polarization in an Intellectual Community a Necessary Phenomenon?

A case could be made that the polarization of orthodoxy and heresy, as a Hegelian dialectic or a "Kuhnian" paradigm clash, has been inevitable and necessary; that in psychoanalysis as in general, the seeds of integration are to be found within the fruit of heresy. Historian Edward Peters's comments on the etymology and history of the word "heresy" are consistent with this idea:

The Greek word *hairesein* originally meant simply "to take," but its frequent occurrence in discussions of competing philosophical schools in a pluralistic intellectual culture soon gave it the more specific meaning of "choice," and later the still narrower meaning of a "choice" among different schools and movements of philosophy. In these senses there was nothing pejorative about the word, particularly since there existed no philosophical school that made universal claims to a monopoly of truth. . . . Among Jews and Christians, however, the term began to acquire an exclusively pejorative sense . . . via . . . the powerful Judaeo-Christian conviction that in the realm of certain beliefs there was no option for plurality of opinion . . . that those who held beliefs that the community or its leaders found objectionable were not exercising permissible free choice in an intellectually or spiritually pluralistic society, but attacking God and dividing the indivisible community of believers. (1980, pp. 14–15)

The Conflict's Id Origins

Thus heresy originally had the positive sense of a free choice, an open-minded assertion of intellectual autonomy, and only later took on the negative sense of hostile assault on the community. It is safe to assume that both senses are present in the motivation of every heretic. In the positive sense heresy invites and strives for integration. Truth may be pluralistic. In this sense it is motivated by the heroic Promethean meanings of the unconscious fantasy that drives it. In the negative sense it is motivated by the murderous and incestuous oedipal aspects of that fantasy. It is embattled and rejects integration, becoming simply the mirror image of the close-minded dogmatism it opposes, as Alexander pointed out in the case of Horney.

In summary then, the first of the two factors accounting for the persistence and acrimony of the controversy between orthodoxy and heresy in psychoanalytic history is that it is fueled by a conflictual unconscious fantasy that was originally Freud's but is to some degree Everyman's, the fantasy scenario being ostracism of the iconoclast–scapegoat–hero. This fantasy represented an unresolved conflict for Freud between his need to attack authority and his need to respect and obey authority. Anyone who has spent an hour in a psychoanalytic institute recently can attest that this conflict is alive and still unresolved in the minds of psychoanalysts today.[7]

ORIGINS OF THE CONTROVERSY IN CONFLICTING PHILOSOPHIES

Guilty Man versus Tragic Man: Nature versus Nurture

This explains the bitter intensity of the ongoing controversy from below, from the side of the id or, as Bettelheim suggests we should call it, the It (das Es). To discuss the second factor involves approaching the question from above, from the side of the superego (the "I that stands above"—das Überich); that is, from a discussion of the overarching Weltanschauungen that are at issue in the controversy.[8] As I have already suggested, the same conflicting philosophical premises have underlain every new edition of the ongoing debate between psychoanalytic orthodoxy and heresy. Not only Kohut, but all the other psychoanalytic heretics

I have mentioned were condemned for discounting the importance of the drives and exaggerating the importance of interpersonal factors, whether in the form of internal object relations, faulty parenting, cultural influences, the curative effects of the real relationship with the analyst, or some combination of these. Considering the stubbornness with which it has resisted resolution, it is not surprising that the controversy involves points of view, the intrapsychic (guilty man) and the interpersonal (tragic man), which participate in a controversy much larger than psychoanalysis, that of nature versus nurture (see Overton, 1973). To understand from above how psychoanalysis became embroiled in this philosophical debate, we must again go back to Freud.

Freud's Philosophical Conflict

Freud's unresolved struggle at the level of the "It" between iconoclasm and authority had its counterpart at the level of the "I that stands above" in an unresolved conflict between two different *Weltanschauungen*, the heretical nurture philosophy of the interpersonal frame of reference and the orthodox nature philosophy of the intrapsychic frame of reference. Whether he was enacting the role of revolutionary or rabbi, these two conflicting philosophic currents, embodying the heretical Freud and the orthodox Freud, actually pervaded all his thought, leaving a subtle but profound inconsistency in even his greatest works. The conflict is most clearly evident in his repudiation first of the seduction theory (Freud, 1906), and much later (Freud, 1926) of his first, It-centered theory of anxiety. These two changes reflect the two sides of Freud's ambivalence about the nature–nurture question. Is man what he is because of his innate biological constitution or because of the impact of his environment, especially the way he is raised.

The seduction theory held that psychoneurosis was due to the delayed impact of a traumatic sexual seduction in childhood, memory of which had been repressed. Cure required the recovery of this repressed memory. This was the original psychoanalytic theory. It emphasized the nurture side of the nature–nurture duality, in a form which can be generalized: "psychopathology is caused by childhood trauma." Here was the first appearance of tragic man in psychoanalysis. Freud abandoned the seduction theory in favor of the view that the seductions that were eventually remembered by his patients were not actual events but rather childhood wishes stemming from the child's innate sexuality. This view continues to be that of orthodox psychoanalysis today. It can be generalized in the form: "psychopathology is caused by infantile sexuality, preserved in the unconscious fantasies of the Oedipus complex." The emphasis here is on the nature side of the duality, man's innate sexuality leading inexorably to the Oedipus complex. This was the first appearance of guilty man.

Garcia (1987) suggests that Freud's views on the etiological importance of the seduction theory were more balanced than is generally thought, and it would not be unfair to say that some shifting statements he made about it over the years betrayed an ongoing ambivalence.[9] However, there is no question that Freud did reject the seduction theory as incorrect and decided that in the interplay between innate disposition and accidental experience, disposition was primary:

> [A] mistaken idea had to be overcome which might have been almost fatal to the young science. Influenced by Charcot's views of the traumatic origin of hysteria, one was readily inclined to accept as true and aetiologically significant the statements made by patients in which they ascribed their symptoms to . . . seduction. When this aetiology broke down under the weight of its own improbability and contradiction in definitely ascertainable circumstances, the result at first was helpless bewilderment. Analysis had led back to these infantile sexual traumas by the right path, and yet they were not true. The firm ground of reality was gone. . . . At last came the reflection that . . . if hysterical subjects trace back their symptoms to traumas that are fictitious, then the new fact which emerges is precisely that they create such scenes in *phantasy*. . . . This reflection was soon followed by the discovery that these phantasies were intended to cover up the autoerotic activity of the first years of childhood, to embellish it and raise it to a higher plane. . . .
>
> With this sexual activity of the first years of childhood the inherited constitution of the individual also came into its own. Disposition and experience are here linked up in an indissoluble aetiological unity. For *disposition* exaggerates impressions which would otherwise have been completely commonplace and have had no effect, so that they become traumas giving rise to stimulations and fixations; while *experiences* awaken factors in the disposition which, without them, might have long remained dormant and perhaps never have developed. The last word on the subject of traumatic aetiology was spoken later by Abraham [1907], when he pointed out that the sexual constitution which is peculiar to children is precisely calculated to provoke sexual experiences of a particular kind—namely traumas. (1914, pp. 17–18)

Seduction Theory versus Libido Theory: The I and the It

Freud's repudiation of the seduction theory ushered in the long period of his It psychology. Parallel with the shift in emphasis from sexual trauma to innate sexuality, Freud began to develop his libido theory as a way of describing this innate sexuality, its development and vicissitudes. The cornerstone of the libido theory was Freud's first theory of anxiety. It held that anxiety was the toxic transformation of sexual excitement that could not be discharged normally. The libido theory also held that motivation was the result of the physiological need to seek the state of lowest energy by discharging excess drive tensions. But Freud's mind did not come to rest here. In the middle of an ambitious attempt to formalize and extend his libido theory in a series of metapsychological papers, he abruptly abandoned the enterprise and the libido theory itself. Between 1920 and 1926 he launched into a series of revolutionary works that changed psychoanalysis dramatically from a reductionistic It psychology to a much richer I psychology. In the culminating work of this period, *Inhibitions, Symptoms and Anxiety* (1926), he brought nurture back onto center stage when he renounced his first anxiety theory. Discarding the idea that anxiety was produced directly from the It, a toxic vicissitude of innate sexuality, Freud now proposed that anxiety was a response of the I to the anticipation of an external danger situation that had actually been experienced in childhood, either abandonment, loss of love, castration, or social ostracism.

The shift in emphasis from autonomously erupting It forces to the unconscious memory of childhood danger situations was clearly a move back toward the seduction theory and its unconscious memory of childhood trauma. But this kinship between Freud's second anxiety theory and his seduction theory is not widely recognized. The reason, I believe, is that the overall tone of *Inhibitions, Symptoms and Anxiety* is again one of ambivalence about the relative importance of nature (internal, neurophysiologic danger) and nurture (external danger of physical or psychological trauma). Freud reinstates external reality, but then mitigates its importance by saying that the danger situations were only dangerous because they threatened to provoke a buildup of unsatisfied drive tensions. In one place he declares that castration is feared because it would lead to "being helplessly exposed to an unpleasurable tension due to instinctual need" (1926, p. 139); in other words, the external danger really represents an internal one. But in another place he says the opposite, that "an instinctual demand often only becomes an (internal) danger because its satisfaction would bring on an external danger—that is because the internal danger represents an external one" (1926, pp. 167–168).

This ambivalence may be seen as an attempted integration. Freud was trying to bring together the nurture emphasis of his heretical period with the nature emphasis of his orthodox period. But the fact that these conflicting philosophies were also implicated in an unconscious conflict, with its fantasy of ostracizing the heretic, stood in the way of integration. During both his heretical (seduction theory) period and his orthodox (libido theory) period, Freud had externalized the inner conflict and struggled against outward enemies, first the disapproving Breuer and the scientific establishment he stood for, then the disloyal Adler and Jung. In

Inhibitions, Symptoms and Anxiety, the struggle became clearly internal. Freud was trying to be a heretic to his own orthodoxy, which put him in the untenable unconscious position of needing to ostracize himself. In the end he tried to be heretic and orthodox at the same time, claiming to have replaced his old "incorrect" anxiety theory with a new one, but at the same time holding on to the old theory in the form of the contradictory idea of "actual-neurosis." He remained caught up in either–or categories, vacillating over whether internal danger or external danger is more fundamental, deciding here (psychoneurosis) one way and there (actual neurosis) another:

> And . . . why should it not be possible for . . . traumatic moments to arise in mental life without reference to hypothetical situations of danger—traumatic moments, then, in which anxiety is not aroused as a signal but is generated anew for a fresh reason. Clinical experience declares decidedly that such is in fact the case. It is only the *later* repressions that exhibit the mechanism we have described, in which anxiety is awakened as a signal of an earlier situation of danger. The first and original repressions arise directly from traumatic moments, when the ego meets with excessively great libidinal demand; they construct their anxiety afresh, although, it is true, on the model of birth. The same may apply to the generation of anxiety in anxiety neurosis owing to somatic damage to the sexual function. We shall no longer maintain that it is the libido itself that is turned into anxiety in such cases. But I can see no objection to there being a twofold origin of anxiety—one as a direct consequence of the traumatic moment and the other as a signal threatening a repetition of such a moment. (1933b, pp. 94–95)

This is not the comfortable shifting back and forth between complementary frames of reference that I have described in the thinking of Bettelheim. Rather, it was an ambivalent compromise formation. It fell short of the integration of complementarity, according to which both points of view would be understood to apply to every case.

The Problem of Evil

But it was not only fixation at the level of unconscious fantasy, a phenomenon of the It, that stood in the way of the integration of intrapsychic and interpersonal perspectives. There is something incendiary in its own right at the level of the *Weltanschauung*, something about the spiritual–moral assumptions (a phenomenon of the "I that stands above") underlying the nature–nurture question, that seems inherently controversial. Ultimately, the debate revolves around the question of the origin of evil in the world and whether human nature is fundamentally good or evil. Those who argue for the primacy of nature claim, explicitly or implicitly, that evil originates in man, in his innate original sinfulness, or in his innate instinctual drives, and that human nature imposes unavoidable limits on the perfectibility of society. Those who argue for the primacy of nurture claim that evil originates in a corrupt society, that man is originally innocent until corrupted by that society, and ultimately that evil can be eradicated by improving society. The fact that people become so violently invested in this debate has something to do with the subject matter. As I learned at the Orthogenic School, people simply have strong feelings about evil and who is responsible for it, feelings that cannot adequately be explained as a function of the strength of unconscious conflict. In fact it may make more sense to explain the strength of unconscious conflict as a function of the participation of these feelings in it. There is something irreducible about evil and our reaction to it.

But the situation in psychoanalytic controversy is even more complicated, and resolution is made even more difficult by the fact that the orthodoxy–heresy split involves not only the nature–nurture question but also the mind–body problem, with its own set of strong polarized feelings. In fact, it has frequently been Freud's materialism, more than his emphasis on the intrapsychic, that dissident analysts have objected to. Alexander alludes to this in his description of Horney's attempt "to expel (the) Satan" of the libido theory and its "vague and mystical biological substance." It is also evident in Kohut's (1977) distinction between his own "self psychology" and Freud's "mental-apparatus psychology," a distinction that entails an obvious disparagement and repudiation of Freud's mechanistic metapsychology.

The Mind–Body Problem

It may ultimately have been Freud's materialism that prevented him from appreciating the complementarity of the intrapsychic and the interpersonal and achieving a balance in his theory. The tripartite model of his structural theory (Freud, 1933a) would otherwise have been open to such an integration. The major structures of the Freudian personality, the It and the I (including the "I that stands above"), can be viewed as complementary, with the It representing the intrapsychic (instinct) and the I representing the interpersonal (culture). The equation of the It and the intrapsychic is essentially definitional. That between the I and the interpersonal is in accord with Freud's own emphasis, on the I as "earmarked for representing the demands of the external world" (1933a, pp. 77–78) and on the "I that stands above" as the internalization of parental authority (pp. 61–62) and ultimately of culture (pp. 66–67). But for an interpersonal–cultural I to stand in a truly complementary relation to an intrapsychic It, it would have to have equal and independent status, a possibility at odds with Freud's materialist *Weltanschauung*. Even with his strong emphasis on the I in the 1920s, Freud could never admit it as an equal partner to the It, which he continued to view as the foundation and most important part of the psyche. Based on his allegiance to the epistemology of nineteenth-century physical science, Freud viewed the I as ultimately reducible to the It. In order to conceptualize the I and its world of interpersonal experience he needed mentalistic concepts, which he could not accept as having scientific status equal to that of the physicalistic concepts of the libido theory and the constancy principle. The fact that he could conceptualize the It in such physicalistic terms meant to him that it was closer to the bottom line, the "real scientific" explanation of psychic phenomena.

But this linkage of the intrapsychic It with materialism is not an inevitable one, and ultimately it was constraining for Freud in the same way as his first anxiety theory. In conflict with his *Weltanschauung*-based need to describe the It in terms of the (unobservable) biophysical energies of "instinctual cathexes seeking discharge" (1933a, p. 74), he also wanted to include in it the peremptory unconscious wishes of clinical observation, which are capable of mentalistic but not of physicalistic description. Unlike "instinctual cathexes seeking discharge," such wishes in the It contain elements of mind as well as body, and indeed Freud tried to take this into account by calling them the *mental* representations of instinct. This was the more progressive, heretical current in his thinking: giving mentalistic and physicalistic concepts equal status in the explanation both of drives in the It and of interpersonal influences in the I. But to do so inevitably entailed understanding the mind as more than an epiphenomenon, put Freud at odds with himself and his own orthodox nineteenth-century-science materialist *Weltanschauung*, and led to the kind of unresolved ambivalence so evident in his *Inhibitions, Symptoms and Anxiety*.

Had he pursued the heretical implications of his notion of unconscious wishes, Freud would have had to face the internal contradictions in his conception of the It and ultimately the irreducibly mentalistic character of the I. This in turn might have made more plausible the idea of human needs not reducible to tension discharge and suggested the possibility that the "drives" (in the sense of peremptory unconscious fantasy-based motives) are complex blendings of biological needs (from the It), spiritual needs (from the "I that stands above"), and interpersonal influences (from the I). If the drives are understood in this way, love, for instance, could be conceived of as including elements of both body and mind: *libido*, describable in physicalistic terms, and *agape*, not reducible to a biological description. But the orthodox position, wedded to materialism, has never admitted this kind of dualism, and is forced to sneak the mental–spiritual dimension in the backdoor by describing *agape* as a "sublimated" derivative of *libido*. Freud's reductionistic explanation of religion as a vicissitude of man's instinctual cathexis of the father (1933c) is in the same vein. His unwillingness to accept the notion that a religious *Weltanschauung* might address a spiritual reality not encompassable by scientific description is typical of the orthodox point of view that phenomena of the I are secondary to and derivative of processes in the It.

It may be said that all Freud's major theoretical revisions of the 1920s were expressions of the resurgence of his heretical thinking, that the introduction of the concepts of Eros (1920), of the I and the "I that stands above" (1923), all tended toward the reassertion of the interpersonal. But they also implied a new *Weltanschauung* that Freud was not ready to acknowledge, constrained as he was by the three factors I have described: (1) the inevitably close (definitional) association of the intrapsychic with the It; (2) his not so inevitable (*Weltanschauung*-based) need to construe the It in physicalistic terms; and (3) his view of the I as derivative and his assignment of "ontological primacy" to the It *because* it was more amenable to the kind of physicalistic explanation he aspired to.

In summary then, Freud originated both the heretical interpersonal and the orthodox intrapsychic points of view in psychoanalysis and developed a structural theory that had the potential to integrate them. He fell short of integration, however, because his conceptualization of the psychic structures remained mired in philosophical inconsistencies (related to the mind–body problem) that he could neither recognize nor resolve, inconsistencies that became evident in his confused definition of the It (1933a) and especially in his ambivalence about how to understand the origin of anxiety. Had Freud been able to follow out the more radical implications of the interpersonal emphasis of his I psychology, as he started to do in *Inhibitions, Symptoms and Anxiety*, he might have discovered the complementarity that was nascent in his structural theory and taken psychoanalysis beyond the *Weltanschauung* of nineteenth-century physics to that of twentieth-century physics. He began this process, but could not complete it.

Waelder's Synthesis and the Historical Working Through of the Conflict

It is my contention that Freud's inability to achieve a stable synthesis from the dialectic between his own orthodoxy and his own heresy has had profound repercussions for the subsequent history of psychoanalysis. The unconscious fantasy that was initially Freud's became, in effect, the unconscious fantasy of psychoanalysis. Freud's unresolved conflict, initially externalized in his struggles with the orthodoxy of the "compact majority" and with the heresies of Adler and Jung, then internalized as an ambivalent struggle with himself in *Inhibitions, Symptoms and Anxiety*, has become reexternalized and repeatedly reenacted in schisms between the orthodox group, adhering to nature, the instinctual drives and the inevitable Oedipus, and various heretical groups espousing nurture, motives not reducible to animal instinct, and some form of the seduction theory. This may be thought of as a kind of group regression in response to the anxiety-laden ambivalence of Freud's 1926 theory. The two warring factions have in effect *defused* the tension—alleviated Freud's anxiety—by each taking half of Freud's ambivalence, with the ostracism of the heretic serving as a kind of group repression:

> If the ego [read *orthodoxy*] succeeds in protecting itself from a dangerous instinctual impulse [read *Eros, synthesis, complementarity*], through, for instance, the process of repression, it has certainly inhibited and damaged the particular part [read *heresy*] of the id concerned; but it has at the same time given it some independence and has renounced some of its own sovereignty. This is inevitable from the nature of repression, which is, fundamentally, an attempt at flight. *The repressed is now, as it were, an outlaw; it is excluded from the great organization of the ego* [emphasis added[10]] and is subject only to the laws which govern the realm of the unconscious. If, now, the danger-situation changes so that the ego has no reason for fending off a new instinctual impulse analogous to the repressed one, the consequence of the restriction of the ego which has taken place will become manifest. The new impulse will run its course under an automatic influence—or, as I should prefer to say, under the influence of the compulsion to repeat. (1926, p. 153)

Thus, whenever a new impulse toward synthesis arises from the collective id of psychoanalysis, it has a tendency to run its course under the "automatic" influence of our group repetition compulsion to ostracize the heretic.

It would be a mistake, however, to think of this process as pathological. It has been a problem, but it has also been a solution. In fact, there is a tantalizing anomaly of psychoanalytic history that argues for the inevitability, perhaps the cultural–evolutionary necessity of this orthodoxy–heresy struggle: The struggle had occurred despite (and oblivious to) the fact that the complete synthesis of Freud's two anxiety theories, of the intrapsychic and the interpersonal points of view, and of the It and the I, was actually achieved in 1930 by one of Freud's own disciples:

The immediate occasion of the following exposition is the new concept of the theory of anxiety which Freud has given us in his book *Inhibitions, Symptoms, and Anxiety* (1926a). In his earlier concept, Freud assumed that anxiety erupted from the id as the immediate result of the tensions of excessive, unsatisfied needs, and that the ego was, as it were, a defenseless victim. The new concept modifies this; Freud states that in a situation of danger, of threat of future excessive, unsatisfied tension, the ego's anticipation of this state may result in the experience of anxiety. This anxiety is at the same time a signal which causes a readjustment of the organism for the purpose of avoiding the danger, for example, by flight or by suitable defense measures, thus fulfilling a biological function. This new concept naturally was not intended to set aside or replace the earlier concept, nor did Freud mean that anxiety might come about at one time in this way and at the next time in the other way. *Undoubtedly it meant that in each concrete case both theories—anxiety sweeping over the ego, and anxiety formed as a danger signal by the ego—represent two sides of one actual phenomenon, described one time from the side of the id and the other time from the side of the ego. This twofold method of observation gives rise to the conjecture that this method might be applicable to all psychic phenomena, and that a twofold or perhaps, generally speaking, a manifold approach to each psychic act would be not only admissible but even required by psychoanalysis.* [italics added]

In the id, according to psychoanalysis, there is gathered together everything by which a person is driven, all inner tendencies which influence him, every *vis a tergo*. In the ego, on the other hand, reside all man's purposeful actions, his direction. . . . In its division between a person's ego and id, psychoanalysis recognizes the two aspects of his being driven and his being directed. (Waelder, 1930, pp. 68–69)

These opening paragraphs of Robert Waelder's *The Principle of Multiple Function* resolved in one stroke the ambivalence that had plagued Freud for 40 years, recasting that ambivalence in the framework of complementarity. But amazingly, no one noticed, least of all Freud. Indeed, three years after Waelder's paper appeared, and Waelder's assertion to the contrary notwithstanding, Freud continued to maintain that anxiety arises "at one time in this way and at the next time in the other way" (see above, p. 139). Presumably out of deference to Freud, Waelder actually misrepresented him, giving Freud the credit for the integration that was in fact his own. It is simply not true that Freud was not trying to replace the old concept with the new, and nowhere does Freud suggest that both concepts apply to every case of anxiety.

Unlike Freud, Waelder was very likely aware of Bohr's principle of complementarity, first described in 1927 (Bohr, 1934).[11] In fact, the principle of multiple function is no less than a psychoanalytic version of Bohr's epistemological principle. Multiple function, like complementarity, teaches that to be properly understood, every psychic phenomenon *must* be looked at from two mutually exclusive and apparently incompatible points of view. This is what Waelder means by the "twofold method of observation" in psychoanalysis. The question then of whether the It or the I is primary, or is the source of anxiety, is based on a misunderstanding. We can make either one appear to be primary simply by changing our observational focus. Anxiety is not produced by the It *or* by the I. Rather, the It *and* the I offer two equally valid conceptual frameworks for talking about the (unitary) production of anxiety. Danger does not arise from instinct or experience. Instinct *and* experience are the two epistemic faces of one danger.

Waelder corrects the imbalance in Freud's structural theory by adding to Freud's picture of the passive (quasi-epiphenomenal) ego, the "loyal servant of the id" (Freud, 1933a), a picture of the ego as an independent center of (purposive) initiative:

> But this passive role does not exhaust the work of the ego. The ego does not simply accept orders and carry them out. Rather, it generates an activity of its own toward the outer world as well as toward the other forces in the individual himself. This activity of the ego is characterized by an attempt to assert itself, to succeed, and to assimilate in its organic development the outer world as well as the ego-alien forces in the individual . . . it seems that, from the beginning, the ego also makes efforts to bring its instinctive life under its central guidance. . . . The ego evidently takes an active stand toward its instinctive life; it has a tendency to master it, or rather to assimilate it into its organization. (Waelder, 1930, p. 70)

In applying the principle of complementarity to biology, Bohr had argued that a full biologic description required *teleological* as well as *mechanistic* explanations. This may have inspired Waelder's distinction between purposive (ego) and instinctual (id) processes, as he elaborated in 1967:

> the ego was well-recognized in the mid-20's as an equal partner in the adventure of life—on the clinical level of discourse at any rate. Whether it can be recognized as an equally fundamental element in a general theory of the mind, however, is a different question because the "ego" is a concept of a different kind from, say, "instinct," "drive," or "id." A drive is a force like, say, gravity; it pushes things in a particular direction with a certain intensity. It is what the medieval philosophers called a *vis a tergo*, a force pushing from behind. But the ego can be so described only on the lowest level of its activities, viz., that of reflex action; in its higher operations it is a *problem-solving agent* and thus a *teleological* concept. It explains psychic activities in terms of the purposes they serve. It is a close relative of Aristotle's entelechy, the preexisting form which guides the development of plant or animal according to nature; or a relative of the medieval physician's *vis medicatrix naturae*, the healing power of nature. (1967, p. 340)

Waelder's problem-solving ego is an ego of adaptation, which he called "the center of the personality" (1930, p. 387) fully ten years before Hartmann's (1939) *Ego Psychology and the Problem of Adaptation*. But Waelder so understated this radical extension of ego psychology that it was all but ignored, and it is still Hartmann who is generally thought to have introduced the notion of an independent ego of adaptation. This is ironic (but consistent with Hartmann's status as "pope" of the orthodox camp) given that Hartmann's ego psychology in the end was even more constricted by Freud's materialism than Freud's was (Apfelbaum, 1965, 1966). Waelder, on the other hand, was explicit that his teleologic view of the ego as problem-solving agent was incompatible with Freud's materialism, though typically he managed at the same time to avoid directly challenging Freud's view:

> (Freud) always tried to find explanations in terms of forces, tensions, conditioning by past experience, and the like. It is characteristic that in earlier times he speaks less of the "ego" than of "*ego instincts*"—a term suggestive of forces, vectors. Basically, it has probably always remained his view though . . . he grew progressively more tolerant of teleological concepts in later years. . . . Freud's hesitation to admit the "ego" as an equal to the drives, not only on the level of clinical theory but also as one of the fundamental facts of nature, reflects his reluctance to accept teleological explanations as the last word; it reflects the ethos of modern science. It can be criticized *on that level* by those who are either prepared to challenge the whole modern approach to nature—the exclusive alloplastic orientation, the constant striving for domination—or are willing to resign themselves to definite limits of predictability and accessiblity to influence in matters of life; but within the orientation of modern science, Freud's hesitation is justified. (1967, pp. 342–343 and 346)

Waelder's synthesis was never recognized as such by Freud and remains unrecognized for what it is today, although the paper containing it has managed to become a psychoanalytic classic. The principle of multiple function is most often referred to in passing and thought of as no more than an elaboration on Freud's idea of compromise formation. George Klein (1976) and Pine (1985) take it much more seriously, but they too fall short of recognizing its full epistemological and ontological significance. That such a powerful idea has managed to "hide in plain sight" for so long is largely due to Waelder's conscious decision to avoid any direct or open disagreement with Freud. He knowingly chose the path of evolution rather than revolution. To the extent that he wanted to support and strengthen psychoanalysis as a humanizing force in twentieth-century culture, he succeeded. To the extent that he wanted to resolve Freud's "problem of anxiety," he failed, but it was a qualified failure. The principle of multiple function acted like a good if somewhat premature interpretation: a lengthy process of working through would be necessary before it could be heard and used. This working-through process has occurred, I believe, in the *agon* of the orthodoxy–heresy dialectic, whose compulsive repetition is the expression of Freud's still-unresolved ambivalence on the one hand and the attempt to master it on the other. It is as if the two sides have agreed, "We're going to keep doing this until we get it right." As the dialectic has progressed, voices like Waelder's, Bettelheim's, Alexander's (before he succumbed to the lure of heresy), and, increasingly, the object-relations theorists' have sounded the tone of integration to the point where it is now clearly audible as the *basso continuo* of the psychoanalysis Waelder described as "a kind of polyphonic theory of psychic life."

NOTES

1. This of course does not mean that they are not also scientific disputes. Indeed, it is now well known from the work of Kuhn (1962) that there are conflicting philosophical premises at the root of the most obviously "scientific" controversies.
2. Students of Greek and Shakespearian drama will rightly object to this terminology, saying that the tragic nature of man has to do precisely with his guilt (over *hubris*). On the other hand, it is true that Oedipus and Hamlet were not blessed with the most empathic of parents.
3. See Frattaroli (1991) for a discussion of how Freud's intolerance of this iconoclastic aggression led to what I argue is a misreading of Hamlet's oedipal conflict.
4. This interpretation is entirely consistent with Freud's own (1900) interpretation of his Irma dream, in which he describes himself as inclined to blame everyone else for any ill effects of his own theory and practice.
5. His alliance with Fliess during this period, a much more likely candidate for ostracism than Freud himself, could also be seen as in part representing such a masochistic need for punishment.
6. He was also one of the first psychoanalysts to refer explicitly (Alexander, 1960) to Bohr's principle of complementarity in his writing.
7. On the other hand, as the years pass since Freud's death, and the influence of his immediate disciples, also dead, is waning in the analytic institutes they founded, things do seem to be loosening up a bit, and resolution of the conflict now seems attainable.
8. I am using the term *superego* here in the broad sense, as defined by Waelder (1930, 1934, 1960, 1965). See also Frattaroli (1991) for a detailed discussion of Waelder's conceptualization and its advantages. I will for the most part use the terms "the It," "the I," and "the I that stands above" for id, ego, and superego because, as I hope will become evident, they convey better the progressive, integrative sense of Freud's structural theory.

9. It may have been because of this ambivalence that nine years elapsed between the time (Freud, 1897) he first wrote Fliess about abandoning the seduction theory and the time he first announced the change in a published paper (Freud, 1906). His letter to Fliess shows clearly the inner turmoil that the change entailed:

> Now I do not know where I am, as I have failed to reach theoretical understanding of repression and its play of forces. It again seems arguable that it is later experiences which give rise to phantasies which throw back to childhood; and with that the factor of hereditary predisposition regains a sphere of influence *from which I had made it my business to oust it* [emphasis added]—in the interests of fully explaining neurosis.
>
> Were I depressed, jaded, unclear in my mind, such doubts might be taken for signs of weakness. But as I am in just the opposite state, I must acknowledge them to be the result of honest and effective intellectual labour, and I am proud that after penetrating so far I am still capable of such criticism. Can these doubts be only an episode on the way to further knowledge?
>
> It is curious that I feel not in the least disgraced, though the occasion might seem to require it. Certainly I shall not tell it in Gath, or publish it in the streets of Askalon, in the land of the Philistines—but between ourselves I have a feeling more of triumph than of defeat (which cannot be right). (1897, pp. 216–217)

10. The parallel between the ego repressing the outlaw id on the one hand and orthodoxy banishing the heretic on the other suggests that the structural theory itself may be viewed as a derivative of Freud's unconscious fantasy of ostracizing the iconoclast–scapegoat–hero. Abend (1979), despite his disclaimer that such linkages with unconscious fantsy "do not of necessity invalidate the theories or the clinical judgments derived from them," suggests that we should be cautiously mistrustful of theories so linked. I disagree, on the grounds that there is no theory, including Freud's and Abend's, that is free of such linkages. The principle of multiple function applies.

11. Although he did not explicitly refer to Bohr in his writing until the year after Bohr's death in 1962, the theme of complementarity, not identified as such, is present in Waelder's work from 1930 on. Waelder had received his Ph.D. in physics in 1920, when Bohr's model of the atom had center stage, and just before the major theoretical breakthroughs that led to a more or less finished quantum theory by 1927. Although he had left physics for psychoanalysis in the early 1920s, it is scarcely imaginable that Waelder would not have kept up with developments during this epoch-making period, and he would certainly have learned of Bohr's principle and of its epistemological import (which Bohr emphasized right from the start).

REFERENCES

Abend, S. (1979). Unconscious fantasy and theories of cure. *Journal of the American Psychoanalytic Association.* 27:579–596.

Alexander, F. (1940/1961). Psychoanalysis revised. In *The Scope of Psychoanalysis 1921–1961.* pp. 137–164. New York: Basic Books.

Alexander, F. (1946). The principle of corrective emotional experience. In F. Alexander and T. French (eds.), *Psychoanalytic Therapy*. New York: Ronald Press.

Alexander, F. (1950). Analysis of the therapeutic factors in psychoanalytic treatment. *Psychoanalytic Quarterly* 19:482–500.

Alexander, F. (1960). *The Western Mind in Transition*. New York: Random House.

Apfelbaum, B. (1965). Ego psychology, psychic energy, and the hazards of quantitative explanation in psycho-analytic theory. *International Journal of Psychoanalysis* 46: 168–182.

Apfelbaum, B. (1966). On ego psychology: A critique of the structural approach to psycho-analytic theory. *International Journal of Psychoanalysis* 47:451–475.

Bettelheim, B. (1960). *The Informed Heart*. Glencoe, IL: Free Press.

Bettelheim, B. (1967). *The Empty Fortress*. New York: Free Press.

Bettelheim, B. (1969). *The Children of the Dream*. New York: Macmillan.

Bettelheim, B. (1976). *The Uses of Enchantment*. New York: Knopf.

Bohr, H. (1967). My father. In S. Rozental, (ed.), *Niels Bohr: His Life and Work as Seen by his Friends and Colleagues*. New York: Wiley.

Bohr, N. (1934). *Atomic Theory and the Description of Nature*. Cambridge, England: Cambridge University Press.

Bohr, N. (1958). *Atomic Physics and Human Knowledge*. New York: Wiley.

Campbell, J. (1949/1975). *The Hero with a Thousand Faces*.

Dewald, P. (1976). Transference regression and real experience in psychoanalysis. *Psychoanalytic Quarterly* 45:213–230.

Folse, H. J. (1985). *The Philosophy of Niels Bohr: The Framework of Complementarity*. Amsterdam: North-Holland Personal Library.

Frattaroli, E. (1991). A New Look at *Hamlet*: Aesthetic response and Shakespeare's meaning. *International Review of Psychoanalysis* (in press).

Freud, S. (1897/1954). Letter of September 21, 1897. In M. Bonaparte, A. Freud, and E. Kris (eds.), *The Origins of Psychoanalysis: Letters to Wilhelm Fleiss, Drafts and Notes: 1887–1902*. New York: Basic Books.

Freud, S. (1900/1953). The interpretation of dreams. In J. Strachey (ed. and trans.), *The Standard Edition of the Complete Psychological Works of Sigmund Freud*, Vols. 4 and 5. London: Hogarth Press.

Freud, S. (1905/1953). My views on the part played by sexuality in the aetiology of the neuroses. In J. Strachey (ed. and trans.), *The Standard Edition of the Complete Psychological Works of Sigmund Freud*, Vol. 7, pp. 271–274. London: Hogarth Press.

Freud, S. (1914/1957). On the history of the psycho-analytic movement. In J. Strachey (ed. and trans.), *The Standard Edition of the Complete Psychological Works of Sigmund Freud*, Vol. 14, pp. 3–66. London: Hogarth Press.

Freud, S. (1920/1955). Beyond the pleasure principle. In J. Strachey (ed. and trans.), *The Standard Edition of the Complete Psychological Works of Sigmund Freud*, Vol. 18, pp. 1–64. London: Hogarth Press.

Freud, S. (1923/1961). The ego and the id. In J. Strachey (ed. and trans.), *The Standard Edition of the Complete Psychological Works of Sigmund Freud*, Vol. 19, pp. 3–66. London: Hogarth Press.

Freud, S. (1925/1959). An autobiographical study. In J. Strachey (ed. and trans.), *The Standard Edition of the Complete Psychological Works of Sigmund Freud*, Vol. 20, pp. 3–74. London: Hogarth Press.

Freud, S. (1926/1959). Inhibitions, symptoms and anxiety. In J. Strachey (ed. and trans.), *The Standard Edition of the Complete Psychological Works of Sigmund Freud*, Vol. 20, pp. 77–175. London: Hogarth Press.

Freud, S. (1933a/1964). The dissection of the physical personality: Lecture XXXI from New Introductory Lectures on Psycho-Analysis. In J. Strachey (ed. and trans.), *The Standard Edition of the Complete Psychological Works of Sigmund Freud*, Vol. 22, pp. 57–80. London: Hogarth Press.

Freud, S. (1933b/1964). Anxiety and instinctual life: Lecture XXXII from New Introductory Lectures on Psycho-Analysis. In J. Strachey (ed. and trans.), *The Standard Edition of the Complete Psychological Works of Sigmund Freud*, Vol. 22, pp. 81–111.

Freud, S. (1933c/1964). The question of a Weltanschauung: Lecture XXXV from New Introductory Lectures on Psycho-Analysis. In J. Strachey (ed. and trans.), *The Standard Edition of the Complete Psychological Works of Sigmund Freud*, Vol. 22, pp. 158–182. London: Hogarth Press.

Garcia, E. E. (1987). Freud's seduction theory. *Psychoanalytic Study of the Child* 42:443–468.

Holton, G. (1970). Roots of complementarity. *Daedalus* 99(4):1015–1055.

Kernberg, O. (1976). *Object Relations Theory and Clinical Psychoanalysis*. New York: Jason Aronson.

Kerberg, O. (1980). *Internal World and External Reality: Object Relations Theory Applied*. New York: Jason Aronson.

Klein, G. S. (1976). *Psychoanalytic Theory*. New York: International Universities Press.

Kohut, H. (1977). *The Restoration of the Self*. New York: International Universities Press.

Kuhn, T. S. (1962). *The Structure of Scientific Revolutions*. Chicago: University of Chicago Press.

Loewald, H. (1960). On the therapeutic action of psychoanalysis. *International Journal of Psychoanalysis* 41:16–33.

Modell, A. (1968). *Object Love and Reality*. New York: International Universities Press.

Modell, A. (1984). *Psychoanalysis in a New Context*. New York: International Universities Press.

Overton, W. F. (1973). On the assumptive base od the nature–nurture controversy: Additive versus interactive conceptions. *Human Development* 16:74–89.

Peters, E. (1980). *Heresy and Authority in Medieval Europe*. Philadelphia: University of Pennsylvania Press.

Pine, F. (1985). *Developmental Theory and Clinical Process*. New Haven: Yale University Press.

Segal, H. (1979). *Melanie Klein*. New York: Viking Press.

Waelder, R. (1930/1976). The principle of multiple function: Observations on overdetermination. In *Psychoanalysis: Observation, Theory, Application*. New York: International Universities Press.

Waelder, R. (1934/1976). The problem of freedom in psychoanalysis and the problem of reality testing. In *Psychoanalysis: Observation, Theory, Application*. New York: International Universities Press.

Waelder, R. (1960). *Basic Theory of Psychoanalysis*. New York: International Universities Press.

Waelder, R. (1963/1976). Psychic determinism and the possibility of predictions. In *Psychoanalysis: Observation, Theory, Application*. New York: International Universities Press.

Waelder, R. (1965). *Psychoanalytic Avenues to Art*. New York: International Universities Press.

Waelder, R. (1967). Inhibitions, symptoms, and anxiety: forty years later. In *Psychoanalysis: Observation, Theory, Application*. New York: International Universities Press.

Winnicott, D. W. (1958). *Collected Papers: Through Paediatrics to Psycho-Analysis*. New York: Basic Books.

Winnicott, D. W. (1965). *The Maturational Processes and the Facilitating Environment*. New York: International Universities Press.

5

Bettelheim's Contribution to Anthropology

ROBERT A. PAUL

BETTELHEIM'S UNMASKING OF MALE'S WOMB ENVY is as fundamentally profound to our society as Freud's presentation of female penis envy. Yet Bettelheim's discovery has met with resounding silence in our psychoanalytic community, and a few tut-tuts or titters in the anthropological community. Paul sets the intellectual record straight by demonstrating that the ethnographic data *following* Bettelheim's book confirms it—a rare opportunity in the social sciences.

Paul reviews the fundamentals of Bettelheim's argument: previous psychoanalytic theory held that ritual penile mutilation was a residuum of castration. In contrast, preliterate societies treat this rite as a mastery of an existential dilemma—boys do not have a definitive marker of puberty onset, unlike girls' menarche; as such, male mutilation "induces" menstruation and assimilates female reproductive powers.

When presenting the recent ethnographic data, Paul remarks that these "people act as if they read Bettelheim's book before they set about making up their culture."

Then Paul takes a challenging synthetic step after citing critiques of Bettelheim's work and Bettelheim's critiques of Freud. He suggests that these apparently disparate theories are complementary: like any creative act (rit-

ROBERT A. PAUL • Graduate Institute of Liberal Arts, Emory University, Atlanta, Georgia 30322.

Educating the Emotions: Bruno Bettelheim and Psychoanalytic Development, edited by Nathan M. Szajnberg. Plenum Press, New York, 1992.

ual, symptom, fine art), it is multiply determined. A powerful, painful act like male adolescent genital mutilation is kept alive by serving the psychological needs of the initiates, the initiators (adult males), and the women being imitated. The act contains the male wish to be powerful like the woman, the wish–fear to be castrated (to win the father's love), and the wish to face neither of these eventualities.

As Bettelheim said in his book, he believed that it was an antithetical response to Freud's thesis. As a new synthesis, he hoped it would provide a stimulus for new thinking, a new antithesis. This is how good scientific thinking proceeds—and how we become a better society.

Paul's chapter establishes womb envy as a phenomenon that exists in faraway preliterate societies—Melanesia, New Guinea, and Australia. What does this mean for contemporary America? As James Boon suggested in his critical study of anthropology, Westerners can learn much about others by traveling to exotic foreign locales; or they may learn little, by labeling these rituals and people as savage. In psychoanalysis, one may travel temporally far back to childhood in order to understand better one's contemporary thoughts, feelings, and beliefs; or one may use such reminiscences only to excuse, to mask one's contemporary motives and actions. What implications do such foreign mutilations have for us?

If womb envy is pervasive in contemporary American society, as I believe it is, we do not have comparable socially homogeneous and accepted rituals to mark the onset of boys' adolescent voyages and to bind their anxieties about such envy. Further, even in preliterate societies, we could justifiably (not self-righteously) ask: male mutilation may have an adaptive function to bind anxiety about womb envy, but at what cost, in terms of cultural defensive styles and possibly the overt subjugation of women? As a compromise formation, does the ritual partially bind anxiety, leaving some anxiety to find outlet in intrapsychic constriction and/or interpersonal restriction, such as demeaning women in order to bind one's envy?

And the more difficult question: to what extent and how do women contribute to the constellation of womb envy, other than the anatomical difference that engenders our psychological need to envy the other's prowess (whether penis, womb, intellect, or muscle)? The destructive power of coveting was recognized in the Ten Commandments.

These issues have far-reaching implications for our society that cannot be elaborated here. Freud believed that for each gender a fundamental issue was difficult, perhaps impossible to come to terms with: for men, their homoerotic yearnings, genetically derived from father; for women, their penis envy. The subsequent generation of analysts, such as Blos, demonstrated that both issues can be addressed successfully in late adolescence. They took up Freud's concern as a challenge. We ask the reader to speculate with us what it would mean for our society if male womb envy could be worked through and how this could be done in a psychoanalytically informed manner. This would truly be an act of culture, one as formidable as the draining of the Zuider Zee.

INTRODUCTION

Genital Mutilation in Boys

Bruno Bettelheim's *Symbolic Wounds* (1954/1968) is an attempt to understand the ethnographic phenomenon of male initiation rituals involving genital mutilation found in many widely dispersed societies throughout the world, using insights gained through the observation of the spontaneous actions of children living in the Orthogenic School in Chicago. In assessing the importance of Bettelheim's theoretical contribution to the anthropological understanding of initiation rituals, my chapter will run the following course: after presenting the main arguments of *Symbolic Wounds* in summary fashion, I will demonstrate the extent to which Bettelheim's view that in performing genital mutilations on initiated boys, men are expressing envy of the female powers symbolized by menstruation is empirically borne out by the ethnographic data. I will then juxtapose Bettelheim's idea with an apparently contradictory theory according to which male initiation rites are intended not to imitate women, but to purge men of whatever female components they may possess as a result of their early socialization by women so as to induct them into adult male society. By closely examining the psychodynamics involved in the ritual symbolism of male initiation rites, I will then show that these two views may indeed be reconciled, so that Bettelheim's theory may be seen after all as a necessary component of our ways of thinking about initiation.

Anthropology's Resistance

Before getting to the body of my essay, however, I must take note of the fact that Bettelheim's ideas have encountered considerable resistance from anthropologists concerned with initiation rites, not so much because of their specific psychodynamic formulations, but rather because psychodynamic explanations as such are unacceptable to many anthropologists. There were, I believe, sound and legitimate reasons why the founding figures of modern anthropology, Boas and Durkheim, wanted to differentiate the study of culture and society from the study of individual psychology, and so insisted that explanations of social and cultural phenomena that appealed to psychological principles were not valid.

Rituals and Symbols as Collective Phenomena

There is no doubt that rituals and ritual symbolism are more than simply the expression of individual motivations, and that they need to be seen as collective phenomena subject to explanations or interpretations that address the collective level. Too literal an adherence to these precautions, however, has led many anthropologists to ignore what is to me the self-evident fact that while the totality of a ritual extends way beyond the realm of personal motivation, yet ritual cannot exist without the deep and meaningful engagement of the intentions, wishes, and anxieties of those who participate in it; and that such engagement is achieved most effectively when the themes reflected in the symbolism and actions of ritual reflect and address themselves to the strongly felt psychodynamic motives and conflicts animating those involved. Public symbolism is not identical with private fantasy; but on the other hand, it is powerless unless it draws upon the latter and redirects it toward its own social and cultural agenda, as Victor Turner (1967) argued so persuasively in *The Forest of Symbols*.

I therefore disagree strongly with those theorists of initiation rites who reject Bettelheim's argument simply because it is psychodynamic, failing to see that explanations at the level of social reality and individual psychology not only do not contradict each other, but are necessary to each other. It would be a misrepresentation to assert that anthropology has uniformly rushed to embrace Bettelheim's ideas.

Thus, for example, Karen and Jeffrey Paige (1981), in their very ambitious book on reproductive ritual, offer a political argument for the practice of circumcision. Correlating the practice with the presence in a society of strong fraternal solidarity and the dilemma of fission in lineages, they take pride in the fact that their explanation renders moot all the various psychodynamic theories put forward to explain the practice:

> The dilemma of fission . . . unlike the dilemma of Oedipus, is rooted in the social structure of adult society. If the dilemma of fission is the source of circumcision . . . it will not require a theoretical detour through infant personality, Oedipal rebellions against the primal father, or neurotic primitives. (1981, p. 125)

In a less smug but no less adamant vein, Fried and Fried (1980), in their similarly ambitious study of rituals of life cycle transition, characterize their interpretive strategy thus:

> While not entirely rejecting psychological explanations of ritual behavior, we prefer to deal with such behavior in economic and social contexts. Rather than seek universal human meanings in such institutions, we prefer more

limited statements that provide for change as the economies and social arrangements of peoples undergo alteration. (1980, pp. 169–170)

More forthright in setting forth its biases and presuppositions without even any need for supporting argument is this quotation from a recent book-length treatment of ritual by La Fontaine (1986). Specifically addressing Bettelheim's thesis, she writes:

Anthropologists do not accept the assumption that the institutions of any society can be identified with the fantasies of disordered adolescents. Behavior in non-Western societies cannot be explained by comparing them with children, let alone with psychotic children. Nor can the obligatory formalized action of a ritual, which is not created anew each generation but is part of a long tradition, be convincingly explained as springing from individual fantasies. (1986, p. 112)

To take one final example illustrating a rather extreme instance of this mentality, let me cite Mary Douglas's (1966) rejection of Bettelheim's theory of genital operations, which she opposes not on its merits, but simply because it is a matter of foundational belief in the discourse of British social anthropology that public facts do not admit of private explanations, and that any ritual fact must therefore be understood as a reflection of social structure. She writes that when Bettelheim

argues that rituals which are explicitly designed to produce genital bleeding in males are intended to express male envy of female reproductive processes, the anthropologist should protest that this is an inadequate interpretation of a public rite . . . What is being carved in human flesh is an image of society. And in the moiety- and section-divided tribes he cites, the Murngin and Arunta, it seems more likely that the public rites are concerned to create a symbol of symmetry of the two halves of society. (1966, p. 116).

This view is no more plausible, but certainly a good deal less entertaining, than the notorious hypothesis put forward by Singer and Desole (1967) according to which it is not the vagina the Australians seek to imitate when they subincise a penis, but rather the bifid phallus of the kangaroo, whose great sexual prowess they rightly admire.

(A rather more persuasive argument has been advanced by Walter [1988] to the effect that the subincised penis is intended to resemble the not yet fully formed genital of the male fetus, since the point of Australian initiation is quite literally to achieve a second, male birth.)

My own response to Douglas would be that if it is indeed the case that the subincised penis is an image of the dual organization of society—as it may well be—then this image is compelling to those involved in the ritual *because* society itself is seen on the model of the relations between the sexes and because powerful psychological motivations are generated by the ritual actions and then attached to the social realm, thus inspiring renewed commitment to the now more deeply felt structural principles of society.

Summary of Symbolic Wounds

What, then, are the individual fantasies and conflicts that initiations mobilize with their symbols and action? It is to this question that Bettelheim has made his innovative and lasting contribution. Let me present, stripped to simplicity for the sake of clarity, the main arguments of Bettelheim's (1954) *Symbolic Wounds*:

1. Psychoanalytic thought has held, until now (1954), that circumcision as an initiation or related ritual, and genital mutilations similar to it, are derived from the castration complex, which in turn derives from the crime of the sons against the father in the primal horde. On this interpretation, circumcision is a symbolic residue of the actual castration practiced by the primal father in his jealous wrath; circumcision thus expresses paternal aggression and in this way enforces the incest taboo.

2. This theory implies that the initiation rites of preliterate peoples are the result of unrestrained id impulses (paternal aggression) and are destructive or neurotic in character; whereas in fact perhaps they ought to be viewed as constructive, ego-based attempts at mastery of certain existential dilemmas.

3. As for what these dilemmas are, we are given a clue by the behavior of some schizophrenic children observed at the Orthogenic School, who themselves initiated a shared secret ritual of self-inflicted bleeding at the time in puberty when the girls began to menstruate, raising anxieties in the boys, with no such definitive sign of sexual maturity, about their own ambiguous status.

4. The examination of ethnographic cases shows that in many instances, either explicitly or implicitly, the aim of genital mutilation at initiation is to induce males to menstruate, or in some other way to master or assimilate, at least symbolically, the apparent female capacity for reproduction.

5. Therefore, it may perhaps be supposed that the existential dilemmas addressed by initiation rites are these: since males, unlike females, have no definitive sign of sexual maturity comparable to menarche, therefore the distinctions between child and adult, and between male and female, are rendered conceptually and emotionally problematic for males.

6. In an effort—misguided, of course, but no less valiant than the efforts of schizophrenic children to achieve ego mastery through apparently bizarre symbolic contrivances—to master the envy of women and

their menstrual and reproductive powers that males feel at pubescence, societies institute initiation rites for the benefit of the initiates themselves, so that in symbolically mimicking female reproductive functions they can express and master anxiety.

7. This theory assumes that rituals, including initiation rituals, serve psychological purposes for all concerned, the initiates, the initiators, and the women of the society; whereas orthodox analytic theory has assumed that circumcision and related practices, including nose or ear piercing, extracting a tooth, scarification, and so forth are an expression of the counteroedipal wrath of the fathers alone, to which the initiates are subjected against their will and interests.

8. This theory also casts doubt on the anthropological theories that assert that the aim of initiation operations is simply to instill tribal lore or to mark the passage from one social status to another. In the former case, learning is better achieved through supportive rather than intimidating techniques; and as for the latter, why mark a social passage with such painful, even brutal methods?

9. Other corollaries follow as well:

a. Circumcision may have been instituted at the instigation of women, as occurred among the school children.

b. Secrecy surrounding men's rites is designed to disguise the fact that the male claim to female powers is doomed to failure.

c. Female circumcision may be partly a result of men's ambivalence about female sex functions and partly a reaction to, or imitation of, male initiation.

Many more points are made in this concise and seminal book, but I believe the ones set forth above do at least adequate justice to the main argument, and may serve as the basis for further discussion.

I will raise at the outset, only to dismiss it, the possible criticism that the book seems dated in many ways from the contemporary vantage point. How could this not be so? Every field has its fashions and trends, and they change. *Symbolic Wounds* is no more or less guilty of this fault than any other book from the same era, and by the canons of the time, rather than the retrospective standards of the present, it needs no defense.

We cannot expect that Bettelheim, or anyone else, should have found *the* explanation of initiation rites. First, because like all social facts, such rites are multifunctional and over determined so that the truth of one theory need not negate the correctness of a rival theory; and second, because there is no clear unified category of initiation rites, or genital mutilations. Each case is different and occurs in a different social and historical context, as well as in a different cosmological framework. The same action may be interpreted and understood in different ways in different cultures; while apparently disparate practices may express closely related underlying meanings. Is subincision to be lumped together with circumcision and classed as "genital mutilation"? Or are they, in fact, quite different operations with entirely different significance? Problems of this kind are unavoidable in comparative cross-cultural work, and since Bettelheim wrote, we have become much more aware of them. We therefore must not expect that Bettelheim has cracked the riddle of initiation with a stroke; but this has little bearing on whether his insights have led to greater understanding of a broad range of cultural phenomena.

ETHNOGRAPHIC SUPPORT

That having been said, I can state that in the light of subsequent ethnography, executed with the attention to detail that has since come to be expected of the observation of ritual symbolism in our field, Bettelheim's central hypothesis only seems to grow in plausibility and indeed predictive power, since so much corroborative material was not yet available to him. It was already evident in the Australian data on which he relied heavily that the natives themselves frequently expressed themselves this way: they made no bones about the fact that in opening an incision on their penis shaft, they were creating a vagina for themselves and menstruating through it. A plethora of more recent data from New Guinea and other parts of Melanesia, South America, and to a lesser degree other ethnographic areas strongly supports the idea that in many societies, especially technologically simple ones such as hunter–gatherers and rudimentary horticulturalists, men assert that they can achieve, at least symbolically, the reproductive status of women; that they often do this by mimicking menstruation in some more or less direct way; and that they do it in ritual settings that initiate boys, who previously belonged to a female-dominated domestic world, into a secret society of adult males. On entering this all-male world, they have revealed to them not only practical learning but a body of mythical lore surrounding the origins and nature of society, wherein it is quite often supposed that while males are certainly superior to women, and very different from them, yet the secret of their superiority rests in their possession of patently female powers and characteristics, which in fact originated with women, or were stolen from women, or which are in danger of being usurped by women if revealed to them.

By way of illustration, let me cite the recent ethnography, *Anxious Pleasures*, by Thomas Gregor (1985), a rich study of the sexual lives of the Mehinaku Indians, who live by fishing and gathering on the banks of the Xingu River in the Brazilian forest. Gregor writes of them as follows:

For the Mehinaku, menstruation is the most anxiety-charged of the physi-ological characteristics of women. Caused by deadly fauna living in the vagina, menstrual blood is associated with wounds, castration, poison, disease, stunted growth, and enfeeblement. Yet there are a number of occasions in which men symbolically menstruate, the most significant of which is the ritual of ear piercing. (p. 186)

During this initiation rite, boys are strengthened by abstemious behavior and separation from women, and are expected to go through the painful operation on the ears with fortitude. They quite consciously equate ear piercing not only with genital mutilation, but with menstruation:

According to the Mehinaku, the ear-piercing ceremony is the equivalent of the ritual that occurs at the onset of a girl's first menses. Both ceremonies focus on blood and seek to staunch its flow as rapidly as possible . . . . "Ear piercing," as Ketepe [a Mehinaku informant] puts it, "is menstruation. The Pihika ceremony is like a girl's first menses." When pressed further, Ketepe recognizes that menstrual blood and blood from the boys' incisions are not identical: "The boys kid a little when they menstruate. It's not real menstrual blood." (1985, p. 188)

Further, in his analysis of the initiated male's ritual regalia, Gregor notes that

the headdress, ostensibly a crown of masculine adornment, caps an alto-gether different view of a well-dressed Mehinaku. His earrings are conferred in a ritual in which he menstruates. The feathers for his earrings were in mythic times taken from the vagina of the Sun's wife. And his prominent headdress is symbolically associated with women's labia. Fully adorned, the Mehinaku male is an ikon of female sexual anatomy. (pp. 192–193)

Gregor's Mehinaku material is by no means atypical; the anthro-pological reader immediately registers many parallels, not only from elsewhere in South America but from Melanesia and Australia as well. Obviously, many of Bettelheim's contentions are borne out by these data. Not only is the boys' initiation a mimicking of menstruation, to which it is explicitly equated, it is also regarded as having originally belonged to women. Men clearly envy and emulate menstruation and other symbols of female sexuality, as their regalia makes clear. And the informants them-selves are aware that despite their claims, they are really only engaged in make-believe; and so women are strictly excluded from the proceedings.

In another part of the vast Amazonian world, in the Vaupés region of Colombia, the Barasana Indians described by Stephen Hugh-Jones (1979) initiate their boys at a festival called "He House," after the "He" instru-ments, the various trumpets and long flutes that play a major symbolic role in the ceremony. The He instruments represent the ancestral anaconda and other mythical ancestors of the Barasana. In normal times, the instruments lie hidden in the mud of the river bank. By bringing them up into the longhouse, the men reenact the primordial events when the anaconda created the Barasana by vomiting them up. As the instruments are displayed and played, the boys are conjoined to this mythic lineage.

According to Barasana myth, in ancient times the women once succeeded in stealing the He instruments from the men for a while. When that happened, the men became like women, that is, they began to cultivate crops and to menstruate (Barasana men normally fish and do not cultivate). The reason the women were able to carry out this dastardly rebellion was that the men were lazy and refused to get out of their hammocks when their fathers told them to bathe in the river. The women, overhearing this command, seized the opportunity to steal the He instruments from the river themselves. As Hugh-Jones notes in his perceptive analysis:

> This refusal to bathe in the morning can be linked to menstruation in two respects: first, it has connotations of laziness . . . connected with confinement during menstruation and after He House. Second . . . the most common way of describing a menstruating woman is to say she is "one who does not bathe" . . . Hence the men in the myth were behaving as if they were menstruating. (1979, p. 127)

Hugh-Jones argues that the instruments are the symbols and means of the subjection of women by men, so that their possession entails dominance in the society. He adds that while in this society men certainly are ritually dominant, in fact

> the question as to who creates remains unresolved and in private the men will admit that in this respect their victory over the women was at best double edged. (p. 128)

In the ritual itself, men, especially the shamans, manipulate not only symbols of masculinity, principally the He instruments, but also symbols of femininity, especially a beeswax gourd, the analysis of which is far too complex for me to assay here. In any event, it is clear that in doing so, they are attempting to claim control over both the masculine and feminine roles in reproduction.

It is not surprising, then, to find that not only among the Barasana, as analyzed by Hugh-Jones, but among neighboring peoples as well, the shamans themselves, who preside over the ceremonies, are described as being like menstruating women. As Hugh-Jones writes:

> At the onset of puberty a girl becomes "opened up" and from then on she is opened up during each menstrual period. Shamans are also opened up in that . . . their activities are associated with oral and anal incontinence. [Much of the ceremony revolves around the use of emetics and purgatives.]

Shamans . . . are confined in special enclosures during He House just as women are so confined during menstruation. (1979, pp. 125–126)

But not only the shamans but the initiates also are likened to menstruating women. They are kept in enclosures and said to be lazy, which as we saw is a condition associated with menstruation. During the initiates' confinement, the women do men's work, thus reenacting the mythic episode when women usurped the He instruments and men menstruated. According to Hugh-Jones's interpretation, far too intricate to be adequately recapitulated here, the essential feature of maturation for both sexes is regarded as the "opening up" of orifices. This renders them sexually fertile; but the flow thus induced must also be tightly controlled, especially in women, or the unbridled *élan vital* will prove unmanageable and destructive. In girls, this opening up is achieved physiologically through the fact of menarche. In boys, it is accomplished by the action of the He instruments, which are themselves long hollow tubes through which air is made to resonate in imitation of the ancestral anaconda, as well as being quite clearly phallic in their connotation.

The Barasana data thus touch on another theme raised by Bettelheim in his book, namely the relation of male continence and incontinence to fantasies of male–female reproductive power. As Dundes (1976) has shown more recently in his analysis of the ritual instrument known as the bull-roarer, initiates are often not only feminized in initiation, but also equated with feces. The symbolic connection arises through the typical male fantasy of anal birth, which is one way of conceptually mastering the problem of how men can imitate women's reproductive capacity. The emetics and purgatives of the Barasana may thus, like the anal plugs of the Chaga, be linked, through the ideas of oral and anal flow and its control, as metaphorical transformations of the menstruation wishes to which male envy of women leads.

I could multiply examples here, but there is no need to do so. It seems obvious from the data so far discussed that these people act as if they read Bettelheim's book before they set about making up their culture. Yet let me introduce the typical, but by no means inconsequential, anthropological caveat that while Bettelheim's hypothesis seems clearly at work in both the instances of the Barasana and the Mehinaku, this not only hardly exhausts all that can be said about them, but it also fails to recognize that the cultural elaboration of the core ideas in these two societies lead to quite different and in some ways incomparable results. Thus, while the Barasana have flutes, beeswax gourds, and make a big to-do over "open" versus "closed" as conceptual categories, the Mehinaku do no such things; while the Barasana do not pierce their ears or perform any mutilation at all, but rather subject themselves to whipping, vomiting, and diarrhetics. Indeed, the skeptic might claim that despite appearances, the Barasana do not fit Bettelheim's hypothesis, since there are no wounds, symbolic or otherwise, associated with their initiation rituals; and even in the Mehinaku case, piercing the ears is by no means self-evidently identical to genital mutilation, except perhaps to the eye of the psychoanalytic observer (and of course to the Mehinaku themselves!).

These and other similar caveats aside, I believe it is fair to state that Bettelheim's grasp of the dynamics underlying ritual complexes of the kind I have briefly outlined here was profound and prescient and retains validity to this day. Having established in what ways the theory is essentially correct, in my view, I will now devote some attention to a critique of those aspects or corollaries of it that remain problematic.

CRITIQUES OF BETTELHEIM AND RESPONSES

Child Rearing with Prolonged Father Absence

One of the main alternative psychodynamic theories of harsh initiation rites—one no doubt influenced by Bettelheim's work, but significantly different from it as well—is that proposed by Burton and Whiting (1961; see also Whiting, et al. 1958; and numerous other works). Their approach involves a statistical correlation of those societies in which harsh initiation is practiced with certain child-rearing patterns. These authors agree with Bettelheim in doubting the psychoanalytic dogma that puberty rites are outlets for counteroedipal wrath intended to instill castration anxiety, and they agree with him further that the question that is paramount in puberty rites is the establishment of correct and unambiguous sex role identity. Their hypothesis is that child-rearing patterns that foster prolonged father absence, especially polygyny, which necessarily leads to this situation, result in excessive identification of male infants with their mothers. Puberty rites are intended to rid boys of the infantile female identification, by severing them rudely from the maternal world, inducting them into the male society with a rough hazing, and symbolically purging them of female features.

Lidz and Lidz (1977) advance a parallel argument about male menstruation. While noting their agreement with Bettelheim in many respects, they argue that the problem of separation–individuation underlies other, later dynamic developments, and that in the process of individuation, "the child internalizes something of his mother and thus acquires a basic feminine component that remains at the very core of his self" (p. 27). In those societies where mother–child symbiosis is strong and prolonged, initiation rites are necessary to overcome the "pull of the wish–fear for reunion with the mother and reengulfment by her" (p. 27), as well as to undo the male's maternal identification and provide him with male equivalents of what in a woman a man might envy, by way of compensation for his loss.

Response

This theory is thus in some ways the opposite of Bettelheim's: far from making men like women, menstruating or otherwise, ritual mutilation at puberty seeks to rid them of whatever female aspects they may yet possess. Burton and Whiting's theory has been widely supported, not only in their own research, but by subsequent studies. Does this provide refutation of Bettelheim's view? I think not. Helpful data are supplied by the great reams of ethnography, unavailable to both Bettelheim and Burton and Whiting, which have emerged in recent decades from the anthropological exploration of Papua New Guinea.

In one New Guinea group, the Sambia, studied by Gilbert Herdt (1981), the male initiation rite has two main central features. One is a very painful nose bleeding and the other is fellatio performed by the initiates on older men for the ostensible purpose of ingesting growth-enhancing semen. The explicit aim of both these ritual acts, according to the Sambia themselves, is to purge initiates of female characteristics and make them wholly men. So far, this is entirely consistent with the Burton and Whiting hypothesis. Throughout much of New Guinea, blood, or an excess of blood, is associated with females, while semen is obviously male. Therefore the meaning of this rite seems self-evidently to be that female blood is drained out of the boys, while at the same time it is, in effect, replaced with an infusion of male substance.

Herdt cites three reasons the Sambia give for nose bleeding, in order of importance: (1) punishing initiates for insubordination; (2) removing the bad blood and bad talk of one's mother; and (3) learning not to fear bloodshed in war. No mention is made of the envy, control, or imitation of the female reproductive function, which indeed is greatly disparaged. The first reason given, punishing the initiates for insubordination (presumably the sheer act of growing up is a rebellion in itself) in fact seems most consistent with the counteroedipal castration hypothesis rejected by both later authors, while the second reason, purging the initiate of the bad blood of women, is clearly consistent with the Burton and Whiting hypothesis. The third reason, having to do with warfare, supports the view of Young (1962) and others that initiation's *raison d'etre* is to induct

recruits into male corporate groups in societies where warfare is a necessary aspect of male life.

Yet in the data there is support of Bettelheim's position as well, for the
men are claiming, in separating themselves radically from women, that
they are able to procreate entirely by themselves; and indeed the chief
myth associated with the initiatory cult is one that Herdt convincingly
analyzes as being centrally about what he calls male parthenogenesis.
Michael Allen, who in his own earlier study of Melanesian initiation rites
(1967) had rejected Bettelheim's psychodynamic hypothesis in favor of the
sort of social structural, political analysis favored by Australian anthropologists in those days, has, in a later publication (Allen, 1984), come much
closer to supporting Bettelheim's point. Citing Dundes (1976), whose
article on the bull-roarer was itself influenced by Bettelheim's work, Allen
points out that while the rites do indeed make men out of the boys, they
nonetheless do it in the paradoxical way of feminizing the initiates. We
already say how, according to Gregor, the Mehinaku, in their full male
attire, are a veritable symbolic representation of the female genitals. Just
so, despite their disclaimers,

> in many areas of Papua New Guinea . . . boys identify with women by
> equating penile incision with menstruation [in the Sambia case nose piercing
> is substituted for penile incision], while the senior men identify with
> mothers by making possible the novice's "rebirth." In semen-ingesting areas
> . . . novices may identify with the passive role by their passive intake of
> semen (Allen, 1984, p. 120)

He goes on, very astutely, to point out that the bloodletting syndrome
is one in which the men identify with women primarily as creatures who
menstruate and give birth, while the semen-ingesting syndrome places the
emphasis on the imitation of women's capacity to receive semen and give
milk. Thus in the two rites, which are typical of different parts of New
Guinea, but are combined among the Sambia, men are in fact identifying
with two aspects of women: on the one hand, menstruating women and
reproductive mothers, and on the other hand, wives and nurturant
mothers.

So while the Sambia give verbal support both to the orthodox castration theory and the Burton–Whiting mother-identification theory, an analysis that goes beyond the informants' own report and observes the total
symbolism of the rituals certainly seems to lend very broad support to
Bettelheim's view that in ritual men seek to gain and control the natural
endowments of females. As Herdt (1987) himself points out, the sexually
ambiguous symbolism of Sambia ritual allows male society to offer the

initiate "female" substitutes, subsumed within the male world, for the lost maternal identification and/or symbiosis.

These considerations lead me to believe that perhaps the various theories are not really in competition, but stand to one another rather as did the images of the elephant entertained by those notorious blind men of the Orient; that is, each presents a part of the total system as if it were itself the whole, or at least its crucial element. Since Bettelheim's theory was conceived as an attack on the "orthodox" Freudian theory, let me therefore focus my attention on the relation between that theory and both the Bettelheim and the Burton–Whiting theories.

That Bettelheim's book is indeed intended as a revision of Freud, in a manner not unlike that proposed by Harold Bloom for the creative poet seeking to escape the influence of his strong precursor, can hardly be doubted. His chapter entitled "Challenge to Theory" is primarily directed at Freud and his "primal horde" theory, while his final chapter begins with the claim that his book has two purposes, the first

> to suggest that Freud's interpretation of these customs is subject to grave doubts, as are interpretations of those who followed him and saw in ritual circumcision mainly a desire to create castration anxiety. (1954/1968, p. 161)

while the second purpose is to propose his own theory that would be more "in keeping with the facts" (p. 161). This reading of Bettelheim's own motives is lent confirmation by the reparative dedication of the book, which reads "To the memory of Sigmund Freud whose theories on sex and the unconscious permit a fuller understanding of the mind of man."

Freud's Lack of Theory for Circumcision Rituals

Let me begin my consideration of this matter by pointing out that Freud in fact developed nothing that could be dignified as a "theory" of circumcision rituals. His remarks on the subject are all scattered offhand comments made in other contexts, not attempts at a systematic analysis. Bettelheim is quite right to take to task those slavish epigones of Freud who took these casual remarks as gospel truth. Chief among these is Reik, whose analysis of puberty rites (1946/1962) appears to be the actual target of Bettelheim's critique. But Bettelheim tends to set up Freud's theory as a straw man, more in need of debunking than it actually deserved. He ignores the fact that Freud's comments were by and large restricted to the practice of circumcision among the Jews; when he did mention Australian data, it was only in the most superficial way and without any attempt at serious interpretation. This being the case, a number of points can be made from the perspective of the present, when all these arguments are to some extent curiosities of intellectual history rather than burning issues.

1. In an appendix on infant circumcision, Bettelheim expressly notes that what he has to say applies mainly to preliterate peoples of Australia, Africa, and elsewhere, and *not* to the Jewish practice of infant circumcision. Indeed, he gives Jewish circumcision pretty much the same interpretation as did Freud, namely, that it represents an evolutionary development in civilization in which a ritual generated in one context and with one sense became adapted to a different purpose in a different social setting, expressing heightened superego demands leading to greater repression and hence to the enhanced redirection of libido into the work of civilization. Whatever one may think of this evolutionary view, it confirms that on the question of circumcision specifically as it is practiced by the Jews, Bettelheim and Freud are essentially in agreement. But since Freud was not talking about circumcision in any but the Jewish context, for the most part, then Bettelheim's theory is rather an addition to, rather than a replacement for, the castration theory he attributes to Freud.

2. Were he an anthropologist, Bettelheim would have been aware that his theory that rituals can change their meaning in the direction of greater superego function is exactly what Robertson Smith (1889/1972) had proposed long before in his analysis of sacrifice in his great book, *The Religion of the Semites*. Freud himself, unlike many of his followers, relied heavily on this work and incorporated its main insights into his own theory of the origins and history of culture.

3. Not only is his opponent a straw man, in that he actually agrees with him, but he is further a straw man in that none but the most dedicated acolytes of Freud, and certainly no anthropologists (other than Roheim, for awhile), ever took the primal horde theory very seriously in the first place, at least not as a literal piece of prehistory (Reik again is the chief exception). I speak with some authority on this subject, since I myself have published one of the most sympathetic articles (Paul, 1976) on *Totem and Taboo* in the entire anthropological literature; and even I certainly do not believe in the historical reality of the primal crime.

4. It cannot be stressed enough, I think, that circumcision and subincision (or superincision) ought to be viewed as radically different operations rather than simply classed together as genital mutilations. The object of the former, removal of the foreskin and exposure of the glans, is generally understood by natives and analysts alike as a ridding of the penis of its anomalous passive, enclosing, moist female character and fully establishing it as an active, intrusive, dry male organ. Subincision, by contrast, creates a deep scar on the underside of the penis shaft—in

superincision the wound is on top of the penis—which, when healed, may be thought to resemble a vagina in that it is in the genital region and represents an aperture which may be made to bleed periodically through reincision. I therefore believe that what Freud had to say about Jewish circumcision and what Bettelheim has to say about subincision in Australia may really be two different kettles of fish.

5. But now let us look more carefully at what Freud actually said about castration anxiety. Bettelheim argues that in orthodox Freudian theory, the purpose of initiation rites is thought to be the instilling of castration anxiety in initiates; so that they are seen primarily as an acts called forth in response to the destructive, aggressive drives of the fathers. Bettelheim, by contrast, wants to argue that perennial customs ought to be understood as constructive activities of the ego, not the id, serving positive functions for all concerned.

But Freud believed that castration anxiety originated in boys during the oedipal period, around 5 years of age, in a manner partly predetermined by phylogenetic inheritance. He could not, therefore, possibly have held simultaneously that rituals performed in puberty instill castration anxiety, since by his account such anxiety is already there. On the contrary, it seems to me that from a Freudian perspective, the essence of circumcision in adolescence is that while it *rearouses* and heightens an *already present* castration anxiety, the ritual allows for mastery and resolution because it in fact *stops short* of actual castration, repeats the dreaded trauma in modified form, and allows the ego to see that what it fears is not fatal after all. The initiate emerges from the ritual strengthened precisely because he has survived castration and emerged with a phallus which, while heroically scarred, is still functional. So in a Freudian view, genital mutilation should not be caricatured as an explosion of raw id; this is in any event contrary to Freud's approach to ritual, as I will now show.

6. Freud's approach to ritual in general was never that rituals could represent unrestrained id impulses, but rather that they are, both in the case of the compulsions of neurotics and the organized rites of cultures, compromise formations that enact both id wishes and ego and superego constraints simultaneously.

Thus, for example, Freud's interpretation of the totemic feast is that it at one and the same time reenacts the primal murder and cannibalism, by slaughtering and eating the sacrificial beast, *and also* represents punishment for the crime, through the death and sacrifice of that self-same victim. In an analogous way, initiation rites, in a Freudian interpretation, would express, even just for the fathers, *both* a wish that the boys be castrated *and also* a simultaneous wish that they not be castrated. This can be symbolically achieved by a partial cutting of the initiate's penis, which still leaves it operational; which is indeed what is accomplished in most genital mutilation.

7. It is a narrow view that it is only the fathers who might wish for the initiates to be symbolically castrated. For as Freud argued, most notably in *Inhibitions, Symptoms and Anxiety* (1926/1959), a primary anxiety in the ego, dread of castration by the superego figure, apparently arises by two opposite routes. On the one hand, castration is feared as a talionic punishment for oedipal wishes and fantasies. But on the other hand, the boy himself desires castration as one outcome of the observance of the oedipal primal scene, in that the boy wishes to be loved by the father and to conceive by him, and so recognizes that he must become like his mother, that is, undergo castration and become a woman. Little Hans typified the first syndrome, the Wolf Man the second.

Therefore we may argue that symbolic castration in initiation rites or elsewhere need not be inconsistent with the unconscious infantile wishes of the initiates themselves, which may very well be to become "women" and to become pregnant by the beloved father. Schafer points out that even mistreatment at the hands of parental figures has pleasurable aspects that are actively desired, including "sustained contact with parental care, or . . . nonabandonment" (1960, p. 181), as well as gratification of moral masochism. Thus Schafer reminds us that for Freud, "each punishment of the superego signifies feminine (castrated) pleasure in relation to the father" (1960, p. 182).

Even more explicitly for our present purposes, Brenner points out the active wishes that may be satisfied on the part of initiates:

> [p]enile mutilation, like communion, combines morality and masochism. Among the motives for submission to and identification with parental moral demands, wishes for libidinal gratification play a significant role in both circumcision and subincision. (1982, p. 133)

Synthesis

Having posed the matter in this way, it now becomes clear to us how the Freudian castration theory, the Burton–Whiting theory, and the Bettelheim theory can all be seen as forming a coherent synthesis. For by this account, the wish to be castrated, the wish to have female reproductive powers, and the simultaneous wish to be freed of these wishes would come together and could be perfectly realized in an initiatory genital mutilation. In undergoing the operation, one could realize the wish to be castrated and to become like a woman, able to menstruate, be penetrated by a phallus, and bear children; and at the same time, through the paradoxical measure of becoming like a woman, act upon and master one's primordial mother identification and thus free oneself to become an adult male with control over one's complete bisexual nature. As Burton and Whiting argue, this syndrome should be most pronounced in those for whom a primary identification with the mother was most salient. This synthetic interpretation would make sense of a great many aspects of initiation ritual, such as, for example, the New Guinea rites that require homosexual unions between older men and novices. Homosexuality, in this view, could be seen as itself a compromise resolution of the antagonism between unisexuality and bisexuality in that it is done only among the men and is considered a male phenomenon; but it also creates among the men a metaphorical replication of the total heterosexual society.

It is, in any event, quite counter to what is found in the ethnographic record to suppose that real paternal aggression is absent from initiation rites. In their discussion of initiation among the Awa of New Guinea, Newman and Boyd (1982) write as follows:

> The patriclansmen of each boy are especially aggressive during the initial proceedings. So great is their hostility toward the boys that they are not allowed to be directly involved in the purging ritual lest they handle a nosebleeder, vomiting cane, or bamboo blade in such a manner as to inflict serious injury on their young relatives. (p. 283)

That this aggression is not only real, but experienced by the novices as such, is made plain in this quote from a Hausa man recalling his own circumcision:

> We then realized what was to happen and we got sick. We threw up. Some of the boys lost control of the bladder and bowel. They cried. Our older brothers, uncles, and fathers held us . . . The barber grabbed my penis, pulled the foreskin forward and with one quick move he cut it off. I screamed. (Fried and Fried, 1980, p. 68)

This seems a far cry from a ceremony designed by the boys themselves to help master their concerns about the differences between men and women. These boys, it seems to me, are quite deliberately subjected to what can only be described as a castrating attack by their older male relatives, including their own fathers. It is my argument that since they are, after this ultimate realization of their worst fears is induced, not castrated after all, it is precisely this that gives the ritual its power to make men of them.

The point is illustrated in a beautiful example of symbolism from among the Nuer people of the upper Nile (Beidelman, 1966). These warlike men initiate their sons not only with quite extensive and bloody scarification, but also with the presentation of two gifts which ever after will be viewed as identical with the youth himself. One of these is a war spear, the other an ox. Since the war spear is explicitly given phallic connotations, while an ox is quite literally castrated, this presentation epitomizes what, in my view, is the message of initiation insofar as it utilizes the theme of the threat of castration: with the spear, the boy is symbolically given an adult phallus, while with the castrated beast, his manhood is taken away. Thus the wish of the men to castrate and not to castrate and the wish of the boys to be castrated and not to be castrated is fulfilled through the creation of symbolic metaphors of the self, the ox, and spear. In genital mutilation, the same wishes are fulfilled by means of an act on the body that symbolically both *does* and *does not* castrate the initiate. But in affirming that castration anxiety does indeed play a role in the genesis of the symbolism of many initiation rites I am by no means denying the validity of Bettelheim's theory, which I feel is established beyond reasonable doubt. For castration is understood in the unconscious as making a woman out of a man. The separation of men from women and the seizure of female reproductive power can only imply that the men become like women and menstruate. Indeed the crux of the analysis rests in the two-edged aspect of menstruation itself, as it must appear to the male unconscious. It is on the one hand a sign of the greatest boon, the female power to reproduce, while it is simultaneously the mark of the greatest sacrifice, the loss of the phallus. It is in this ambiguity, so amply capitalized on by the ritual symbolism in the ethnographic record (a sample of which I have cited here), which makes it possible to argue that when men envy menstruating women and dread castration by the father, it is all the same psychological complex that is involved, one into which Bettelheim and others have offered us penetrating glimpses.

CONCLUSION

It has been my intention in this chapter to reexamine Bettelheim's contribution to the theory of male initiation rites presented in *Symbolic Wounds*. I have suggested that Bettelheim was farsighted, indeed ahead of his time, in emphasizing the aspect of male psychodynamics in which awe before and desire for the power of the feminine is a strong motivating force. More recent ethnographic studies have confirmed that such themes resonate throughout the symbolism and acts associated with male puberty rituals. I have also showed that, while Bettelheim's view is not complete, taken together with other views that might at first glance be taken to contradict it, the theory of male menstruation envy is one essential element of the psychodynamics revealed in the symbolism of initiation rites.

Bettelheim deserves credit for the leap of imagination that enabled him to move from observing the spontaneous gestures of disturbed children to insight into much more widely distributed human conflicts. And his part in helping rectify the false impression that women envy men, but not vice versa, can now be seen as an important step in the history of psychoanalytic anthropology.

References

Allen, M. (1967). *Male Cults and Secret Initiations in Melanesia*. Melbourne: Melbourne University Press.

Allen, M. (1984). Homosexuality, male power, and political organization in North Vanuatu: A comparative analysis. In G. H. Herdt (ed.), *Ritualized Homosexuality in Melanesia*. Berkeley: University of California Press.

Beidelman, T. O. (1966). The ox and Nuer sacrifice: Some Freudian hypotheses about Nuer symbolism. *Man* NS1:453–467.

Bettelheim, B. (1954/1968). *Symbolic Wounds: Puberty Rites and the Envious Male*. New York: Collier Books.

Bettelheim, B. (1974). *A Home for the Heart*. New York: Knopf.

Brenner, C. (1982). *The Mind in Conflict*. New York: International Universities Press.

Burton, R. V., and Whiting, J. W. M. (1961). The absent father and cross-sex identity. *Merrill-Palmer Quarterly of Behavior and Development* 7:85–95.

Douglas, M. (1966). *Purity and Danger: An Analysis of Concepts of Pollution and Taboo*. New York: Praeger.

Dundes, A. (1976). A psychoanalytic study of the bullroarer. *Man* NS 11:220–238.

Fried, M. N., and Fried, M. H. (1980). *Transitions: Four Rituals in Eight Cultures*. New York: Norton.

Freud, S. (1926/1959). *Inhibitions, Symptoms and Anxiety*. New York: Norton.

Gregor, T. (1985). *Anxious Pleasures: The Sexual Lives of an Amazonian People*. Chicago: University of Chicago Press.

Herdt, G. H. (1981). *Guardians of the Flutes: Idioms of Masculinity. A Study of Ritualized Homosexual Behavior*. New York: McGraw-Hill.

Herdt, G. (1987). Transitional objects in Sambia initiation. *Ethos* 15:40–57.

Hugh-Jones, S. (1979). *The Palm and the Pleiades: Initiation and Cosmology in Northwest Amazonia*. Cambridge: Cambridge University Press.

LaFontaine, J. S. (1986). *Initiation: Ritual Drama and Secret Knowledge Across the World*. Manchester: Manchester University Press.

Lidz, R. W. and Lidz, T. (1977). Male menstruation: A ritual alternative to the oedipal transition. *The International Journal of Psychoanalysis* 58:17–31.

Newman, P. L., and Boyd, D. J. (1982). The making of men: Ritual and meaning in Awa male initiation. In G. H. Herdt (ed.), *Rituals of Manhood: Male Initiation in Papua New Guinea*. Berkeley: University of California Press.

Paul, R. A. (1976). Did the primal crime take place? *Ethos* 4:311–352.

Paige, K. E. and Paige, J. M. (1981). *The Politics of Reproductive Ritual*. Berkeley: University of California Press.

Reik, T. (1946/1964). The puberty rites of savages. In *Ritual: Four Psychoanalytic Studies*. New York: Grove Press.

Robertson Smith, W. (1889/1972). *The Religion of the Semites: The Fundamental Institutions.* New York: Schocken Books.

Schafer, R. (1960). The loving and beloved superego in Freud's structural theory. *The Psychoanalytic Study of the Child* 15:163–188.

Singer, P. and Desole, D. E. (1967). The Australian subincision ceremony reconsidered: Vaginal envy or kangaroo bifid penis envy. *American Anthropologist* 69:355–358.

Turner, V. (1967). *The Forest of Symbols.* Ithaca, NY: Cornell University Press.

Walter, M. A. H. B. (1988). The fetal and natal origins of circumcision and other rebirth symbols. In G. N. Appell and T.N. Madan (eds.), *Choice and Morality in Anthropological Perspective*, pp. 213–237. Albany, NY: State University of New York Press.

Whiting, J. W. M., Kluckhohn, R., and Anthony, A. (1958). The function of male initiation ceremonies at puberty. In E. Maccoby, T. M. Newcomb, and E. L. Hartley (eds.), *Readings in Social Psychology*, pp. 359–370. New York: Henry Holt.

Young, F. W. (1962). The function of male initiation ceremonies: A cross-cultural test of an alternative hypothesis. *American Journal of Sociology* 67:379–391.

6

From the Orthogenic School to the Reservation
Acculturation of a Psychoanalyst

ROBERT BERGMAN

THIS IS AN ETHNOGRAPHIC ACCOUNT of a seventeen-year sojourn among the Navajo. Unlike the anthropologist, Bergman did not go to study the Navajo; he went to work and live with them.

Many previous psychoanalytic forays into other particularly preliterate cultures were disastrous for psychoanalysis and possibly for the host culture. The anthropological psychoanalyst suffered from the *hubris* of interpreting the foreign culture in terms of his or her home culture. A metapsychology (of libido, ego, id superego)—one already intellectually flawed, as Cohler argues in this volume—was used to transform foreign beliefs, meanings, and actions into psychoanalytic thinking.

Bergman avoids this fault. He uses instead the psychoanalytic ability to create and understand meanings between individuals in order that they better understand each other and themselves. As Alfred Flarsheim, a Bettelheim student, remarked, with each analysis, the analyst can expand the frontiers of his or her personality.

ROBERT BERGMAN • 2271 N.E. 51st Street, Seattle, Washington 98105.

Educating the Emotions: Bruno Bettelheim and Psychoanalytic Development, edited by Nathan M. Szajnberg. Plenum Press, New York, 1992.

Bergman begins with the problems of talking differently. The Navajo conversational style, their pragmatics and syntax, differs from the Euro-American. Whereas Freud had to work with his patients to free associate, to become "free of" the reluctance to speak in non sequitur, the Navajo demonstrate a comfort with the latter in daily conversation. Direct statements or requests are considered rude, anathema, except for rare emergencies.

Bergman takes us through the travails he was presented with: mediating Navajo–white marital tangles; reuniting families whose members had been psychiatrically hospitalized; getting proper civil service positions and titles for the Navajo who were already performing the significant jobs; working with (occasionally against) the U.S. government to improve conditions; and humanizing the boarding schools. Finally, as an elegant example of how two cultures successfully interface when pursuing a common task—better education for the children—he demonstrates how the Navajo staff recognized that their bitter memories of their own boarding school stays resulted in their treating the children harshly, an example of what we would refer to psycho-analytically as identification with the aggressor.

Many of Bergman's examples have much to do with what happens when culture meets culture: with a marriage, between a tribe and American culture, between an analyst and his patients or co-workers. Bergman writes in a disarmingly simple style, belying the sophisticated process he engaged in. At the end of his chapter, we learn how he helped reinvigorate a community: in a cold school setting the parents built a native hogan so that the children would feel more at home. Bergman finishes his account, saying that he put himself out of work. But his work is carried on by the Navajo. This is also how a good analyst should feel at the end of a successful analysis: that the analysand develops greater autonomy and can do without the analyst.

INTRODUCTION

The Navajo are among the most studied people on earth. In order to hold all the published works describing Navajo culture, a library shelf would have to be at least 50 feet long (Werner *et al.*, 1983), and the most complete bibliography of Navajo topics in print in 1969 (Correll *et al.*, 1969) is 326 pages long. In 1966, psychiatrists as well as anthropologists had published work on the special needs as well as the strengths of the Navajo people (Kluckhohn and Leighton, 1946; Leighton and Leighton, 1966). On the other hand, no organized program of psychiatric care for this group of more than 100,000 people had ever been established prior to that time. It became my job to organize a Navajo mental health program then, and I came there almost directly from Bettelheim's Orthogenic School, where I had worked as a counselor during my psychiatric residency.

I was part of the Division of Indian Health (later, the Indian Health Service) of the United States Public Health Service. When I arrived, though no psychiatric program existed, there was a substantial and fairly comprehensive system of clinics and hospitals serving the Navajo people. It had been put together rapidly following the 1955 decision of Congress to take the responsibility for health care from the Bureau of Indian Affairs and assign it to the Public Health Service. At the time of this transfer, health conditions were so bad that the Public Health Service had concentrated at first on such major problems as the high infant mortality rate and the high prevalence of tuberculosis. These problems were not solved but were much smaller than they had been after a decade, and it was decided that the time had come to devote some resources to mental health (Bergman, 1983).

There were not many resources at first. I was not only the chief of the mental health program; I was also its only member. It was just as well that I did not have more than myself to manage at the time because despite the vast literature available to me, I had no way of understanding many of the practical necessities of doing psychiatric work there and only a little help in knowing where or how to begin. The area is vast: 17,200,000 acres—about the size of West Virginia—and occupies major parts of Arizona, New Mexico, and Utah. The population is spread more or less evenly over the land, and in 1966, paved roads were still far away from most people's homes (Navajo Nation Fax, 1988). The Navajo people were impoverished. The traditional Navajo reliance on raising livestock and the growth of the population in the first part of this century had led to overgrazing, and a poorly conceived and horribly administered government stock reduction policy in the 1930s had almost destroyed the old economy and had left nothing adequate in its place (Aberle, 1983). Faced with these daunting problems, I began to try to find my way.

Navajo medicine people teach their apprentices in arduous, personal discussions that usually last past the middle of the night (Kluckhohn and Wyman, 1940). So when I left the Orthogenic School 20 years ago and began to study the Navajo healers, I felt right at home. That is how Bruno Bettelheim taught us counselors: late-night staff meetings. One of the Navajos' suspicions of me was that I would be ignorant and literal minded from excessive reliance on books, which they regarded as dangerous to proper intellectual development. Books discourage improvement of memory. Real life is too personal and shifting to be described truthfully in anything but dialogue. I know that Dr. Bettelheim valued books, but he shared their opinion about the advantages of dialogue. In reviewing my work in the Southwest, it seems to me that I was constantly using what I had learned from Dr. Bettelheim—some of it from his written works but more of it from those arduous, personal discussions often lasting past the middle of the night, the Orthogenic School staff meetings. My account in this chapter is to describe my journey from the milieu of the Orthogenic School in a foreign land of emotionally troubled children to my sojourn among the Navajo people, a land of culturally jarred normal children and parents.

DIFFERENT WAYS OF TALKING

Navajo Belief: All Behavior Is Meaningful

When I first moved to the reservation, I was often puzzled by what the people around me were doing, but I carried with me Dr. Bettelheim's voice saying, "I only know three things, and one of them is that if I saw things the same way as the other person, I'd do the very same thing he's doing." It was not the usual way for white people to think about Indians. If the Indians behave oddly, it is easy to understand why: they behave that way because they are Indian. But in the staff room of the school, I had learned the habit of assuming that all behavior is meaningful and that I could understand the meaning if I worked hard enough at it, and so I came to realize the people—especially people at cultural boundaries—avoid noticing that they cannot understand each other. If something seems wrong, the fault is not with their inability to catch on, but with the other person being stupid or crazy or of a different culture. Generally, people think they understand everyone just fine, but that lots of people appear to behave senselessly—especially mental patients or people of a different culture.

Navajo Speech

In the beginning of my work as the psychiatrist for the Navajo Area of the Indian Health Service, my patients would show up, chatting amicably with family and friends. Then they would sit down with me and say nothing. I was used to mute people, but not people singling me out as the only one with whom they were mute. White co-workers, and even some Navajo ones, would reassure me that it was nothing personal: Indians were just like that—very silent. However, when I picked up Navajo hitchhikers as I drove around the reservation, they talked incessantly. Ultimately, I learned my patients considered me boorish and ignorant. They were treating me properly as a boor. Like the boor I seemed to be, I failed to get the idea. When people did talk—even the hitchhikers, their associations seemed psychotically loose. The younger people's conversations moved from subject to subject with what seemed sensible connections: they were adjusting to what they had learned were white ideas of how you should talk (Levy, 1963).

I am no longer sure how long it took me to catch on, but it was only after listening to Navajo people talk in chapter meetings that I really got the idea. The tribe is divided for political purposes into local units called chapters, which are self-governing by a process like town meetings. I was surprised at the first meeting by this business of loose associations. Someone would talk about the need for something to be done about the road to the chapter's well. Other people would nod in agreement, but the next speaker would talk about the rug auction. The supposedly laconic Indians went on talking for hours and hours and sooner or later all the threads of the discussion were taken up again.

Free Association and Non Sequitur

What is it that psychoanalytic free association is "free of"? One of Freud's main achievements was to help his patients overcome their reluctance to utter non sequitur that left them in the dark as to why something was coming to mind. European speech, unlike Navajo, has greater blindness to the nature of ordinary mental processes: it does not take good will, attentiveness, and understanding as much for granted. We claim frequently that we are paying attention to each other. If I want to tell a friend about my plans for a trip, and he is telling me about an interesting clinical case and happens to mention that his patient once lived in New York, it gives me the chance to say, "Speaking of New York . . ." I appear to demonstrate that I really was listening to his account when, in fact, I was just waiting to get in my two cents. If the friend were Navajo, I would not bother with the connection. It would seem strange to him anyhow. If I would like a *non-Indian* friend to give me a ride, I might say, "If you're going to be leaving soon, I wonder if you could take me along?" To a Navajo friend, I say, "It's a nice day." He might reply, "I'm going to town in a little while. Would you like to go along?" To a Navajo person, the white-style requests would sound demanding. Someone uncultured to Navajo ways would probably miss the Navajo form entirely or would feel that it was unpleasantly indirect.

Navajo and Direct Speech

But there is an additional reason for the subtlety. When this egalitarian tribe subsisted by hunting, gathering, raiding, and herding, cooperation was maintained among large networks of family and friends. In an emergency one needs to command cooperation. Therefore, direct requests for assistance are felt as compelling: only in emergencies can direct requests be granted without disorganizing resentment. One's inconvenience must be justified by the other's need and balanced by a memory or an expectation of being helped as readily by the other. Otherwise, direct requests are too heavy-handed. If I say, "It's a nice day" (wanting a ride) and my friend is too busy to give me a ride, he could say, "I was thinking of hauling water this afternoon." I would never mention my wish for a ride, because if I did, my friend would have to take me unless I convinced him that I really did not need to go, and it would be hard to do that without confusion and hurt feelings.

Until I learned about this, I made a fool of myself over and over. When I found myself severely anxious and baffled, I had a way of thinking about what was going on. Years before as a counselor at the Orthogenic School I had learned that I did not need to defend myself by blaming the children. Dr. Bettelheim suggested that I look at my behavior through the eyes of the child. What had I done that alarmed or interfered with what the child needed to do. While still in a panic, feeling as though I were crazy or stupid, starting to see the Navajo as crazy or stupid instead, I could calm down based on my past experience. I would assume that everyone was behaving intelligently based on what he or she thought the others were up to. We were misunderstanding each other to some extent. Although difficult to sort out, I knew that sorting was necessary and possible.

Eventually, I would sort out situations that other people thought were crazy. I was once referred a patient who the reservation medical doctors had come to hate. The patient made their lives miserable by coming to the clinic once or twice a day every day for months to complain bitterly that she was seriously ill and that they were not helping her. When I met her, it was clear that she was as angry and distrustful of the hospital and doctors as they were to her. A Navajo co-worker and I took several hours to talk with her. We began without coming to the point in the white way. Instead we followed the Navajo way of talking about who the three of us were and what friends and relatives we had in common, where we lived, and in general what we had been doing. In that context the story began to emerge.

About a year earlier she had come to the hospital to give birth to her first child. The labor had been complicated and she had been flown to a large hospital for specialized care, but she had never learned what exactly was wrong. It proved impossible to save the fetus, and after some time she was told that it was dead. The delay before the stillbirth was horrible for her, and afterward, no one told her why it had happened. It may be that the obstetrician thought he had told her through an interpreter,[1] but it was common for doctors to jump to conclusions about who translated what. The woman was eager to become pregnant again, but she was worried that there was something basically wrong with her that would prevent her from ever successfully bearing a child. Her menstrual periods had become irregular. She went back to her local hospital for advice. The doctor who saw her asked a nurse's aide to interpret, not realizing that an old disagreement between the women's families made it awkward for them to be talking: they neither liked nor trusted each other. Because the doctor asked her directly (in a non-Navajo style), the aide would not refuse the assignment or explain her difficulty. As far as the doctor heard, the only trouble was menstrual irregularity. He did not know about the stillbirth nor her fears of infertility. He prescribed birth control pills to regulate her cycle. The instructions as they got across were, "Take the pills until you bleed, then stop taking them for five days and then start over again." She followed the instructions. After about a week, she had some spotting in spite of the drug, and so she stopped it and bled for five days; when she started again, the same thing happened. When she went back to the hospital complaining that her period was still irregular, the doctor thought correctly that she was probably not using the pills properly and told her that she should be sure to take them as directed.

The patient could see easily that the doctor was not taking the problem very seriously; he thought she was too stupid or careless to take medicine properly. She did not know, however, that the white man's medicine depends on a correct history to reach a correct diagnosis. Traditional Navajo medicine people diagnose their patients without asking any questions. She *had* learned that the more startling the complaint, the more seriously the white doctors regard it. Since she felt they were not paying attention to her, she produced ever stranger and frightening complaints. After a few weeks of this, she and the clinic staff detested each other and no one knew what was happening. When we figured it all out and explained the irony of having taken birth control pills when she wanted to get pregnant again, this struck her as funny. It was a relief to her antagonists as well, and they were able to make peace.

NAVAJO–WHITE MARITAL TANGLES

Misunderstandings between Indian and non-Indian people in non-marital relationships became a mainstay of my practice, particularly Navajo–white marriages. Often underlying the spouses' complaints was a disagreement about how to spend time together, particularly on special occasions. Each would think that the other's preference revealed a lack of regard. Navajo people usually grow up in extended families with many people sharing the child care; they remain attached to groups of people as well as to individuals. If the couple is planning an anniversary, for example, usually the Navajo spouse will want to get together with lots of friends and relatives and the non-Navajo will suggest spending romantic time alone. Unfortunately, the Navajo spouse believes that the other is ashamed of him or her and does not want to have the family see them together. The non-Navajo concludes that the other does not feel that he or she is special and would rather be with other people. The couple may be sophisticated about both cultures, yet may not understand what is going on and be jealous (for non-Navajo) or hurt (for Navajo).

WITHIN-FAMILY NAVAJO TANGLES

Unraveling my own and other people's cross-cultural misunderstandings was a good preparation for a more difficult task: working out the tangles that Navajo families get into when cultural change interferes with traditional patterns of interaction. In one community where I worked over a number of years, several people in one extended family accused each other of witchcraft. They experienced an unusually high incidence of illness and other troubles. People who had cared for one another for years had become enemies. It was possible to trace much of what was wrong to one incident. The home community is in a remote and particularly traditional area. Only one member of the family had made his way in the off-reservation world. He was a noted silversmith, who earned a fairly regular cash income by selling his work and later by working in a jewelry store in Scottsdale, Arizona. The others subsisted by herding and collecting welfare assistance. The silversmith came home from the jewelry store one summer and invested his savings in sheep. He asked his brother to take care of them for the fall and winter. It was a particularly bad year and by the time he came back the following summer, his relative had eaten all his sheep. From his point of view, it would have been reasonable for them to eat some of them and to keep some of the lambs as their own, but as it was the money that he had earned by lonely, hard work far from home had been wiped out by his brother's carelessness and selfishness. The family thought him selfish, since he easily earned what seemed like vast amounts of money while they had almost none. They were shocked that he begrudged them his sheep, which he appeared to have acquired so easily. They did not see that the disagreement was about the balance and reciprocity between earner and traditional subsistence herder. We could repair some of the damage and reach some new understandings, but many of them remained angry and suspicious.

Unfortunately, there were many such cases as more people worked for wages. Often the outcome was a split of the family and realignment of friends and relatives into factions in and outside of the cash economy. No doubt the traditional (noncash) subsistence will gradually become rare.

CONFLICTS WITH THE CIVIL SERVICE

From Each According to His Ability

Most Navajo wage workers are employed by government agencies in relatively low-level positions, but they usually knew what was going on in the agencies. When I went from the Orthogenic School to my new office in Window Rock, Arizona, the Navajo capital, my ideas of how work forces should be constituted, trained, and supervised had become strongly Bettelheimian (as is said in Navajo). The most important work should be done by those most qualified to do it; they should receive the training and support needed to do the job. I supposed that almost anyone would agree with that statement. Indeed, the civil service system officially states that it exists to ensure that outcome. But from my Orthogenic School training I could pay attention to what was happening instead of to the myth of what was happening.

The Paranoid Mailbox Man Becomes a Clinician

Shortly after I came on the job, I was invited to meet the public health nurses. Since I was the first psychiatrist to work there, no one (including me) knew precisely what I was going to be doing. One of the nurses asked if I would consult about staff members' mental health problems. I said I would and asked what kind of problems she had in mind. She said that one of the drivers (interpreters) seemed to be paranoid. A few days before, she had asked him to make a set of mailboxes for the field health office. He had built and labeled them. When asked why he had assigned himself the lowest box, he responded that this reflected his status. When I asked her who had the lowest status, she said that there was no such thing. I met that man as soon as possible and was as impressed by him in person as I had been secondhand. In general he and his fellow drivers were an impressive group. They did most of the field health work. The nurses, who did not know their way around, could not speak the language, and understood little about their patients' drivers, rode along and legitimized the drivers.

By civil service rules, people could not be hired as guides and interpreters, nor at that time could people be hired as paraprofessional health workers. But there was a civil service slot for drivers.[2] So these men were hired as drivers, even though drivers were not needed: the word "interpreter" was enclosed in parenthesis so that it appeared that regulations were not violated.

In those days, when I went out to visit mentally ill people and their families, my situation was similar to that of the public health nurses. I could not speak the language, but I could see that my presence made people nervous. The driver (interpreter) tried to calm them down, pretending that I was talking "through" the interpreter. No simple description of what was happening among us is possible, but when it worked well, it was a collaboration between someone ("the driver") who understood the language and the manifest situation and someone (myself) who could help him think about the different levels of meaning of what was said and done. Since my presence was complicating, and on-the-spot supervision had its limitations (as well as advantages), I thought that I could dispense with my immediate presence. After more than a year of struggling with the personnel system, I helped set a precedent to hire people to do what they were already doing and to help them to learn to do it better, that is, to be the mental health clinician.

Harry Bilagody, who made the mailboxes, was one of the first three mental health workers in the Indian Health Service. The model I had in mind for that position was that of the Orthogenic School counselor (Bettelheim, 1974). Like the counselors, the mental health workers were chosen for both their capacity to understand patients' needs and for their capacity to learn and to grow. At the school, some fellow counselors had been psychiatrists and psychologists, some had not. There seemed to be no correlation between professional training and how we did our work. In psychiatric hospitals, as a doctor, I had done the easy and clean work and had gotten most of the credit. At the school, we all did the dirty work and doing the dirty work well was recognized as essential to the children's healing. The Navajo patients, like the children at the school, were frequently in desperate straits. They needed more than psychotherapy. In the Navajo mental health program, we believed that meeting the patients' basic needs was essential to their getting better. Most of them had been subject to years of contemptuous treatment by the petty tyrants, reservation bureaucracies, both Indian and white. It was a strong indictment of the overall system that our program was regarded by many people as a marvel of humanitarianism simply because we treated people with normal courtesy. Unfortunately, it was hard to maintain a standard of ordinary decency and common sense in the midst of the fossilized agencies. A century of condescension was hard to change or to live down. The mental health workers were unusual people, less prone to the identification with the aggressor, that is, not mistreating other Navajo people, which is common in reservation offices. However, it took constant attention to the attitudes and relationships among ourselves to keep it that way. For it was often against regulations for people to act decently: we were permitted to drive 40 miles to ask a family to visit a patient in the hospital, but to drive them to the hospital was an offense punishable by a month's pay.

I had the support of my Public Health Service superior, Emery Johnson, M.D., in draining and redraining the encroaching sea of institutionalized hostility. Like Bettelheim, he worked to ensure that the organization he ran spent its energy on achieving its purpose instead of on maintaining and aggrandizing itself. Once, an executive of another agency asked Dr. Johnson to stop me from taking part in a trial. When the man said, "I can't understand how a federal officer can testify against the government," Dr. Johnson answered, "You don't understand. He's not testifying against the government. He's testifying for the Indians. If the government is against the Indians, that's too bad."

Reuniting Families

In effect, parts of the government and many other entrenched institutions were against the Indians, and the mental health workers often got in the middle. In our early years, we devoted considerable effort to bringing Navajo mental patients home from the state hospitals where many had spent years in misery and loneliness. It was important to the family to accept and to cope with the burdens of caring for the long-missing person. Katherine Hillis, another of the original three mental health workers, once visited such a family and explained to them how they would receive the patient's social security check to help pay his expenses. The family responded that it would not go far because the prices in the trading post were so high. In those days it was common for Navajo people to receive government checks at the local trading post, endorse them, and never see any cash at all. It was all applied to their account with the trader who thereafter had a monopoly on their business. Navajo who could not speak English were afraid to try to cash their checks elsewhere; some did not realize that it was possible. Ms. Hillis suggested that this family cash their checks at another store and spoke to the manager. He had never thought of doing business with the Navajo, could see the possibilities, and agreed to cash checks without charge or obligation. We were pleased that prices at the local trading posts came down; and we believed that change also improved the mental health of the community.

Acculturation: The Navajo and the Psychoanalyst

In the early years we spent one day a week meeting with each other. This took much time and resources. Some traveled 180 miles to attend. There was some individual training and supervision, but most of it was done in group meetings modeled on Orthogenic School staff meetings. We had detailed discussion of incidents that were hard to understand or had gone wrong. We tried to feel our way into the perceptions of all the participants.

I introduced the idea that unconscious reactions can interfere with therapeutic work. For example, the Navajo staff had struggled to reach their position of relative autonomy in the white system. Some of their patients were envious, which, in turn, provoked the staff member's guilt. One confronted her fellow Navajo with long-winded, critical lectures about how the patients could better themselves. As she became in touch with her guilt, and talked with us, she could drop these hostile educational efforts. On the other hand, the same person helped me see myself through Navajo eyes. She pointed out that when I went into a hogan to visit people I had never met, I would introduce myself and state the purpose of my visit in the first sentence as I came in the door. She explained that I came across as an alarming loudmouth who was probably going to try to push people around. I learned to come in quietly, to find a place to sit, to talk about something impersonal, then to introduce ourselves, including where we were from and who was related to whom, who I knew who might be related to them. Ten or fifteen minutes after I arrived, I could tell why I had come. My informant speculated, "You want to tell them right away because you think you need an excuse to be there. In the Navajo way you don't need an excuse to visit someone."

I learned about signs and symbols of power. Once, when we were bringing a consultant to Window Rock to conduct a special training session, Mr. Bilagody, the one who first taught me about sensitivity to status, asked if we were going to give out certificates to those who completed the session. "It's only a week," I said. "I've seen certificates for shorter courses than that," Harry answered. "What would you do with a certificate?" I asked. "Frame it and put it on my wall. So people will respect me a little more." "But I don't have any certificates on my wall and people respect me," I said peevishly. He responded, "Everyone knows you have diplomas and certificates, and so your now putting them up has class." We got the certificates.

We also got diplomas. After I became national chief of mental health programs for the Indian Health Service, we set up mental health worker positions. The paraprofessional could attend college and graduate school while working for the government. As a result, a number of Indians entered the mental health professions.

The Boarding Schools

On my last day at the Orthogenic School, Dr. Bettelheim asked me what I was going to do on the reservation. I said that I did not know, but that I had learned that here were close to 30,000 Navajo children attending poorly run boarding schools and I hoped to be able to improve the situation (Emerson, 1983). He told me that a long time ago he had some acquaintance with the government's Indian school system and had been unable to influence it. "Good luck," he said. I spent a major part of my time in the next ten years looking for that luck.

Administrative Sabotage

At first I thought that it was going to be relatively easy. Contrary to my expectation, the school administrators seemed eager for suggestions. They had seen my kind many times before and had learned that the best way to get rid of us was to agree with us. So I was invited to visit, consult, and learn about the reservation's many boarding schools. I had heard that they were bad. For at least 50 years, the Indian schools had attracted the alarmed attention of child welfare organizations and experts. Many had suggested that the basic trouble was that the children were living in institutions instead of being at home. I had just come from a fine children's institution. I did not share that prejudice, but I also had very definite ideas about what was needed to make a boarding school worth living in. These schools did not come close.

They were new and shiny. Most had been built after World War II. Before that time, most parents had successfully opposed the government attempts to enroll their children. During the depression, there was not much money for schools. With the war, many Navajo were in uniform, others worked in two defense plants nearby the reservation. At that time, the formerly prosperous herding economy had been destroyed by over-grazing and stock reduction, an unsuccessful government program, through bad planning and mismanagement, had deprived many people of their livelihood. Those who had learned English and had seen the outside world during the war came home convinced that getting a white person's education was economically necessary. During the 20 years following the war, the percentage of Navajo children attending school went from negligible to almost 100%, about half in boarding schools (Emerson, 1983).

Reasons for Boarding Schools

The official explanation for boarding was that the roads were inade-quate to transport the students back and forth daily. This made no sense. People were adept at getting around. When the Navajo started Headstart schools throughout the reservation, children even in the most inaccessible places were bused daily in Headstart vans. When those children turned six, many were sent to boarding schools. No one seemed to notice the contradiction. There were instances of children enrolled in the boarding schools who lived near children attending day school. Building and operating the dormitories was much more expensive than buying school buses, running them, and paving roads.

The real reasons seemed simple and unpleasant. Most families did not have enough to eat. Children were fed in boarding schools. The children could have been fed less expensively at home. But to increase welfare support to so many able-bodied people on welfare would have meant an apparent change in the principles of welfare distribution and official recognition of how bad the reservation economy was. Beyond that, closing boarding schools would have worsened the reservation economy: the schools were the major employer of Navajo people. Most had grown accustomed to the boarding schools and few wanted to question their existence.

The children led miserable lives. School started for most at six. Some families, in order to have a younger child cared for, would lie about his or her age, sending them to boarding school at four years of age. The school buildings were new and well-maintained, the classrooms well-equipped, but the dormitories looked like warehouses. The architecture, designed in Washington, was unsuited to the climate, the terrain, and the culture. Indian schools look just the same from Oklahoma to Alaska, and to Navajo children they look nothing like home and a lot like jail. Most of the dorms were designed to house 180 children, and most were beyond capacity. There was a large living room, a large playroom, and two large dorm "wings," rooms divided into partially separate cubicles each with two double bunks. Each child's private space was his or her bunk, the child could not hang wall decorations next to that bunk, and had no privacy anywhere ever.

The dorm staff was as inadequate as the buildings, despite and sometimes because of being Navajo. There was usually one dorm staff on duty per 80 children. At that ratio, the best surrogate parent in the world could have done little good, and these people were not even supposed to try to be surrogate parents. The Bureau of Indian Affairs Branch of Education officially mandated that the dorm staff, although called instructional aides, were to maintain order and wash the floors. They were not to counsel. If a child was in distress, they were to refer him or her to a teacher counselor, who often could not speak Navajo.

Usually the instructional aides did try to comfort and help the children, but they did not do it well. Most of them had attended boarding school as children. They had convinced themselves that the awful experiences of their school days had been good for them. For instance, until the late 1960s, children were punished for speaking their own language. The instructional aides thought that it was impressive not to know Navajo: they would pretend that even when their English was poor. The children were marched everywhere they went, kept quiet at all times, and severely punished for infractions. Many Navajo men told me that Marine boot camp was easy because it was so much nicer than boarding school. After two or three years of effort, we tried to soften the regimentation. Instead, the entrenched bureaucracy was replaced with chaos. Supposedly following our suggestions, rules were mostly abandoned. *Devil's Island* became *Lord of the Flies*. Bullying, previously a quiet problem because of the few adult staff, became a noisy and ever-present problem.

At the different schools, ineffectual plans were instituted and new forms of regimentation were introduced under the guise of pseudoscientific psychology. One white master's-level counseling graduate, the head of guidance (as the dorm administrators were called) at a large school, instituted a scheme she called behavior modification. Each time a child made his or her bed without being told, or smiled politely and said good morning in English, or did any of a number of other things, a reward, a slip of paper, was handed out. The children with the most slips of paper at the end of the year would be given a wonderful reward. The reward was not specified, but it was hinted that it would be a trip to Disneyland. Naturally, the child bullies stole or extracted most slips of paper. This they did with impunity because there were so many children and so few aides that the aides could not tell the children apart and did not know to whom they had given slips. Justice was served in the end. The funds for the project disappeared. There was no reward.

Even after the rule against speaking Navajo disappeared (along with all the other rules), Navajo was not the language of even the beginner classrooms. Teachers who could not speak Navajo tried to teach children who could not speak English how to read and write it. The children were bewildered by their so-called education. They felt that someone was crazy. The healthier ones knew it was not them: they thought of the white world as stupid and hostile. Less healthy or secure children concluded that there was something seriously wrong with themselves: they were so incapable that there was no chance in life for them. Since they were away from home most of the time, they had few opportunities to speak Navajo with anyone who had more than a child's competence in the language. In the school they failed to learn to speak English well even if they stayed 12 or 13 years. So there are two or three generations of Navajo people, many of whom speak no language fluently, and their speech made it sound like they did not think very well either.

Changing the System

Two schools, a tiny minority, did better. At the Rough Rock Demonstration School and at the Rock Point School, children were taught to read and write Navajo while being taught to speak the foreign language, English. The results were good and the method has been spread to several other schools in the intervening 20 years. The person most responsible for that improvement was Wayne Holm, the director of the Rock Point Community School. The Rock Point School, with which I was associated for years, improved their dorm life while pursuing another basic solution: they helped the families feed their children, closed the dorms, and bought buses. I, as a former counselor, concentrated on the dorms at other schools. Few regarded the dorms as important. When I met with the dorm people and told them that before I came to Navajo I had worked as an instructional aide in a school in Chicago where the instructional aides were as important as the teachers, they were amazed.

It did not do much good. I did not get to any one school very often. Even when I made some impression, the aides felt overwhelmed and discouraged by the number of children. So I tried to find ways to change the system. In 1967, I was invited to speak on the psychological problems of boarding schools at a meeting sponsored by the Committee on Indian Health of the American Academy of Pediatrics. I knew that the national leadership of the Bureau of Indian Affairs and its branch of education would be there. I was enraged with them. I wrote as strong a statement as I could. Reading it to myself, I found new reserves of indignation and strengthened the attack. Afterward, the acting commissioner of Indian Affairs approached me smiling. He had enjoyed my talk. It was all too true. "Unfortunately, we can't do anything about it," he said. "Would you join us for lunch?"

I kept trying. One effort lasted for a while. In September 1968, I read in the *Navajo Times* that Secretary of the Interior, Morris Udall, would be coming to the Tribal Fair, accompanied by his assistant secretary for Indian Affairs, Will Rogers, Jr. I had the idea that Mr. Rogers was someone who could make things happen. On the day of the visit, I stationed myself where the official party was likely to pass. I shoved my way through the crowd and handed him my two papers on boarding schools. He read the papers and sent them down through channels demanding a response. The Bureau of Indian Affairs proposed a model dormitory project to be operated jointly with the Indian Health Service. I would be in charge.

It took several years for it to happen. The Special Senate Subcommittee on Indian Education, set up by Robert Kennedy, later chaired by his brother, and with Walter Mondale's interest, appropriated the funds.

In the spring of 1971, I walked into the little children's dorm at the Bureau of Indian Affairs school at Toyei, Arizona. I was the new boss and the few instructional aides had gathered in the living room to meet me. We would hire more. Soon after I arrived, the 200 children came back from eating lunch in the dining room—a separate building. As they entered the children removed their shoes. I asked why. One of the aides said, "No one is allowed in here with shoes on. They make marks on the floors." Noticing that adult staff wore shoes, I took my shoes off. After some discussion of who rules apply to, I asked whether the floors or the children were more important. The aides responded cordially that the answer to that depended on whether I was really in charge: would the school administration criticize the aides for listening to me? By now, the children had disappeared into the dorm wings. I asked what they were doing. "They're taking a nap." "No they're not," I said. "They're bouncing on their beds and whispering to one another." "Oh," said one of the aides and went into the boys wing and yelled, "Stop bouncing and whispering! Fall asleep!" The others explained that a first grade teacher had complained that the children were falling asleep in class and had demanded that a noon nap be instituted. I said that sleep was the children's criticism of the teacher and that it was the teacher's problem to solve with them in the classroom. The next day, the teacher berated one of the aides because she had heard that the nap had been abolished. I intervened, repeating that the children are more important than floors or even teachers.

I found myself as a white man in the awkward yet necessary position of asking the adults to care for the children more than the adults cared for what they thought were the white man's rules.

Our model project involved just the dorm personnel. This would complement Wayne Holm's changes in teaching methods. The dorm building was terrible. We had no money for construction, but the dorm parents, as we called them, were tribal members and, therefore, had a right to reservation trees. That summer with newly hired staff members, we went to the forest, and felled trees and built a hogan in the dorm. When the children arrived, they found a more familiar place they could go into any time they liked. Constructing the hogan as a group established a pattern of cooperation and cohesion along Navajo lines. Two of the house parents were talented painters. They covered the walls of the living room and the corridors with murals of Navajo life and mythology. We asked the children to decide on the colors for their dorm wing cubicle walls. The many different, mostly very bright colors improved the feeling of the setting.

Much of that first summer was spent in training sessions. When I asked the dorm parents what was the purpose of the school, their original answers focused on discipline. After many hours of discussion many confessed that they hated school because of the discipline. It had done more harm than good. Once that barrier was breached, there came a flood of anger. People told story after story of what had happened to them in boarding school. Only then were they ready to talk about what education should be. Ideas about how the children should be cared for still did not come easily at first, because it was still hard for the staff to get over the feeling that this was school and that at school common sense did not apply. Although many of them were parents and good ones, in the school setting it was second nature to look for some culturally inconsistent white rule to tell them what to do.

On the other hand, I had my own rigid ideas about how everything had to be native Navajo. The children and the house parents corrected me. I told the kids that they could name their dorm wings and their groups. The boys and the girls groups met and promptly reached a consensus. The boys, to my satisfaction, named themselves the Mustangs and their home, Mustang Lodge. The girls said that their domain was to be called Hollywood and that they were the Stars. I almost vetoed that before the house parents convinced me that I should keep my word about letting the children choose freely. I said that I thought that it would be better if the girls chose names that were closer to their own identity. One of the house parents asked if I wanted to keep all of my own old traditions. Although Jewish, I had no desire to keep kosher. I got the point.

RÉCHERCHÉ

Looking back on my years with Indian schools now, it seems to me that the efforts to make a difference worked well in some times and places. Our bothering the system probably humanized it to some extent and may have hastened the demise of the boarding schools. Most Navajo and other Indian children attend day schools, which have plenty of problems of their own, but the cast of characters has changed. By now most of the main players, good or bad, are Indian. The day of the white do-gooder is pretty much over and the problems of the present are left in the hands of Indian mental health professionals, many of whom are descendants of Bettelheim's Orthogenic School.

Notes

1. The percentage of patients who did not speak English was very high in those days, but it was civil service policy that no one was to be hired as an interpreter. It was assumed that anybody who could more or less speak both languages could be used to talk to a patient, just as a telephone could be used to talk to someone somewhere else. That idea was crucial in what had gone wrong. People are not telephones.
2. People could be hired as interpreters to work in foreign countries, but the rules forbade people within the United States from being paid to translate the language of their own communities.

References

Aberle, D. (1983). Navajo economic development. *Handbook of North American Indians* 10:641–658 (Smithsonian Institution, Washington, DC).

Bergman, R. (1983). Navajo health services and projects. *Handbook of North American Indians* 10:672–678 (Smithsonian Institution, Washington, DC).

Correll, J., Watson, E., and Brugge, D. (1969). *Navajo Bibliography with Subject Index.* Window Rock, AZ: The Navajo Nation.

Emerson, G. (1983). Navajo education. *Handbook of North American Indians* 10:659–671 (Smithsonian Institution, Washington, DC).

Kluckhohn, C., and Leighton, D. (1946). The Navajo. Cambridge, MA: Harvard University Press.

Kluckhohn, C., and Wyman, L. (1940). An introduction to Navajo chant practice. *Memoirs of the American Anthropological Association* 53.

Leighton, A., and Leighton, D. (1966). Elements of psychotherapy in Navajo religion. *Psychiatry* 4:515–523.

Levy, J. (1963). *Navajo Health Concepts and Behavior.* Window Rock, AZ: United States Public Health Service.

Navajo Nation FAX 88. (1988). Window Rock, AZ: Navajo Nation.

Werner, O., Manning, A., and Begishe, K. (1983). A taxonomic view of the traditional Navajo universe. *Handbook of North American Indians* 10:579–591 (Smithsonian Institution, Washington, DC).

7

Secrecy and Privacy in a Psychodynamic Milieu

The Individual and His Community

NATHAN M. SZAJNBERG

THIS LAST CHAPTER teases apart two confounding issues in contemporary society: the difference between secrecy and privacy and the balance between privacy and a sense of integration with one's community. The setting within which this chapter explores these issues is the mental hospital—a community, for better or worse, where it is often a challenge to seek privacy, and where staff secrecy can be corrosive.

I discuss developmental levels of secrecy, leading up to privacy, a simple sense of solitude, as Bettelheim put it. The latter, privacy, has had a waxing and waning history in Western thought. Perhaps the value of privacy and the need for it has passed: the adolescent with perpetually earmuffed Walkman headphones, listening to heavy metal music, may be blocking out the adult world not for privacy, but to commune with the thousands of adolescent compatriots, who, the teenager fancies, may be listening in also. The magnetism of crowded discos or street corners* may be moving back to the public expression of private activities portrayed by Brueghel. But even if privacy is a passing phase in American culture, it is worth studying for what it means or meant to us, and possibly so that we may learn where we are heading.

---

*William Whyte (1988). *City.* New York: Doubleday.

NATHAN M. SZAJNBERG • 24 Chapman Road, West Hartford, Connecticut 06107.

Educating the Emotions: Bruno Bettelheim and Psychoanalytic Development, edited by Nathan M. Szajnberg. Plenum Press, New York, 1992.

Further, what is the balance between privacy and a sense of community? The latter is severely attenuated in secular, heterogeneous American culture. Communities are now rarely centered around the white-spired church or the synagogue, nor around the workplace. To a great extent, our living communities are determined by income—one's neighbor earns about the same as other neighbors. Such common fiscal bonds are weak, for they do not embody personal, moral values, such as how to live one's life or raise one's children, let alone to live in a more heterogeneous populace. Some cities try to rectify the problems of community homogeneity by busing children, as if children could solve the problems of developing a more heterogeneous community after their elders have failed.

Developing a sense of integration with one's community, what Goethe* discussed in his autobiography, has lain fallow in much of psychoanalytic literature. This chapter only begins to touch on this issue, suggesting that there need not be opposition between an autonomous individual and a sense of belonging to one's community. It is hoped that this chapter on privacy, as this book, will be a step toward developing a greater sense of community.

INTRODUCTION

A long-term psychiatric unit is purposefully an odd place. It is drastically different from the everyday world. The latter is complex: we change our physical and psychological settings or roles as we move from home to work to recreation, from being a parent to being an employee or employer or colleague. In a psychoanalytically oriented milieu, we soften external responsibilities such as paying bills, caring for children, and working in order to permit patients to refocus on their inner lives.

The Milieu

The first purpose of such an odd setting is clinical—to help disturbed patients find better lives. However, a second purpose is to serve as a social laboratory, just as the analytic consulting room—that other odd, rarefied dialectical setting—serves as a laboratory for learning about man's inner world. In the very controlled setting of a psychiatric institution, we can learn about how individuals relate to each other and to their community. There is a long-standing tradition for this including Goffman's compassionate critique of individuals in a state insane asylum, to Maxwell-Jones's

---

*Johan Wolfgang von Goethe (1974). *The Autobiography of Johann Wolfgang von Goethe.* Chicago: University of Chicago Press.

Britishly cool outline of what makes a therapeutic community, to Bettelheim's lifework on milieu therapy for children. It is possible to extrapolate from these settings to learn about our own society. Foucault (1973) taught us about our intolerance of insanity in particular, ironically since the Enlightenment, by studying the evolution of insane asylums.

In this chapter, I will focus on one area of tension in contemporary society—the relationship between secrecy and privacy, and, by extension, between private and public and between the individual and his community. I suggest that the intrapsychic tension can be played out within an individual's intimate community. And a mental hospital community, for better or worse, is intimate. Therefore, I will explore these psychological concepts—secrecy and privacy—within the arena of the psychiatric milieu.

Our Ambiguous Definitions of Secrecy and Privacy

There is ambiguity in definitions of secret and private that reflect our psychological cloudiness in distinguishing them. The root for private is from Latin, *privatus*, "apart from the state, deprived of office, of or belonging to oneself" (Webster's, 1971). But the definitions muddle matters as we read further. The first definition of private is "intended for or restricted to the use of a particular person or group or class of persons." Yet its third definition is "secret," listed as a synonym! The first two definitions of secret support our daily lay use: "1. kept from knowledge or view, concealed, hidden . . . 2. remote from human frequentation or notice." For the psychoanalyst, the second definition may refer not only to geographic remoteness but also to the anomie that can be found in the confines of a bustling city. Both of these definitions capture the idiomatic "under one's hat," "close to one's chest," "*entre nous*," "within these four walls," "for your eyes only," "under wraps," "buttoned up," or "holding one's tongue." But surprisingly, the dictionary lists "genital" as a synonym for secret, when colloquial American speech would be *private* parts.

Because the dictionary underlines the ambiguity, runs counter to common usage, we need turn to a psychological analysis to understand the distinction between secret and private. Vignettes from psychodynamic milieus help us to differentiate these as states of mind and to place the capacity for secrecy and privacy as a developmental accomplishment. And the milieu demonstrates how such states of mind are played out in the interpersonal realm of a community. If the milieu is a good holding environment, as a patient moves through regressive phases (and this may occur repeatedly and microscopically in one day as well as macroscopically over an extended stay), we can best understand such regression in developmental terms.

Indeed, I will try to persuade the reader that the capacity to keep a secret is a significant developmental achievement: it does not come "naturally" and it can be facilitated. Even in a psychotic individual, it represents a way station en route to a bounded self-representation; that is, the ability to feel one's boundaries as a person. However, secrecy (as distinctly opposed to privacy) among the milieu's staff results in disruption and unrest in the milieu. The milieu therapist (nurse, caretaker, therapist) must feel free to maintain privacy, while abstaining from keeping secrets from his or her colleagues and the patients.

As a thought experiment, we can tentatively articulate the psychological characteristics of the secret:

1. The secret is a valued bit of external knowledge, which can be internalized.
2. The secret-keeper must feel that he and at least one other (the potential secret-seeker) and even onlookers need to be aware that a secret exists, even though the latter are not aware of its (valuable) content.
3. One creates an intrapsychic, teasing tension that this secret knowledge can be lovingly shared or, conversely, hostilely withheld. There is also another tension: if the secret is "guessed" against the keeper's wishes, one's ego boundaries are threatened. The intrapsychic tension is played out in the community.

I will start with the disruptive nature of secrets that are kept among the staff, which was my impetus for writing this chapter. In the second part of the chapter, I will observe the differential reaction of the milieu of the two kinds of secret-keepers, staff versus patients. I will offer vignettes that place secrecy on a developmental line leading to privacy. This, I hope, will help us derive a psychologically clearer distinction between secrecy and privacy. I will close with examples that distinguish between requests for so-called privacy in some patients who have not yet developed a consistent psychological capacity for doing so: instead, there are underlying feelings of poor self-regard and the need to keep this *secret* from others. In contrast are such patients who have developed a sense of privacy, the ability to enjoy simple solitude.

SECRECY AMONG THE MILIEU STAFF: DESTRUCTIVE CONSEQUENCES

Others have described how disagreements among a staff will disrupt the patients' community. Stanton and Schwartz (1954) wrote from a sociological perspective. From a psychological perspective, Searles (1965) wrote that a psychotic patient's projections of his or her disrupted inner world can result in fragmentation and disagreement among caretakers. The patient, unable to articulate an early experience, communicates it by raising certain feelings in the staff, what can be technically referred to as a form of the repetition compulsion. As such, it must be recognized and analyzed in order for the therapeutic setting to return to equilibrium. In fact it is as if the patient were saying (if only he or she could put it into words), "This is how embattled, disrupted my inner world feels. How well can you handle these polarized, warring feelings?"

This general principle can be applied to concealment among a staff. It has two sources: the idiosyncratic need everyone has to some degree to maintain secrecy, and the countertransference, which represents the milieu therapists' identifying with the patient's need for secrecy creating chaos in the milieu.

The secret withheld is thought to be crucial and directly related to the milieu's functioning. In this sense, this information differs qualitatively from something held privately, which, although it can be shared with others, is indirectly or benignly related to the functioning of the milieu. Often, what is held cryptically is a hostile act under the guise of privacy.

For instance, for some months the "secret" of an alleged extramarital affair between two senior staff members was kept by their close circle of friends. During this time, two psychotic patients allegedly had intercourse "surreptitiously" on one occasion, despite the usually cautious attention of the staff. In addition, several female patients began to sleep in various conference rooms or living areas, rather than in their own bedrooms. The staff, who called this "sleeping around," were puzzled by it and felt overwhelmed at trying to keep up with who was sleeping where at night. Because of their need to repress their knowledge about the senior staff, the milieu staff repressed their own parapraxis, while revealing to others that the staff knew preconsciously why patients were "sleeping around." Other patients stayed awake and vigilant during much of the night.

The closely held secret was known in fact by many staff members. Yet, they would not tell each other that they knew. One major reason, cited in retrospect, was that this was a "private affair" that lay outside the realm of the milieu. One new staff member was shocked to see the two in an alleged amorous embrace at an off-unit party. When she tried to discuss what she had seen with a colleague, she was encouraged to keep it secret. This continued for several months. Only after the two involved resigned did the staff openly disclose and discuss the affair and realize its widespread effects on the unit. After the staff discussion and without needing to reveal details to patients, there was no more "sleeping around."

This vignette highlights two characteristics. First, how the claim to privacy was used to vindicate the secret. Paradoxically, many staff members knew about the affair, while denying that it was rather publicly known. Second, how the secret's existence and effect on the patients was denied. It is difficult to describe to the reader the almost palpable release of tension among the staff and patients when the "secret" was openly disclosed among the staff. In the second example, the same appeal to privacy was used to safeguard information allegedly vital to the milieu.

A new staff member, who was anxious about whether she could work well in a psychodynamic milieu, called the clinical director aside secretly to say that she knew that a staff member was thinking of leaving. She presented the information implying that the staff member was pivotal to the existence of the unit. (In fact, he was not.) Yet, she would not say who the person was for doing so would reveal a confidence. Ambivalent, she felt that if she did reveal the identity, either the person could be convinced to stay or the director would have enough warning to recruit a new staff member. Her final appeal was that a person's leaving was his or her private matter. She denied that the secret could have any significant impact on the unit, but she did whisper it to her colleagues.

We can speculate that the fact of having a secret helped this insecure person feel valuable to the milieu. In fact, the man who was going to leave had been disaffected for some time; some of his colleagues had hoped that he would leave. Nevertheless, the staff made no conscious connection between this and the now widespread secret that someone valuable might leave. Instead, they reacted with anxiety that his leaving would jeopardize the unit. Their anxiety lent a desperate air to the milieu, which could be best described as an attitude in both staff and patients that one had better do what one could today, because disaster will befall one at some unknown moment. Once the staff member left, the rest of the staff experienced a sense of relief.

SECRETS AND BOUNDARIES

If you can have a secret, you can have boundaries. Ultimately I am referring to ego boundaries, but developmentally they are preceded by body boundaries (Hoffer, 1949). Both ego- and body-boundary formation can be manifested in the milieu in terms of doors, walls, windows, or, as in the next case, being moved from one psychiatric unit to another.

This vignette reveals the ambivalence and resulting ambiguity about boundaries: how we feel vulnerable when boundaries are poorly felt. The example involves a staff-held secret, but also reflects how a secret may represent feelings evoked by the patient in the staff.

A young woman was transferred to a psychodynamic milieu from another unit, primarily because a boy on the other unit attempted to rape her. This woman reacted to the transfer with ambivalence: she was both resistant yet relieved once transferred. The milieu staff was aware of the reasons for the transfer.

Following transfer, however, "secret" correspondence and telephone calls continued between the two patients with demands from the young man (with his therapist's explicit encouragement) that he should visit this young woman to "work things out." The secret was ill-kept. Notes were put on a elevator and were "discovered" by another patient or a staff member, who sometimes delivered the note. Furthermore, telephone calls had to be connected through the nursing station. Even after the staff openly discussed how frightening it was for this young woman to have been nearly raped and to continue to have contact with this fellow, male staff, in particular, had difficulty intercepting their communications. Intellectually, the staff recognized that the young woman, who suffered from poor body integrity (and poor ego boundaries), clearly needed to be on a different unit. Yet they effectively denied the protective boundary, the walls, the *Reizschutz*, between these two patients.

The staff's difficulty in maintaining a boundary for this patient reflected her own boundary ambiguity, as it was evoked in the staff and re-created in the milieu. Evidence for this ambiguity came from both her individual psychotherapy and the milieu. In sessions, we learned that the young woman both feared and yearned for an attacking sexual intercourse: from her need to merge with someone; from her need to feel charged and excited to enliven the deadness of her spirit. Prior to hospitalization, we knew that she had been raped by different men, yet had acted seductively in vulnerable situations. The male staff remarked to each other (and eventually to her) about her seductiveness. She was not conscious of such behavior. In addition, early in her stay she broached the milieu's boundary by telephoning former boyfriends and shouting out of the windows for illicit reunions with them, some of whom, she said, had previously attacked her. Her Romeos, lacking balconies, carried on from the street below.

TOWARD PRIVACY AMONG THE STAFF

Keeping secrets represents at least tentative ego boundaries. At times, these can be weakened. Then, the staff may feel that they can keep nothing secret—and ultimately private—from the milieu.

Bettelheim (1973) describes the psychotic patient's capacity to hone in on the therapist's personal feelings, insofar as these feelings have something to do with the patient's life. This ability appears uncanny at times, but simply bespeaks the degree to which the institutionalized psychotic patient feels so dependent upon his caretakers (and so uninvested in the matters of the usual demands of social life in the outside world—a job, school, shopping) that he concentrates his energy on assessing the moods of those upon whom he relies. For instance, a patient may be aware that a staff member is thinking of a vacation before the latter announces the fact because of the patient's vulnerability to abandonment.

Some staff may react to this with the sense that, in the milieu, they cannot maintain ego boundaries and the capacity for secrecy and privacy which this entails. Yet, the key is that the patient will be sensitive to those feelings of the staff that are directly related to the patient's caretaking. By its very nature, a secret as I have operationally defined it is a bit of information about the milieu that is valuable to the milieu's functioning as a caretaking environment.

This does not necessarily hold true for privacy, as I believe the following vignette will demonstrate. A staff therapist, sensitive to the issue of secrets and their pathological effect on patients, returned from an exasperating vacation. Anticipating impending marital problems, she went on vacation with the unconscious or preconscious hope that those problems would be resolved. While on a canoe trip, she met with several unpleasant experiences, including a bear prowling through the campgrounds. She returned and announced to both staff and patients how bad her vacation was, including the specifics of the harrowing experiences. She did so because she said that she could not have kept this "secret" from the patients anyhow.

In a certain sense this therapist's rationale was correct. She may not have been able to keep her affective reaction from the patients. However, had a patient commented on her demeanor, she could have clarified that it had to do with private matters, rather than something evoked in her by the patient. As Searles explains (1965), the patient only needs (and wants) to know if he has a correct unconscious perception of reality—does the therapist feel angry, anxious, happy, and so on in reaction to the patient. In this case, this was not so. In fact, the therapist honestly was pleased to be back at work. The ability to keep private the content of one's thoughts can foster a sense in the severely disturbed patient that he too can choose to keep things private, to form ego boundaries.

PATIENTS' SECRETS AS DEVELOPMENTAL ACHIEVEMENTS

Whereas staff secrecy is disruptive to the milieu, patient secrecy is less so, because it is generally centered more on the patient's needs than the milieu's. In addition, staff therapists can address patient secrecy as an adaptive step toward personality rebuilding.

Embryonic Secrecy

Michael knew how to "steal" food and hide the goods, but did not yet have the capacity to keep his stealing secret. The young boy was profoundly obese: he ate voraciously, even to the point of vomiting, then would stuff himself again. His portly frame resulted from a desperate and unsuccessful attempt at creating some body boundaries, some protection from the outside world. He littered parts of himself in a trail from his room throughout the unit. Perhaps like Hansel, he felt that he could find his way back only by following his trail of belongings, which included, indiscriminately, toys, letters, books, clothing, and especially empty cartons of food. He was bursting out of his clothes.

Michael's ego boundaries were similarly amorphous. His loud, raucous voice was heard throughout the milieu. He would come upon several people talking and appear to intrude himself upon them. I say "appear to intrude," because this was not an object-directed, provocative intrusion. When asked to be quiet or told to wait, he would be surprised that people experienced him as intrusive. He simply could not hold himself in: he could not keep himself to himself.

Early in his stay, he asked the clinical director to guess what the best cereal was. Before the director could respond, Michael blurted, "Kellogg's Frosted Flakes." He told me that he had stolen and hidden a cache of the cereal on the unit, even though he had been told and had seen that other patients could eat as much as they wished. We tried to provide supplies of special foods.

The director replied that if this were his favorite cereal, we would supply him and he could store or hide as he wished. He retorted, " You mean I can hide it behind the couch with the other Frosted Flakes?"

Michael felt that he had to sneak his special food, yet consistent with his minimal capacity for boundaries, he could not keep his secret to himself. Although he had some rudimentary ideas that a secret was a special bit of external knowledge (the hiding place and identity of his food), he shared his secret with the director, with whom he had minimal experience: we might expect that he might have been uncertain whether his secret would be protected.

From a developmental perspective, this vignette is familiar. A four-year-old who is starting to struggle with the idea of secrecy is not yet able to keep the secret to himself. He will *tell* his mother that he is making a drawing of her in school for a "surprise" Mother's Day gift.

Stealing represents a denial of ego boundaries, a stage that precedes the capacity for true secrecy (Freud, 1965). Psychodynamically, it is a playing with, a testing of one's ego boundaries. Developmentally, it is captured in the three-year-old's attitude of what is mine is mine and what is yours is mine, too. At this age, the child begins to recognize that something (that desired toy) may not belong to him; taking that toy may precipitate battles between himself and the other child holding it, or it will result in Mama's or nursery teacher's reprimand.

Winnicott (1971) tells us that stealing implies that the child feels he deserves something good, that a good thing resides in an outside world, and the child identifies it as belonging to him. The child becomes anxious when he tries to take possession and realizes that it may be taken from him. The child recognizes boundaries, tries to deny them, yet the tension of boundary formation exists and arouses anxiety. The external world may not agree that what is taken, even stolen, really belongs to the child. Further, as with Michael, the capacity to steal does not necessarily include the capacity for secrets.

Secrecy as a developmental stage can be subdivided. There is an intermediate area between the capacities for stealing and secrecy, in which an object can be taken and *also* be kept secret. We can move further developmentally to a substage in which what is taken is not necessarily an object, but a bit of external knowledge. Furthermore, like stealing, the "loot" can be shared with loved ones and kept from hostile others. In addition, there is tension, intrapsychically and played out interpersonally, that one will be found out. In other words, that one's capacity to keep a secret within one's ego boundaries will fail. Secrecy has anxiety as a necessary component.

The Secret as Shame of a Fragment of One's Self

Mrs. K. portrays how the knowledge of one's craziness is paradoxically kept "secret" from oneself and others, while at the same time hinting at self-awareness. After moving out of a catatonic regression, Mrs. K. peppered the staff with questions about what she should do in every facet of her daily existence. For instance, at dinner she would ask before each forkful of food, "Shall I eat this?" The staff reacted with similar feelings (annoyance at the repeated question), but varied responses. Some would say, "Go ahead," whereupon she would peer back suspiciously while she put down the food, or she would say, "Well, I don't like this." Another staff therapist might remark, "I don't know, would you like to?" She would respond with silence, often eating that forkful.

On one occasion, a staff member responded teasingly, "Mrs. K, someday when you are well, I am going to ask you, 'Shall I eat this,' with each forkful of food I take." Mrs. K. reacted with a blushing smile and set about eating her lunch with gusto. Those present, patients and staff, confirmed that they felt she had communicated that she was aware of the "craziness" of her question, yet played her cards close to her chest. She confirmed much later in her treatment that she had felt as if she had kept her crazy thoughts and feelings walled off from another part of herself.

Mrs. K. was not putting-on her craziness in some conscious manner. Nor, by any means, is every psychotic patient trying to keep his or her psychosis secret, circumscribed from another aspect of the self. But the capacity for holding one's psychosis secret from oneself is a developmental accomplishment for this and other patients, which is on the developmental line to the capacity for privacy (Freud, 1965). From another frame of reference, Mrs. K.'s flicker of nonpsychotic relatedness represents a movement from the position in which "the True Self is . . . acknowledged as a potential and is allowed a secret life" (Winnicott, 1960, p. 143). In her case, the True Self is the healthy kernel within her otherwise interpersonally psychotic existence ("Shall I eat this? Shall I eat that?"). It represents an alienation of a part of her self from the rest of her personality.

This clinical picture is related to the myth of the eccentric uncle who is kept in the closet by wealthy families, while many whisper about his oddness. We can see this in day-to-day practice with some families who manage to keep a grossly psychotic member in the home in the face of the neighbors' and extended family's awareness that something is very wrong.

A sixteen-year-old Latino boy was brought to the hospital at his priest's insistence. For an entire year, the boy had been sequestered at home, out of school and the neighborhood, in spite of his increasing bizarreness and even unsuccessful homicidal actions. Only after the boy began to starve himself in order to murder the devil that he saw standing next to him in the mirror did the family bring him to the priest for an exorcism. Even then, when the priest refused, they trucked the child home. The priest had to force his way into the house and implore that they have the boy see a physician. We can see Mrs. K.'s delusional secret about her own psychosis as an internalization of such family psychopathology.

The latter two vignettes dealt with a patient's secret. By the very nature that it is the patient's, it is not disruptive for the milieu. It is simply another symptom that can be understood in an observational framework that a psychodynamic unit requires. One can treat this as transference material, albeit psychotic, with the degree of secondary process that the observing ego offers: self-reflection, critical thought, integration.

SECRECY MASQUERADING AS PRIVACY: BOUNDARY FORMATION

Bettelheim (1979) points out that privacy may include elements of shame about one's body or self. Patients and the milieu teach us that this is pseudoprivacy that has ulterior motives that better fit under secrecy. Closed doors or pulled curtains may represent fulfilling the need for privacy or shameful secrecy (Bernfeld, 1941).

Demeaning One's Self and Others

Florence's quiet insistence on "privacy" reflects both self-demeaning and other-directed hostility. She had a history of physical and sexual abuse since childhood, including adolescent (voluntary) prostitution. During her long stay in the milieu, she maneuvered to get both patients and staff to ignore or psychologically abuse her in order to confirm her view of the world as destructive and herself as devalued. When a new staff member joined us, Florence asked that he give her a back rub to help her fall asleep. She told him that this was routine. Unbeknown to the regular staff, she pulled her curtains, closed the door, and "got herself ready" for the back rub. Her adolescent roommate (who she resentfully deplored) left the room to rest elsewhere, not telling others what Florence was doing. Florence lay on her abdomen, pulled up her shirt, and called the new staff member to put massage oil on her back. The staff member came to the clinical director to say that he felt uncomfortable about Florence's request. He also felt that he was failing at his job. Much to relief, he was told that erotic back rubs were not given.

In this case, Florence's closed door and pulled curtains reveal both the self-demeaning and shameful view of herself as one who should be treated as a prostitute. It also reveals her hostility: chasing out her roommate and demeaning a naive caretaker under the guise of privacy. Her roommate's quiet acquiescence represented her hostility toward Florence.

Body Shame/Personal Shame

Mona, an adolescent, had waxing and waning periods of self-hatred and shame during which she retreated behind closed doors. She disliked herself so much that when she had the opportunity to select a roommate, she openly stated that she wanted someone whom she despised in order that she not impose herself on someone for whom she cared. Whenever possible, she closed her door in order that she "protect" us from her loathsome presence. She too said that her motivation was a need for privacy.

In Mona's case, her self-loathing was transparent and generalized. It was not expressed focally as shame about specific body parts, as Bettelheim (1979) describes is the case in some societies.[1] Indeed, her shame about her entire body extended to her personality. The many hours she tried to spend alone in her room derived from this self-contempt and resulted in a sense of anomie within a close-knit community. What she called a need for privacy was rather her attempt to keep secret her disgusting self under the guise of contempt for others.

Shame on Me/Shame on You

Mrs. Andrews, in contrast, projected the destructive part of herself onto a severely psychotic roommate. She then closed the door when both she and her roommate were together in order to keep "secret" this projected part of herself from the staff.

A very proper former librarian, Mrs. Andrews valued her "privacy." When she had a roommate who was manifestly psychotic and provocative, Mrs. Andrews treated her with disdain and feared her. She said that someone as "dangerous and crazy" as she herself had been, when she was so paranoid that she once patrolled the hallways of another hospital with a butcher's knife, should be locked away. She projected this destructive part of herself onto her roommate.

As terrified as she claimed to be, whenever the two were in the room together, Mrs. Andrews would shut her door, making it more difficult for the staff to look in on them. She claimed that this was for her privacy. In contrast, when she was alone in the room, she rarely closed the door.

Given her almost palpable terror, Mrs. Andrews was in fact closing herself in a room with a part of herself that was potentially murderous. She wondered whether we would have to tie her down and hide this projected part of herself. In this case, part of her request for what she called privacy was her wish to close off this part of herself from us. This was her true secret, the murderous prowler, kept even from her conscious self.

Please Do Intrude

A patient's request for privacy may inevitably precede severe self-destructive acts. Nineteen-year-old Mindi had a history of childhood schizophrenia with severe self-mutilation, the latter starting about 4 years of age. Although multiply determined, one motivation for self-destruction was her feeling that she was growing monstrous and could destroy others. She would try to cut out parts of her body in order to keep the monster inside of her from growing. Her left forearm and vagina were severely

scarred. She had found ingenious ways of injuring herself. She could spot
a glass sliver on the ground from several yards, then stomp on it with her
sneakers so that it stuck to the sole. She would secret these pieces of glass
in various parts of clothing or body cavities. She would close her door
gradually and turn off the lights just preceding her scarification. In fact,
we learned to predict the severity of such acts by the degree she left her
door ajar. For months, the milieu staff was sensitive to "intruding" upon
her, despite the clear association between the closed door and her self-
destruction. In part, their ambivalence about disturbing her reflected the
countertransference collusion with her death wishes. This is an example of
what Flarsheim (1978) deemed the therapist's unconscious wish for the
patient's death. Of course, the patient was both furious and relieved that
someone cared enough to burst into her room in order to save her from
these secret rituals.

In summary, these case vignettes demonstrate the patient's capacity
for secrecy as a state of mind and developmental achievement. We begin
with Michael, who was developing the emotional capacity for secrecy,
while struggling with the formation of body and ego boundaries. Mrs. K.
indicated her paradoxical awareness of keeping some (crazy) part of herself
away from other parts. Florence, Mona, and Mrs. Andrews teach us how
rooms, doors, or curtains are incorporated into the self, and are early
attempts at self and body boundary formation, even though the need for
these may derive from shamefulness, self-loathing, and the wish to protect
libidinally cathected others from the patient's bad self. Developmentally,
these may represent precocious and/or hypertrophied boundary formation, such as Winnicott (1952) describes in "Psychoses and Childcare."
Each of these cases contain some elements of our initial operating definition of secret as a state of mind: a secret as a bit of knowledge that is
internalized; others need to be aware of a secret's existence, even if the
content of the secret remains unknown to them; both intrapsychic and
interpersonal tensions exist.

It is the last characteristic, the intrapsychic–interpersonal tension,
that makes secrecy (and later privacy) such an excellent paradigm for the
study of how we can respect the individual's right to his own feelings,
thoughts, even solitude, while recognizing the individual's need for a
sense of community. How can the individual develop privacy without the
disruptive tension of secrecy? What are the individual's obligation to his
community in order that, in turn, it will enrich his life?

Before a final vignette on privacy achieved, I would like to remind the
reader what others have written about the psychology of secrecy/privacy.
Bettelheim (1979) suggested that the need for privacy may be historically
brief and culturally bound. He juxtaposes two visual images to demon-

strate this. In nineteenth-century bourgeois Vienna, a mirror was positioned near a window seat so that one could watch the street activities without being seen. The cultural value placed on looking into public scenes without being seen underlies the Viennese psychoanalytic setup: in order for private matters to be revealed, the patient does not look at the analyst nor does the analyst make a spectacle of himself before the patient.

Bettelheim contrasts this with the American suburban street. A large picture or bay window, its shade drawn halfway down, faces the street. From outside it is simple to look in. From inside one cannot easily look out without squatting or sitting down. (Even sitting, often the sofa back is against the window so that the sitter must twist around to look out.) This American proclivity to being seen underlies therapies such as group therapy in which strangers reveal the most intimate matters before each other, often expecting the therapist to do the same. Lest we think this is limited to therapies, our American voyeurism/scoptophilia explains the popularity of Donahue, Oprah, and Geraldo.

There are at least two different motivations underlying the need for what Bettelheim calls privacy: one derives from shame about one's body (elimination should be done in privacy), and this extends to shame about one's self and of others. Our discomfort with our natural functions permeates our social interactions. Personal alienation is extended to interpersonal alienation. The individual's culturally determined internal conflict extends to a society's style and belief system.

The second motivation for privacy is the "need for simple solitude" (Bettelheim, 1979). Historically, the rise of privacy and individualism corresponds with the decline in the feelings of communality associated with the absence of privacy. Privacy, private property, and class structure are intimately related.

Privacy based on alienation implies distrust of others and results in an interpersonal conflict, and for those sensitive to it, an intrapersonal conflict. If there is no consensus from the community about the boundaries of public and private, then the community develops laws to protect these two domains. When we turn to an institution such as the law to regulate interpersonal relations, these relations tend to become alienated and bureaucratized (Weber, 1948). Laws impinge on individualism (an American trait foreseen by de Tocqueville), resulting in a tension we see in contemporary society, whether it is over issues of religion in schools, abortion, or owning handguns.

Bettelheim uses the same word, privacy, to describe essentially different phenomena. This confounds his otherwise far-ranging discourse and insights on the two societies that have been home to him. In addition, Bettelheim alludes to some libidinal underpinnings of privacy, without exploring that and its associated ego functions. Finally in his essay, he does not refer to the problem of public–private, communality–individualism, which are vital issues for him and for us.

Ekstein and Carruth (1972) do not put secret-keeping in a historical or cultural frame. Yet with examples from individual therapy, they persuade us that this is a developmental achievement.[2]

They suggest a developmental line associated with the individual phases beginning with secretless infantile fusion/communion, through secreting with an impulse to conceal or confess, through preadolescent concealing and revealing, to the mature adult's intimacy without confessing and private self without secretiveness.

I suggest that by using the word secret for the different psychic phenomena, Ekstein and Carruth (1972) obscure their otherwise excellent developmental description of the adaptive (rather than only defensive/resistant) value of secret-keeping and its relationship with what we suggest would be better called privacy.

Privacy Achieved: Ruthie

The previous clinical examples describe distortions of privacy. In the milieu, as in society, we face the difficult issue of the balance between public and private and the meaning of optimal privacy as a developmental stage beyond secrecy. Secrets have a progressive thrust. We need to recognize (for the patient may be unaware) that this thrust is toward privacy and self-delineation. Just what is this privacy toward which we strive?

Ruthie was admitted to the hospital after several serious suicide attempts in the wake of her brother's and sister's unfortunately successful efforts. After one year of treatment, Ruthie's attempts stopped. She began to think about discharge and rebuilding her life. She returned to writing poetry, for which she had talent. During the psychotic and suicidal times of her life, preceding and early in hospitalization, her writing had a driven nature. Her favorite writers were suicidal Anne Sexton and Sylvia Plath. Her new writing showed a more comfortable, less driven urge in its creativity. Now when preparing to write, she withdrew to her room and closed the door. This felt comfortable to the staff. There was no sense of tension about this as they felt with the patients discussed above.

Ruthie had two sets of poems. The first set she had written prior to or early in her stay. At that time, she dwelled on her self-loathing and ugliness (although, in fact she was attractive). These poems she now kept secret. The later poems were written in a comfortable manner, as reflections on her recent life journey. These she would share with those close to her. In fact, although they were technically good, she was reluctant to seek publication, simply because they represented her private thoughts. She wished to share these selectively. The former poems reflected the need for secrecy. The latter, the capacity for privacy.

Ruthie teaches us about the intrapsychic development from secrecy to privacy. We learn that those aspects of one's self which are loathsome need to be hidden, need to be secret. Privacy subsumes one's comfortable sense of knowing what one may keep to oneself should one wish to do so.

PRIVACY AND COMMUNITY: TENSIONS REPLAYED IN THE MILIEU

The interpersonal is the complement of intrapsychic privacy. Bettelheim (1979) discusses the tension between private–public and closeness–distance in society. In "Mental Health and Urban Design," he persuades us that anomie can be present if there is too little or too much privacy. The former we find in some urban ghettos. (Some ghettos, however, preserve a sense of warmth, vibrancy, and community.) The latter we find in expansive homes: those wealthy children may later seek closeness in crowded discotheques or communes.

The issue of privacy is temporally and culturally bound. It arose in the last few hundred years, with the rise of private property: it shares etymological fourteenth-century roots with privies, the private bathrooms of the wealthy. We see how there is a psychological–linguistic link between privacy and our toilet activities. The multiple psychological determinants of "privacy" range from shame and self-loathing, which would better fit under secrecy, I suggest, to "the need for simple solitude," which Ruthie demonstrates.

In the milieu, we can see that a patient's capacity for secrecy is a developmental achievement that can be handled in a nondisruptive manner if it is recognized as secrecy and not as an integrated sense of privacy. Closed doors or drapes may reflect shame; adaptively, it also reflects the capacity to create a boundary. Some patients who are self-loathing may not have achieved that boundary. They may feel more vulnerable, even paranoid.

The milieu staff represents parental as well as other transference figures. The clinical examples show that secret-keeping, not privacy, among the staff is disruptive to the milieu. Why so? First and quite simply, staff secrecy may represent an idiosyncratic countertransference. Just as in the consulting room, as Freud taught, this "counter" to the patient's ability and need to transfer infantile feelings onto the staff interferes with that relationship.

Second, and perhaps more complex, staff secrecy may represent a tendency or temptation to control another's perception: this can happen in a total institution if we do not guard against it (Goffman, 1961). It is the sociological counterpart to Searles's idea of the patient's correct unconscious perception of reality: that is, the milieu therapist, like many lay people, may deny the patient's correct perception. Bettelheim (1960) described this in the extreme situation of the concentration camp. In order to maintain control over the prisoner's personality integration, the SS permitted no sign of autonomy, including autonomous perception. If a prisoner saw an SS beating another prisoner and did not avert his gaze, he was punished. Yet, immediately after the beating, the SS might insist that the prisoners take note of the beating. One saw when told to see. Both prisoner and Nazi perceived: the former had to deny perception. The first vignette in this chapter, the "secret" affair known to so many yet denied, is in this category.

Staff secrecy may undermine the patient's developing yet tenuous sense of reality. For instance, one child in a residential center "cured" his counselor of sarcasm. The child, whom the counselor liked, could not bear sarcasm; by its very nature, sarcasm's dissembling tone denies its own content. This confused the child's emerging sense of reality, as he tried to gather what his counselor really meant. Out of caring for this child, the counselor stopped being sarcastic (and later addressed its underlying character trait).

Finally, secrets among the staff may represent a recreation of family psychopathology: deep, hidden secrets are kept from some or all the children or spouse. Children often perceive the feeling that something horrible is hidden; they elaborate imaginatively their own content of this secret, usually with fantasies more frightening and disruptive than the true veiled matter.

Before extending what we learn from the psychiatric milieu to our daily life, let us try to integrate what these patients teach us about privacy and community and the physical structure of the hospital and intrapsychic structure.

Schopenhauer's metaphor of hedgehogs in winter is apt. How can they get close enough for warmth without pricking each other? The patient who has reached a developmental stage of struggling toward privacy can graphically demonstrate the nature of this paradox with his use of doors, hallways, and public areas.

The physical structure of the milieu can be a metaphor for the patient's body and self. We can extend the metaphor of the house as symbolic mother to the dialectical interplay between object and self-representation in both the milieu and the mind. Temporally, as one builds a house, one sets a foundation and major structural members. One follows with the external membrane (roof and exterior walls) to protect from, yet communicate with, the outside. The nature of this exterior depends on the environment. Finally, one partitions functional internal space, creating a tension between separating functional areas while permitting movement among them. Of course, rehabilitating an old house (a more apt metaphor for psychotherapy) takes careful tearing down and painstaking recontruction, so that the final structure uses the strengths, maintains the style of the original dwelling, yet creates a sturdier abode that is more fitting to contemporary needs.

One needs a proper amount of living space so that a patient can begin to construct a sense of boundaries and interpersonal relatedness. De-Lauwe (Bettelheim, 1979) correlated levels of psychopathology with private living areas in France, demonstrating that 10 to 14 square meters per person were necessary. Bettelheim found that American psychotic children optimally need personal areas of 16 square meters per child supplemented by community areas (Bettelheim, 1979).

The same constructing holds for an integrated sense of self. One needs access to all segments of one's personality, while retaining the capacity to create boundaries among parts of one's self, at the same time as one defines oneself in relation to others.

For optimal privacy, one needs the opportunity to keep aspects of one's self (or the unit) separate. For an optimal sense of community, one needs to have fluid access to various areas of the unit, while, paradoxically, respecting and recognizing when boundaries are crossed. In the early part of psychiatric treatment of very disturbed individuals, the patient may need help both to recognize boundaries and to cross them.

The architecture of the milieu can facilitate or inhibit this path from secrecy to privacy. To cite but one example, the glass-enclosed nursing station, surrounded by patients who can see but not hear what is going on inside, who strain to hear or surreptitiously to read lips, affords little privacy for the nurses and certainly none for the patients. Staff within, if they are at all sensitive, become self-conscious about talking, trying to keep their conversations secret from the patients. This was starkly portrayed when a child on an inpatient unit asked why one therapist hated another so much. When asked why he thought this, he said that he had "heard" the first therapist tell a nurse that the other therapist was a son-of-a-bitch (easy to lip-read). I discussed this with the guilty therapist. Although aware that children tended to cluster around the three-sided glass-enclosed nursing station, she remained nonplussed.

How do we extend this knowledge about private versus public, a sense of one's self versus a sense of community, to our lives outside of this very odd community of the mental hospital? We could write off much of what we learned above as limited to people crazy enough to live in an institution. Yet when Aristotle began his treatise on politics, he began with a description of the *family* as a political institution. He recognized how intimately the way we raised our children was related to the way we legislated our community lives. Following Aristotle or Foucault (1973), we can learn that how we treat our most dependent individuals reflects how we see ourselves and our community. In the Soviet Union, at least before *perestroika*, the psychiatric institution served the political ends of the society. In some sense in the United States, when we function poorly, the psychiatric institution serves the economic ends of our society: only the very wealthy or indigent get locked up.

In a psychodynamic milieu, the patient can recreate the existential issues that our society faces. The patient's difficulties may be quantitatively greater, but not qualitatively different. In the consulting room, we have learned about the vicissitudes of individual development. In the milieu, we can learn about the vicissitudes of the individual's inner development and how it dialectically influences and is influenced by the community. We can construct better communities designed for the needs of the individual who has suffered severe difficulties in his development. Our hope is to offer an opportunity for redevelopment, so that not only can his needs be recognized and met (at early narcissistic stages), but also can he later meet his own needs and even contribute toward the needs of the community.

If we listen to our patients and to ourselves, we can begin to define and enjoy the capacity for privacy, that simple solitude, that flourishes in a sense of community, of shared values.

NOTES

1. We know that shame appears at the anal phase of development, is more emphasized in certain societies, and is associated with anal functioning. Yet Erikson (1968) says that psychological modes such as shame center around not only a particular developing erogenous zone, but also can be generalized to other zones to a lesser extent. In this patient's case, the generalization extends to her entire body and parts of her psyche.
2. They review Gross's (1951) libidinal schema for secrecy: secrets and secretions related to the early anal phase, associated with ambivalence about expulsion and retention; the later anal phase's reluctance to give up content; the phallic phase's focus on the process of secreting versus exhibiting; and postambivalent genital privacy, in which the secret becomes a potential gift initially for intimacy and sympathy, later for wooing.

References

Bernfeld, S. (1941). The facts of observation in psychoanalysis. *Journal of Psychoanalysis* 12:289–305.

Bettelheim, B. (1960). *The Informed Heart: Autonomy in a Mass Age.* New York: Free Press.

Bettelheim, B. (1973). *A Home for the Heart.* New York: Knopf.

Bettelheim, B. (1979). *Surviving and Other Essays.* New York: Knopf.

Ekstein, R., and Carruth, E. (1972). Keeping secrets. In P. Giovacchini (ed.), *Tactics and Techniques,* Vol. 1, pp. 200–215. New York: Jason Aronson.

Erikson, E. (1968). *Identity, Youth and Crisis.* New York: Norton.

Flarsheim, A. (1978). The therapist's collusion with patient's wish for suicide. In P. Giovacchini (ed.), *Tactics and Techniques,* Vol. II, pp. 155–195. New York: Jason Aronson.

Foucault, M. (1973). *Madness and Civilization.* New York: Vintage Books.

Freud, A. (1965). *Normality and Pathology in Childhood: Assessments of Development,* pp. 116–118. New York: International Universities Press.

Goffman, E. (1961). *Asylums: Essays on the Social Situation of Mental Patients and Other Inmates.* New York: Anchor.

Gross, A. (1951). The secret. *Bulletin of the Meninger Clinic* 15:37–44.

Hoffer, W. (1949). Mouth, hand and ego—integration. *Psychoanalytic Study of the Child* 314: 49–56.

Searles, H. (1965). *Collected Papers on Schizophrenia and Related Subjects.* New York: International Universities Press.

Stanton, A., and Schwartz, M. (1954). *The Mental Hospital.* New York: Basic Books.

Weber, M. (1948). From Max Weber: *Essays in Sociology* (H. H. Gerth and C. Wright Mills, trans.). London: Routledge and Kegan Paul.

Webster's Third New International Dictionary of the English Language, Unabridged (1971). Springfield, MA: Merriam.

Winnicott, D. W. (1958). Psychoses and Childcare. In *Collected Papers: Through Pediatrics to Psychoanalysis,* pp. 219–228. London: Tavistock.

Winnicott, D. W. (1960). Ego Distortion in Terms of True and False Self. In *The Maturational Processes and the Facilitating Environment,* p. 143. New York: International Universities Press.

Winnicott, D. W. (1971). *Playing and Reality.* New York: Basic Books.

Index